CRITIQUE OF EARTH

CRITIQUE OF
EARTH

The second series of the Gifford Lectures entitled
"Critique of Heaven and Earth"

by

AREND Th. VAN LEEUWEN

*Associate Professor of Christian Social Ethics in the Catholic
University of Nijmegen, (Holland)*

**CHARLES SCRIBNER'S SONS
NEW YORK**

1 3 5 7 9 11 13 15 17 19 I/C 20 18 16 14 12 10 8 6 4 2

Printed in Great Britain
Library of Congress Catalog Card Number 73-1350
ISBN 0-684-13840-9

Contents

Preface

This book contains the second of the two series of Gifford Lectures which I was invited to give at the University of Aberdeen, Scotland, in the years 1970 and 1972. The first series, entitled "Critique of Heaven", was published in 1972. "Critique of Earth" is the title of this second series, thus completing the overall theme "Critique of Heaven and Earth".

In addition to the expression of my sincere gratitude to the Senatus Academicus of the University of Aberdeen for the renewed hospitality I enjoyed during the weeks spent at the University in 1972, I wish to thank the Gifford Lectures Committee at Aberdeen for the generous subvention which paved the way for this second volume to be published.

A. Th. VAN LEEUWEN
Gendt (Gld.), Netherlands, Summer 1974

I

From critique of heaven to critique of earth

"⎯HUS the critique of heaven is transmuted into the critique of earth, the critique of religion into the critique of law and the critique of theology into the critique of politics."

This utterance of Karl Marx is the starting-point of both these series of lectures. Their title, "Critique of heaven and earth", is taken from it; and its interpretation is the compass by which our course is set. The passage was not chosen at random; it comes from Marx's article called *Introduction to the Critique of Hegel's Philosophy of Law*, an article that has achieved renown as the Magna Charta of the critique of religion. Whereas the "critique of heaven" was the subject of the first lecture series, this second series will be centred on the "critique of earth". That is already enough to indicate the connection, the indissoluble connection, between the two series. Just as the beating of a man's heart is felt throughout his body, from head to toe, so here the "critique" is like a single heartbeat pulsating in both parts. The analogy can be taken even further, in so far as the relation takes effect in a dynamic transition characterized by the verb "transmuted into" (*verwandelt sich in*). We have already encountered in the first series the remarkable interaction between the "critique of heaven" and the "critique of earth", a two-way movement in which the passage we have cited functions also in reverse: the critique of earth is transmuted into the critique of heaven. That reminds one of the circulation of the blood, of the bloodstream which returns to

7

the heart, is there "transmuted" and is pumped again through the body.

The reason for thinking of an interaction of some sort lies immediately to hand. In the first place, there is the striking fact that Marx's critique of religion turns out to be part of the critique of law; and, what is more, this article is concerned not with the critique of law in a direct sense but with the critique of the philosophy of law. That would appear to conflict with the statement that the critique of religion is transmuted into the critique of law. Marx pointed out this contradiction himself; for he follows it up at once by saying that the *Critique of Hegel's Philosophy of Law* is not in the first instance attached to the original (namely, law) but to a copy, that is, to the *philosophy* of the German state and German law. Marx is pursuing an indirect method, therefore. Already in the first series we gave thought to the intimate connection between Marx's critique of Hegel's philosophy, on the one hand, and his critique of theology and religion, on the other. Evidently, it is not just the case that the critique of religion issues in the critique of law; but conversely, the critique of law presupposes an indirect method that leads through the critique of religion.

In the present series too, we shall keep running into this problem, only this time approaching it from the other side. There is yet another problem. The pronouncement on which these lectures are based dates from the year 1844. That year constitutes a turning-point in Marx's life and work also, in that it saw the inception of the *Critique of Political Economy*, at any rate in the explicit sense in which that study was to preoccupy him for the rest of his life. That is the reason, therefore, why no mention is made of that critique in the passage cited. The subject comes up, of course, in the article and is considered there; but it does not as yet form the pivot on which the argument is made to turn. The passage quoted speaks only of "law" and "politics" as the subject-matter of the critique of earth, saying nothing about political economy. This again shows the extent to which the passage marks a transition to a new period: the critique of law and politics does indeed *implicitly* embrace the critique of political economy; but the latter has not yet become explicit. Then again, we have here a new

8

pointer to the interaction I was speaking of a moment ago; for evidently, at the level of law and politics we are still only half-way to heaven. Years later, looking back on the developing course of his study of economics, Marx expressed the conclusion reached by his *Critique of Hegel's Philosophy of Law* in these terms: "legal relations and forms of state . . . are rooted in the material conditions of life, which are summed up by Hegel in their totality . . . under the name 'civil society'; the anatomy of that civil society is to be sought in political economy." The transition, therefore, is a dual one, which has to cross over from the critique of heaven to the critique of earth. To put it another way: the critique of law and politics has a distinctive midway position, forming as it does a bridge between the critique of religion, on the one hand, and that of political economy, on the other.

All this serves to indicate the course which this second series of lectures is to take. It will move from the critique of law and politics to the critique of political economy. All the time we shall keep clearly in view the fundamental connection with the critique of theology and religion. Not only shall we repeatedly encounter that connection as the lectures proceed, but the problem of the interaction will come to light and will assume an acute form more especially in the critique of political economy.

In order to get our sights firmly fixed on the transition from the critique of heaven to the critique of earth, and so also from the first to the second series of lectures, we must return once more to Marx's dissertation, which has a central place in his critique of heaven. We have already seen how Marx's way of interpreting the quite distinctive character of Epicurus' theory of atoms stands in direct relation to the analysis of the atomistic character of civil society, which Marx was to develop in subsequent years. In a sense one might even make a connection here with the term "anatomy of civil society", which is the starting-point for the *Critique of Political Economy*. The term "anatomy", dis-section, comes from the same Greek verb from which is derived the word "atom": a-tomos, indivisible. In that sense "anatomy" may be interpreted as the disclosure, by means of analysis, of the atomistic structure, the "an-atomy", of civil society.

9

In his Gifford Lectures on *The Relevance of Science* the German physicist and philosopher, Carl Friedrich von Weizsäcker, has pointed to the abiding and fundamental importance of the theory of atoms propounded by Democritus and Epicurus. Having first considered the areas of correspondence and of difference with modern atomic physics, he concludes that this relation with modern physical science does not really get to the heart of the matter. We would be failing to understand the atomic theory of the ancients if we took it to be in the first place a scientific hypothesis intended to provide an explanation of observed phenomena. Actually, the main development of the sciences in which antiquity most excelled—mathematics and astronomy—was closely connected with the philosophical school diametrically opposed to the atomists, that is, the school of Plato. Essentially, atomism was a philosophy, that is to say, an attempt to solve the speculative problem of Being. Whilst from the standpoint of modern science this may present itself as a weakness typical of metaphysical dogmatism, conversely, modern "scientism", or faith in the scientific method, labours under a similar kind of dogmatism, but without being itself aware of the weakness. Significantly enough, modern quantum-theory confronts physicists with precisely the sort of philosophical questions that the empirical atomism of the nineteenth century thought it could avoid.

Its character as philosophy, von Weizsäcker continues, is just what makes the atomism of the ancient world so amazingly modern. From the standpoint of the modern empirical approach the ancient saying that the atom is *one* would seem to be no more than a rather obscure description of the actual indivisibility of the atom in practice; but ancient atomism interprets the absolute indivisibility of the atom as a self-evident, natural consequence of its ontological quality of being one. Of course, this speculative approach does contrast with modern science, which is based on the quantitative description of phenomena, itself based on the notion of mathematical laws. Even so, the ancient theory of atoms as it related to cosmogony, the idea of the rotating celestial sphere having emerged from a primeval storm of whirling atoms, has had a surprising sequel in modern theories about the origin of the universe. It is the atomists' conception of an infinite universe with an infinite number of atoms forming an infinite number of worlds that seems so amazingly modern. This atomistic cosmogony is in the nature of a scientific myth. Its god is the blind necessity of the atomic collisions. This anti-religious element was thoroughly logical; but it involved the temporary eclipse of the atomistic philosophy in the European tradition. When, in the late period of antiquity, even the intellectuals longed for a religious revival, it was all over with this philosophy. Notably in Christian Europe, atomism was unable to lead more than an underground existence, until, in the first half of the seventeenth century, it underwent a surprising turn of fortune.

"A Catholic clergyman with a considerable scientific reputation and of unimpeachable orthodoxy," we read in Dijksterhuis' study of the "mechanizing" of our view of the world, "feels himself in the grip of its fascination and sees it as his task in life to introduce it into Western thought in a theologically acceptable form. In this he succeeds; and as a result it is quickly elevated to the rank of a respectable theory of which no Christian natural scientist need feel ashamed." This thinker was Pierre Gassendi, with whose work Marx's dissertation evinces a connection.

Dijksterhuis draws a comparison between the way that Pierre Gassendi in the seventeenth, and Thomas Aquinas in the thirteenth century, managed to incorporate something of the ancient world and its mentality into the scientific culture of Christendom. In both cases, opposition on the part of ecclesiastical authority had to be overcome, and certain aspects which Christian thought could not accept—in particular, the uncreatedness and eternal existence of the world—had to be eliminated from the pagan theories. Greater than the likeness, however, is the difference between them. Whereas Thomas, by combining Aristotelean philosophy with Christian doctrine, established a harmony between faith and knowledge, Gassendi, by making a theory with an explicitly materialistic tenor theologically plausible, sowed within the Christian conscious-ness a germ of disquiet and of discord that was to have pre-cisely the opposite effect to what Thomas had been aiming at. One can hardly suppose that Gassendi did not sense this. That he nonetheless gave himself heart and soul to the task of implementing the atomistic way of thinking, and of demonstrating its compatibility with the Christian faith, witnesses to the irresistible power with which a scientific mode of thought was developing, through an inner drive of its own, into an independent authority alongside, and if need be in opposition to, the faith. Gassendi's activity, and likewise that of Descartes, who in respect of the Christian world view stood with his own particular notion of the world just as Gassendi did with classical atomism, is to be regarded "as an attempt pursued with the utmost energy either to prevent or, in so far as it was already a fact, to plaster over the irrevocable and imminent rupture in men's way of looking at the world."

No one in Gassendi's time had a keener, clearer vision of that rupture than the Christian thinker, skilled also in mathematics and in physics, Blaise Pascal. His opposition to Descartes' theory of corpuscles, which is closely akin to Gassendi's theory (*Pensées* 78 and 79: *Descartes inutile et incertain*), was not the product of an Aristotelean-Platonic philosophy, a religious philosophy, but did in fact comprise a rejection of the metaphysical pretensions of Cartesianism. Pascal saw very clearly the consequences of the image of the world presented by the modern natural science (*Pensée* 206: *Le silence éternel de ces espaces infinis m'effraie*, the eternal silence of those infinite spaces appals me); nature is such that it everywhere carries the traces of a God who has perished, both in man and outside man (*la nature est telle qu'elle marque partout un Dieu perdu et dans l'homme et hors de l'homme*). It is this modern awareness which, with an express reference to this thought of Pascal's, the young Hegel (1802) describes as a sense that God Himself is dead. Hegel's speculative philosophy is a comprehensive attempt to heal the breach, to bridge the chasm. By way of his dialectic, the modern sense of God's death is resolved into a speculative Idea of God. Again at the level of human society, the same penetrating gaze enables Hegel to detect the historic break that has occurred in the modern period, the incursion of "civil society"; yet here too the rupture is healed, specifically in the Idea of the state.

At both levels, Marx assails the speculative attempt at accommodation in Hegel's philosophy. In his dissertation he analyses the whole range of subjective problems raised by

Epicurus' theory of atoms, and so offers a new interpretation of an ancient natural philosophy that, with the rise of modern science, was retrieved from its age-old exile, into which a Christian tradition had thrust it. In so doing, Marx radically opposes Gassendi's lukewarm and Hegel's glorious effort to bridge the gulf.

The real importance of Marx's dissertation, however, is not located in the plane of natural philosophy, but resides in the quite distinctive way in which he analyses and interprets Epicurus' atomism. The problems exposed in his dissertation are those posed by modern atomistic society, by what Hegel called "civil society". Thus the critique of heaven, completed in the dissertation, returns in the critique of earth, more explicitly in the critique of Hegel's philosophy of law. At this level too Hegel's speculative attempt at accommodation is torpedoed. Marx chooses his starting-point in that very reality of modern times which with his speculative approach Hegel wanted to deny. From the analysis of Epicurus' atomism he proceeds to the an-atomy of civil society.

Marx took thorough stock of the historical perspective of his critical work against the background of the history of European thought. In direct association with the passage relating the analysis of Epicurus' atomism to that of civil society, Marx gives us in *Die Heilige Familie* (1844) a brief outline of the development of French materialism. There we can see revealed the deeper motives behind Marx's attempt to devise his own quite distinctive form of "materialism". In his sketch one sees, as it were, the historical contours of the critique of heaven and of the critique of earth running across each other. The sketch interests us not in the first instance as a piece of historiography but as a mirror in which the image of Marx's own design is displayed.

The sketch begins at the point where the two lines of critique coincide. The French Enlightenment of the eighteenth century, and especially French materialism, was not only a battle against current political institutions and against the metaphysics of the seventeenth century and against all metaphysics, in particular the metaphysics of Descartes, Malebranche, Spinoza and Leibniz. French materialism comprises two trends or schools, the one originating with Descartes, the other with Locke. The latter school is mainly an element in French culture and has its outcome in socialism. The former school, that of mechanistic materialism, issues in French natural science. Both schools have developed along paths that cross from time to time.

So far as the former school, that of mechanistic materialism, is concerned, its course is briefly sketched by Marx as follows. In his physics, Descartes had regarded matter as being invested with the energy needed to produce itself (*selbstschöpferische Kraft*); the mechanistic process he envisaged as the vital activity of matter (*Lebensakt*). In his physics, matter is the sole substance, the only ground of being and knowing. Now French mechanistic materialism aligned itself with Descartes' physics, as opposed to his metaphysics. His followers were physicists and therefore anti-metaphysicians by occupation.

With Descartes' metaphysics, therefore, the position was quite different. From the very start he was up against materialism—and that in the person of Gassendi, who rehabilitated Epicurean materialism. French and English materialism remained all the time closely associated with Democritus and Epicurus. In addition, there was another contrast between Descartes' metaphysics and the English materialist, Hobbes.

The metaphysics of the seventeenth century (Descartes, Leibniz) still had a positive, profane content. This metaphysics gave rise to discoveries in the field of mathematics, of physics and of certain other sciences; and it looked as though those discoveries were a direct outcome of the metaphysics. That semblance was destroyed as early as the eighteenth century. The positive sciences had freed themselves from metaphysics and had marked off the bounds of their own territory. The whole realm of metaphysics still consisted only in 'beings of thought' (*Gedankenwesen*) and things heavenly, the more so as real existents (*realen Wesen*) and the things of earth were beginning to monopolize attention.

The man who rendered the metaphysics of the seventeenth century and all metaphysics theoretically incredible was Pierre Bayle. His weapon was scepticism, a weapon forged out of the metaphysical spells of sorcery; religious doubt drove Bayle to doubt regarding the metaphysics on which belief was based; and so he subjected metaphysics and its whole history to criticism. He became the historiographer of metaphysics in order to write the history of its demise. But Bayle did more than that. He was the harbinger of the atheistic society, which he heralded by showing that a society consisting simply of atheists is possible, that an atheist can be an honourable person, that man is not degraded by atheism but by superstition and idolatry. Thus Pierre Bayle became the last metaphysician in the seventeenth-century sense of the word, and the first philosopher in the eighteenth-century sense of the term.

Apart from the negative combating of the theology and metaphysics of the seventeenth century, there was need for a positive, anti-metaphysical system. This was provided by the philosopher who stands at the head of the second school of French materialism, the Englishman, John Locke. "Materialism is Great Britain's very own offspring. Even the British scholastic Duns Scotus (whose theology seems to be confused by Marx with William of Ockham's theology) wondered whether matter might not be able to think. To make this miracle come true he had recourse to God's omnipotence, or in other words, he obliged theology to proclaim a materialism of its own. Moreover, he was a nominalist. We find nominalism to be a principal component where the English materialists are concerned; it is in fact the earliest expression of materialism."

Next Marx gives a concise sketch of English materialism and the course of its development. Its real progenitor, the progenitor of all modern experimental science, is Francis Bacon. Natural science he holds to be the true science, and sensory physics the main part of natural science. Democritus with his atoms is one of Bacon's most oft-quoted authorities. Bacon teaches that the senses are utterly reliable and are the source of all knowledge. Science is empirical science, the knowledge of experience, and consists in applying a rational method to what is given by the senses. Induction, analysis, comparison, observation and experiment—these are the principal elements of a rational method. Of the properties inherent in matter, the chief and most excellent is motion.

This brings Marx to the essential core of his historical exposition. In Francis Bacon's case—so his argument runs—"the movement of matter is not simply envisaged as mechanical and mathematical motion, but more as impulse (*Trieb*), vital spirit (*Lebensgeist*), tensile force (*Spannkraft*), as the agonizing (*Qual*) of matter". By his own account, Marx borrowed this latter expression from the German mystic, Jakob Böhme (1575–1624), who was a contemporary of Bacon's (1561–1626). The word *Qual* is almost untranslatable. It means literally "torment", "pain". The meaning is best rendered, I would think, by "pangs", which can refer to birth as well as to death ("pangs of death"). Again, the term *Trieb* in German has quite distinctive associations, which we shall come across in the next lecture, when dealing with Marx's article on the legislation against wood-stealing.

At a crucial point in Marx's argument we again encounter the mystical philosopher, Böhme. In the context of Marx's dissertation we have already met a quotation from Böhme, intended to illustrate Epicurus' doctrine of immortality, which is presented in the form of a theory regarding the eternity of atoms. Marx cites a poem by Böhme in that connection: whoever conceives eternity as time and time as eternity is freed from all discord. And he appends the observation that this teaching does not do away with belief in immortality but helps to explain it and gives it intelligible expression. Now Marx turns once again to this German philosopher and mystic, this time for confirmation in his mother tongue of the views of the English materialist, Bacon. He adds thereto, by way of further elucidation: the primitive forms of matter are "living, individualizing forces of being, inherent in matter, which produce the specific differences" (*lebendige, individual-isierende, ihr inhärente, die spezifischen Unterschiede produzierende Wesenkräfte*).

Obviously, Marx detects in Bacon's materialism the heart-beat of the materialism that is present to his own mind. In Bacon, his argument goes on, "materialism conserves within it, though as yet in a naive fashion, the seeds of many-sided development. In its poetic and sensuous lustre matter commends itself to the whole person (*die Materie lacht in poetisch-sinnlichem Glanze den ganzen Menschen an*). Aphoristic teaching as such, on the other hand, still bristles with theological illogicalities."

Actually, Marx uses an even stronger expression: "In Bacon, *as in its first creator*, materialism conserves within it,

16

though as yet in a naive fashion, the seeds of a many-sided development." How are we to understand this expression? From a historical viewpoint it would appear absurd, for we know that Bacon looks back to the ancient materialism of Democritus. In that context, of course, he is rightly called the "real progenitor" of English materialism; but more than that seems to be meant by the expression "first creator". When we examine it more closely, in fact, the whole passage on the origin of English materialism turns out to be pregnant with theological expressions. It begins with the assertion that materialism is *"der eingeborne Sohn Grossbritanniens"*. On a historical view, this again seems absurd. But here, too, more would appear to be intended than a given fact of history. I previously translated this phrase as "very own offspring (son)", since the adjective *eingeboren* has the meaning of "inborn", "innate" (as one might speak of an "innate" talent or quality), whilst the noun *Eingeborne* means "native". However, a much more obvious thing to do is to take *der eingeborne Sohn* as a biblical expression in the sense in which St. John's Gospel acclaims Jesus Christ to be "the only-begotten Son" of the Father (John 1:14,; 183:18). This rendering would seem at first sight to be absurd, which is why I avoided it in the first instance. But on more careful analysis the incongruity disappears. After all, Marx immediately clarifies the point by going on to say that the scholastic, Duns Scotus, had already contemplated the possibility of a "thinking matter" and had forced theology itself to proclaim materialism. He then describes the nominalism of which Duns Scotus was an advocate as "the earliest expression of materialism".

When we consider the passage as a whole, it must strike us as being a most remarkable materialistic counterpart to the prologue of the Johannine Gospel. What Marx apparently has in mind is a new beginning for materialism in Christian Europe. Theology itself becomes the voice of materialism. Admittedly, materialism was by then many centuries old; it had been inherited from classical antiquity. But just as the Johannine prologue looks back to Genesis 1, and in the Word's becoming flesh makes creation start all over again—or what is the same thing, brings creation to fulfilment, to complete realization in the Incarnation—so Marx gives the materialism of antiquity a fresh start and brings it to its fulfilment in the history of Christian Europe. It is the product of Christian theology. To put it more strongly, it is the way in which matter itself thinks. To put it more strongly still, it is God thinking in the guise of thinking matter, a materialized theology, the Johannine *theos-logos* that has become matter. The thinking of matter is no abstract thinking, but it is *Lebensgeist*, the living spirit of matter. We are reminded of the Spirit of God at the start of creation (Genesis 1:2), of the Johannine "In the Word (*logos*) was life" (John 1:4). This vital spirit is *Trieb*, *Spannkraft*, *Qual*, the *dynamis* which the New Testament ascribes to God, and the "birth-pangs" of the whole creation (Romans 8:22). This vital spirit is the motion, the movement which Marx calls "the chief and most excellent" of the properties inherent in matter (*der Materie eingebornen*). Here we are back with the same term, *eingeboren*, and with its ambiguity, implying both "inborn" and "only-begotten"; for motion is "the chief and most excellent" quality, just as Christ in the New Testament is the *prototokos* (the firstborn) of Mary and, as the risen Lord, the *prototokos* also among the many sons of God to whom the creation will ultimately give birth (Romans 8:19, 29): the firstborn.

The fact that these ideas are taken from Jakob Böhme is in itself a powerful indication of the theological content of this passage; but it is not this connection in itself with which we are now concerned. Marx is not hard at work here unfolding a mystical philosophy of matter; on the contrary, and by way of refuting Bruno Bauer's speculative ideas, he wants to give us as sober and accurate as possible an account of the real history of European materialism. Even so, he does it in a noticeably theological terminology. It is as though Feuerbach's method is being put into reverse. Whilst Feuerbach unmasks theology as covert anthropology, here, on the other hand, is Marx describing the history of materialism in theological terms and speaking of Francis Bacon as "the first creator" of materialism, in whom it yet carried the seeds of an all-round development. In Bacon we are confronted with the thinking of matter. Here the first principle of Descartes' philosophy is inverted. It is not the thinking subject that the *cogito, ergo sum* expresses; but the matter which Descartes' philosophy relates definitively to the status of "object" here confronts us as a thinking subject and

18

says *sum, ergo cogito*. Materialism is not a product of human thinking which assumes a position over against material reality and from that distance and opposition utters statements about it. On the contrary, materialism is the self-reflection of thinking matter, which thinks in the human subject.

It is here that we get to the heart of the matter. After all, for Marx that does not lie in the development of a speculative natural philosophy, the sort of thing that, under the inspiration of Jakob Böhme's Christian-cum-mystical dialectic, for example, had come to full flower in the idealism of Hegel and Schelling. Marx approached the matter from another side. He does not describe the history of materialism as philosophy, but takes his business to be with the history of the natural sciences. Francis Bacon is the true progenitor of English materialism, because he is the true progenitor of all modern experimental science: empirical science, conducted by a rational method. His materialism was not a metaphysics separate and distinct from physics; but it was the self-reflection of thinking matter, which comes to expression in physics. It is this unity of materialism and experimental science that distinguishes English materialism from the French school with its origin in Descartes. For Descartes and other seventeenth-century philosophers such as Leibniz, metaphysics and physics still stood in a close mutual relationship; but this had already been abrogated by the outset of the eighteenth century, so that metaphysics was left completely up in the air.

Marx's opposition to Descartes was operative at two levels: that of metaphysics and that of physics. At the level of metaphysics, he had already aligned himself in his dissertation with Descartes' contemporary and antagonist, Gassendi, who revived Epicurus' theory of atoms and set the metaphysics of classical materialism over against Descartes' metaphysics. Gassendi saw clearly enough the contrariety between Descartes' metaphysics, which proceed from the thinking subject, and his physics, which treat matter as the sole, self-creating and sustaining substance. Marx builds on Gassendi, but goes beyond the limits set by Gassendi in two respects. First, he exposes Gassendi's accommodation with the Christian theological tradition as an inevitable failure. Second, he interprets Epicurus' original notion of the deviation of the atom in a way that makes Epicurus the materialistic counterpart to Descartes: the autonomy which the latter anchors in the thinking subject is secured by Epicurus in physical reality itself. Marx's interpretation, then, acquires a surprising application in the anatomy he carries out of civil society, where the citizens are so many atoms. In my final lecture we shall see this application returning in a quite remarkable version.

For Marx, however, the real problem is not located at this first level, of metaphysics, but at the second level, that of physics. Classical materialism was a philosophy that has turned out to be highly relevant to the modern development of the natural sciences; but it did not rest on empirical science controlled by a rational method. Bacon is the real progenitor of that. It is in Bacon that Marx finds the answer to his fundamental objections to Descartes' physics. Not only is Descartes' physics in flat contradiction with his metaphysics; but, what is more, his physics is very one-sided. It envisages the motion of matter as a mechanical movement pure and simple; Cartesian materialism is a mechanistic materialism, and in that form it has found its way into French science. As over against that, Marx finds in Bacon a view that approaches the movement of matter, not only as mechanical and mathematical motion, but in terms of a primitive and comprehensive essence which he describes as the *Trieb, Lebensgeist, Spannkraft, Qual* of matter. Whereas in Descartes' physics the thinking of matter is the mirror of an abstract, objectivizing thinking, in Bacon we find thinking matter in its origin, as "vital spirit". Matter here is not the framework, the outer shell, of mechanical and mathematical abstractions; but in its poetic and sensuous lustre it makes its appeal to the whole person. In Bacon's thinking, the materialism is still total, it still harbours within it the germ of a many-sided development; indeed, it bristles still with theological illogicalities, it is naive and primitive, it is still prior, as it were, to the modern Fall.

Here we may detect the very heartbeat of Marx's critique, the critique of heaven and the critique of earth. He lays bare the root of that process in modern times which has given rise to an all-pervading mechanistic and mathematical view of the world. The *Critique of Political Economy* starts at this central point, the point where the thinking and being of modern man and modern society have their origin. In the subsequent lectures we shall try to follow this line; and in the last one I shall come back to this central point.

Now we propose to follow further still the course taken by Marx's argument. The many-sided potential of English materialism in its original guise is not realized. As it develops further, materialism becomes one-sided. It is to the credit of the English philosopher, Thomas Hobbes, that like Gassendi he opposed Descartes' metaphysics; but he was unable to offer any resistance to the one-sided tendency of Descartes' physics. Hobbes is the systematist of Bacon's materialism. The bloom fades from sensory awareness and experience (*Sinnlichkeit*), turning instead to the abstract sensationalism of geometry. Physical motion is sacrificed to mechanical or mathematical motion; geometry is proclaimed to be the principal science. Materialism becomes inimical to man. So that the anti-human, flesh-less spirit (*menschenfeindlichen, fleischlosen Geist*) may be conquered on its own ground, materialism must itself shed and mortify its flesh and become ascetic. It appears as a being of mere reasoning intelligence (*Verstandeswesen*), but it consequently develops the ruthless consistency of the reasoning intelligence (*rücksichtlose Konsequenz des Verstandes*).

If sensory experience is the source of all human knowledge, so runs Hobbes' argument, then visual contemplation, thought, representation and so forth are nothing other than phantoms (*Phantome*) of the world of material bodies (*Körperwelt*), which is more or less divested of its sensory form. The thought, the idea, cannot be separated from a matter that thinks; for the latter is the subject of every change. Because only what is material can be observed, can be known, we can know nothing, therefore, of God's existence. Only my own existence is certain. Every human passion is a mechanical motion, which ends or begins. Man is subject to the same laws as nature. Power and freedom are identical.

Hobbes is significant in that he systematized Bacon and thereby "abolished the theistic prejudices of Bacon's materialism". That would seem a logical enough conclusion to Marx's historical sketch; but on closer inspection here is a hidden dilemma that calls for attention. After all, Marx has just been criticizing the one-sided development, to which Hobbes' thinking had subjected English materialism, as the fatal reduction whereby a materialism embracing the whole of physical and human reality is abstracted to a mechanical and mathematical model. It is this very fatality that he reveals in civil society as the reduction of the human person to an ascetic, wraithlike figure, devoted to the worship of abstractions. Physical motion is sacrificed in the interest of mechanical and mathematical motion. Yet in an enigmatic way this would appear to go hand in hand with the "abolition of theistic prejudices" and of "theological illogicalities". Hobbes' atheism is the atheism of civil society. Yet this is just what Marx is determined to oppose. Without seeking to formulate it clearly, the dilemma with which Marx sees himself confronted comprises the question how we are to overcome the fatal tendency to erect a mechanical and mathematical world view without relapsing into Bacon's "theological illogicalities" and "theistic prejudices".

In the remaining part of Marx's historical sketch this dilemma is not resolved. In it he traces the line running from English materialism to French materialism. On English materialism the French conferred *esprit*, they restored to it flesh and blood, gave it balance and grace. In short, the French civilized it. This is the second school of French materialism, which runs from Bacon, through Locke to Condillac and Helvetius. Whereas the first school, stemming from Descartes, issues in science proper, this second school gives rise to socialism and communism. It puts a great deal of emphasis on the outward circumstances of environment and culture as providing the preconditions for the development of human kind. If man is formed by circumstances, then circumstances must be formed in a humane way. If man is social by nature, then he develops his true nature primarily in society, and the potential of his nature is not to be gauged by that of the isolated individual but by that of society. Whilst the socialist, Fourier, takes French materialism as his immediate starting-point, Dézamy develops the doctrine of real humanism as the logical basis of communism. Like Feuerbach in the theoretical field, so French and English socialism and communism in the practical field stood for the materialism that is identical with humanism.

The historical sketch finishes at this point. In the *Thesen über Feuerbach*, which likewise date from this period (spring

1845), Marx goes a step further. There he criticizes all materialism, that of Feuerbach included, because it envisages the
reality present to the senses only in the form of object or of
observation, but not as human sensory activity, praxis, not
subjectively (thesis 1). At the same time he criticizes the Anglo-
French materialism which issues in socialism and communism.
The materialistic doctrine that human beings are the products
of circumstances and upbringing, and thus that changed people
are the products of different circumstances and altered upbringing, overlooks the fact that circumstances are changed
by *people* and that the educator has himself to be educated.
The coincidence of the changing of circumstances and the
human activity can only be conceived as revolutionary praxis
and understood on a rational basis (thesis 3). The standpoint of
the old materialism is "civil", i.e. "bourgeois" society; the
standpoint of the new materialism is human society, or socialized humanity (thesis 10).

These critical theses stand out sharply against the background of the historical outline we have just been reproducing.
What Marx has in view is a total, many-sided materialism
that does in the realm of practice exactly what the original
English materialism had envisaged in the theoretical realm of
natural science: a new materialism capable of overcoming the
fatal reduction of social reality in civil society and of producing
an all-round humane society. This new materialism can be
expressed in the same terms used to describe Bacon's materialism, namely, an empirical kind of knowledge or science that
consists of applying a rational method to what is given by the
senses. It differs fundamentally from the old materialism in
that it starts from what is given to and by the senses as human
sensory activity, praxis. The essential being of man is the
"ensemble of social relations" (thesis 6) and the life of society
is essentially practical (thesis 8). Just as in its first creator,
Bacon, the old materialism carried within itself, though still
in a naive fashion, the seeds of a many-sided growth, so it is
possible to describe the new materialism in analogous terms.
In Marx, its first creator, the new materialism carries within
itself, though as yet naively, the seeds of a many-sided growth.
Only Bacon stands at the outset of a developing process, the
end of which Marx can see approaching. That is why Marx

cannot rest content with a revival of the old materialism; he is faced with the task of transcending it in a new dimension. The process of mechanizing and "mathematicizing" nature has gone hand in hand with the same process applied to society, that is, to human nature. By subjecting this development in the social realm to his critique, Marx simultaneously gets to grips with the analogous development in the realm of nature. He conducts this critique by applying a rational analysis in the area of human nature, on the analogy of Bacon's rational analysis of nature. The character of his rational analysis transcends the rational analysis of nature, just as human nature itself transcends nature. Just as, in Bacon's theoretical materialism, matter is said to think, so, in Marx's practical materialism, human nature—that is, society, which is something essentially practical—emerges as activity, as praxis. And just as natural science by critical analysis changes nature, so does this scientific knowledge of society, by critical analysis, change society: its theory is revolutionary praxis.

With this provisional description of the quite distinctive character of materialism that Marx had in view, I must leave the matter. It is typical that the *Thesen über Feuerbach*, the theses on Feuerbach, are no more than notes, casually jotted down and found later on by Engels among Marx's papers. Furthermore, I have used these theses to supplement and round off a historical outline of the "old materialism", which stops just at the point where Marx's own design begins. Conversely, this historical sketch turned out, as reflected in the Baconian mirror, to yield an image of Marx's vision which the *Thesen über Feuerbach* certainly adumbrate but do not develop. Here we come up against a peculiar difficulty which makes it extremely hard to get at Marx's ideas. In the first series of lectures I referred to his "socratic" method, which he applied to human society as a whole. Although Marx left behind an enormous body of writing, it gives no direct access to the central core of his maieutic method, just as we know Socrates only through the writings of Plato. There are various aspects to this problem. I mention three of them here.

At a philosophical level, the problem is comparable with the one we encounter, for instance, in acquainting ourselves with the thinking of Kant and Hegel, to mention only two philosophers who have a close relation to Marx's method. By using terms like "critique" and "dialectic", one can of course give some indication of the work of these two philosophers respectively; but method, content and result are so indissolubly bound up together that these terms only assume a meaning when we follow the actual workings of their philosophy and from that read off indirectly, as it were, what is entailed in the case of Kant by "critique" and in that of Hegel by "dialectic".

With Marx the problem is duplicated, in that his "critique" and "dialectic" are fundamentally connected with a "materialism" that requires to be understood by strict analogy with the "materialism" of natural science *qua* experimental knowledge under the control of a rational method. Just as we do not get to understand science from the "results" it provides, but only by ourselves conducting experimental research or following it step by step, so one can only get to know Marx's critical method by following closely how it works, which means in effect, tracing the course taken by his "critique of political economy".

This by no means spells an end to our difficulties, however; it is here that they really begin. The fundamental distinction between physical science and social science aggravates the already doubled problem, triples it in fact. The *sui generis* character of the human as opposed to the natural world makes necessary a *sui generis* method, if its secrets are to be unlocked. The difficulty is that of a paradox: on the one hand, we have to dispel the error that we have direct access to the reality that is man—which is after all "our own" reality—through self-contemplation and speculation; on the other hand, the suggestion must be resisted that the human reality might be assessed with the same method as physical science employs in its approach to the reality of nature.

If to all that we add the full tally of mounting resistance and misunderstanding which Marx's "critique of earth" must inevitably arouse, because as terrestrial beings we are ourselves the direct object of that critique, then we shall have some impression of the minefield barring access to Marx's critical method. We shall let be for the present these resistant attitudes and misconceptions, in so far as they are of an "ideological" character; for they only distract us from the essential problem, three relevant aspects of which I have indicated.

For a start, I should point out the fundamental connection of the threefold problem of the "critique of earth", already outlined, with the "critique of heaven". To put it another way, the "critique of political economy" simply cannot be detached from the "critique of theology". Here is a serious impediment for the theologian who is not well up in the special field of economics. We have here a situation with a whole history behind it; and how that situation has come about has already been indicated in Marx's outline of the history of English materialism, which he sees as starting with the scholastic theology of Duns Scotus.

We might also give some account of this course of events in terms of the historical background to the Gifford Lectures, in the context of which these present lectures are being given. The aim of the lectures was defined by Lord Gifford as promoting the study of natural theology. This he defined as "the knowledge of God ... of his nature and attributes, the knowledge of the relations which men and the whole universe bear to Him, the knowledge of the nature and foundation of ethics and morals, and of all obligations and duties thence arising". He was uttering his deep-rooted conviction that this knowledge, provided it is genuinely anchored in feeling and put into practice, is the means to man's greatest wellbeing and the guarantee of his progress.

The foundation document was drawn up by Lord Gifford in 1887. In the period of almost a century which separates us from that time, a process of emancipation and of secularization has taken place, where the modern scientific disciplines are concerned, that has set the aims and purposes proposed by the founder in a radically altered situation. The definition of "natural theology", in particular, can only be understood in the context of a historical background and a course of development which take us back to the theology of the Middle Ages. An illustration of this is the emancipation of economics as a science—an example directly linked with the issue which concerns us now, namely, the connection between the critique of theology and the critique of economics.

In his monumental, posthumously published work, the

History of Economic Analysis, Joseph Schumpeter sketches the origins of the science of economics and its roots in scholasticism. Whereas the economic sociology of the late scholastic period was mainly an elaboration of the doctrine developed in the thirteenth century, "pure" economics was peculiarly the creation of this later period. Within the framework of the systems of moral theology and law developed by the scholastic theologians, economics acquired a distinct if not separate existence. This is why one might describe the theologians of later scholasticism as the "founders" of economics as a science. Indeed they laid for it a firmer basis than did a number of "lay" economists of subsequent generations; a substantial part of the economics of the second half of the nineteenth century would have been developed more rapidly and with less exertion if late scholasticism had been taken as the basis on which to build.

The modern history of the system of natural law exhibits a continuity from scholasticism up to the nineteenth century. Nevertheless, it underwent a gradual disintegration or, at any rate, transformation. If, to begin with, it was a comprehensive system within which all non-juridical subjects were assigned a subsidiary place, in the eighteenth century the flood of material and the opening up of new fields of enquiry and research broke open this outer framework; and "natural jurisprudence" became simply a specialism within a new setting which no longer had to do in the first instance with law. This new entity came to be known, especially in Germany and Scotland, as "Moral Philosophy", where the term "philosophy" was taken in its traditional sense of the total sum of sciences (Thomas' *philosophicae disciplinae*). Thus, moral philosophy comprised, roughly speaking, the social sciences (the sciences of "mind" and "society"), as opposed to "natural philosophy" which included the physical sciences and mathematics. Moral philosophy was the subject of a standard course in the university curricula and consisted for the most part of natural theology, natural ethics, natural jurisprudence and policy or "police", which included economics (economy) and also public finance ("revenue"). Like his mentor at Glasgow University, Francis Hutcheson, Adam Smith taught moral philosophy; and like Hutcheson's work, Adam Smith's *The Wealth of Nations* formed part of a larger systematic whole, from which it had been, as it were, uncoupled. Thus the universal social science of the old scholastics and of the philosophers of natural law continued in a new form. But it was not destined to survive for long. Although during the first half of the nineteenth century moral philosophy still kept its place in the university curriculum, even towards the end of the eighteenth century it had already lost its old importance and position. Its downfall was caused by the same factor that had finally exploded the natural-law system: perpetually increasing specialization. Even Adam Smith realized that he was no longer in a position to continue the work of his mentor in developing a complete system of moral philosophy or social science as a single whole. The time for that had gone. The science of economics now demanded a man's full time and energy.

It is against the background of all this history that the problem with which Marx's life's work confronts us becomes clearly recognizable. Marx was not an economist by profession; but as soon as he had finished his university studies, it was with an almost superhuman degree of effort that he turned to the study of economics and made it his own. This was not something all on its own, but was a necessary outcome of the study he had pursued at the university, namely, that of jurisprudence. Even that professional study, however, Marx had not taken up as a specialism but in conjunction with, and as an aspect of, his philosophical and historical studies. So we can see in Marx's life, from the very outset of his studies, an operative passion for doing "philosophy" in the sense in which the Middle Ages had understood it: that is to say, as the total sum of the sciences. And at the same time he is impelled by what is really a modern enthusiasm to become a specialist in the discipline of economics. Like the boatswain in one of his youthful poems, he tries with heroic determination to row against the stream of modern history and to undo the emancipation of economics as a science. Behind it all is his vision of a human society in which the abstraction of bourgeois existence is overcome and it is once again possible to lead an all-round, human existence.

It is this tendency in Marx's *Critique of Political Economy*—the tendency to row against the stream of modern history—that constitutes the main problem for an adequate assessment of it.

At the same time, implied in the problem is a challenge to theology to undergo such a transformation that it is rendered capable of describing the dimensions of the problem; a transformation that in turn will create a framework in which the problem can be answered; a framework within which the critique of heaven and the critique of earth have a place together. Nowadays we seem to be further away from this than ever, further than was the period in which Lord Gifford set out to promote the study of "natural theology", much further than was the age in which Adam Smith taught moral philosophy.

I am far from deluding myself that the problem is being solved; for the first thing is to see that it is stated as clearly as possible. It is interesting and also encouraging to note that Joseph Schumpeter too encountered this same problem. As the title of his great work indicates, his intention is to describe the history of "economic analysis". He means by this "pure economics"; and he distinguishes this "pure economic analysis" from "the systems of political economy" and from "economic thinking". By "systems of political economy" he understands the setting out of a comprehensive series of economic measures or enactments as regulated by certain (normative) principles, like those of economic liberalism, say, or of socialism, and so forth. Schumpeter regards Adam Smith's *The Wealth of Nations* as one such attempt to devise a system of political economy. As a historian of "economic analysis", Schumpeter is only concerned with it to the extent that Smith's work contains this pure analysis. The rest Schumpeter sees as no more than particular expressions of the ideology of his age and of his country, which for another time and another country is of no value whatever.

The same fate that lay in store for Adam Smith is apportioned in Schumpeter's work to Karl Marx's *Critique of Political Economy*. He praises Marx as a born economic analyst, but is interested only in that element. It necessitates cutting up Marx's work into small pieces and distributing it over a large number of aspects of economics, which are dealt with one by one, in separate chapters and sections. Schumpeter sees nothing wrong with this compartmentalizing method where economists as a whole are concerned; but he makes one exception—and that is Marx. The trouble, as Schumpeter sees it, is that, when Marx's work is dealt with by this method, an essential element is lost, an element indispensable to a proper understanding. In Marx's case, it is "the totality of his vision which as a totality asserts itself in every detail, and that very fact provides the deepest reason why everyone, friend or foe, who makes a study of his work falls beneath its intellectual spell". The recognition here of the *sui generis* character of Marx's work, which cannot be contained within the framework of Schumpeter's historiography and still less within the categories of "pure economic analysis", seems to me a more accurate, fairer representation, and in a sense a corrective to the characterization offered some years previously by the same author. In *Capitalism, Socialism and Democracy* not only is Marxism branded as "a religion", but Marx's doctrine is expounded in four chapters that divide Marx into four: the prophet, the sociologist, the economist and the teacher; a procedural method that guarantees in advance that the *unity* of Marx's work will remain out of the picture.

Karl Popper goes further, and on the basis of this first aspect tries to arrive at a complete evaluation of Marx's work. The second part of his study, *The Open Society and its Enemies*, rejects Marxism as "the purest, the most developed and the most dangerous form of historicism", by which he meant "the claim that the realm of social sciences coincides with that of the historical or evolutionary method, and especially with historical prophecy". Marx was indeed a prophet, a false prophet. Robert Tucker (in *Philosophy and Myth in Karl Marx*) goes further still, and reaches the conclusion that Marx put history in reverse and reduced philosophy to its origins in myth. It is typical of mythical or mythological thinking that "something which of its nature forms part of the inner reality of man is apprehended as existing outside him, that a drama of man's inner life is experienced and is depicted as though it were taking place in the outer world".

With these few examples, which I have purposely chosen from authors who really do make an effort to reach a sound and responsible judgment on Marx's work, I must be content. When we compare Schumpeter's belated recognition of Marx's thought as a totality which eludes the grasp of his "history of economic analysis", with such verdicts as "false prophet" and "mythical thinking", then we have to note a fundamental distinction. The idea that Marx's method confronts us with an unsolved problem for which we need a different kind of approach, different categories, in order to describe it adequately (not to speak of finding a solution), is completely buried under Popper's and Tucker's qualifications. At the close of their studies we see the victorious author in the arena, stooping over his thoroughly defeated victim, Karl Marx.

Against the background of the development of a century of Marxism such a posture is quite understandable. There can be no doubt that Marx's thinking has been turned upside down and transformed into the very thing it was meant to unmask: a total ideology. Iring Fetscher, with texts to illustrate his point, has traced the process step by step (in *Von Marx zur Sowjetideologie*): from Hegel to Marx; from Marxism to Leninism; from Stalinism to neo-Leninism. The author sees no reason in this development to turn further away from Marxism or to reject it; on the contrary, in post-war Germany Fetscher has been an important advocate of a renewed study of Marx's thought; and he is one of the leading thinkers who have promoted an intensive study of Marx in the context of German protestantism.

I said a few things in my first lecture on "the critique of heaven" about the positive significance of the neo-Marxist renaissance in both East and West and about the dialogue between Marxists and Christians that has gone along with it. In the context of the "critique of earth" what have to be pinpointed are the limitations of that dialogue. On the one hand, one can detect on the Christian side a tendency—in line with the old religious socialism but deploying all the apparatus provided by the new theology since the nineteen-thirties—to interpret Marx's critique of religion as a non-essential element in his thinking. On the other hand, there are indications that a latent Hegelian renaissance is forming a bridge by means of which Christian theology and neo-Marxist philosophy may begin to meet. This link would seem to open up to Christian theology the possibility of pushing forward to the position of Feuerbach's critique of religion and towards a politico-economic interpretation—rediscovered partly with the help of Georg Lukacz—of in particular the young Hegel.

As against that, there are still no signs that any real attempt is being made on the theological side to see Marx's critique of political economy as the most important element of his work. I will mention three studies which, though they have differing backgrounds, evince a fundamental concern with the total method of Marx's critique of economics. The French Marxist, Louis Althusser has written (together with Etienne Balibar) a kind of manual on how *Das Kapital* should be read as a *philosophical* work (*Lire le Capital*), and has tried to trace the structure of Marx's critique. From the hand of the Czech philosopher, Jindřich Zelený, there has appeared a study of the "logic of science" in Marx, which examines the structure of *Das Kapital* in association with that of Marx's earlier work (German translation, *Die Wissenschaftslogik dei Marx und "Das Kapital"*). Lastly, also deserving of mention is Helmut Reichelt's study, *Zur logischen Struktur des Kapitalbegriffs dei Karl Marx*, the work of a younger generation of Frankfurt sociologists that marks an important turning-point *vis-à-vis* the prevailing trend in the *Frankfurter Schule* to detach the critical dialectic from the critique of political economy.

There is as yet no evidence that theology is in a position to reply to studies of this kind. What is in any event necessary for that is an intensive encounter between theology and economics. Marx's "critique of earth" impels us towards a transformation of our theological categories and an interdisciplinary critique of our theological method.

2

Reprobate Materialism

IN the preface to his *Zur Kritik der politischen Ökonomie*, 1859, Marx gives a brief account of his studies in political economy and their development. He starts: "My specialism was the study of law, which I found to be even less relevant than the study of philosophy and history. It was in the year 1842/43 that as editor of the *Rheinische Zeitung* I was first faced with the problem of having to talk about so called material interests. The discussions in the *Rheinische Landtag* (The Diet of the Rhineland) on wood-stealing and the distribution of land-holdings, the official argument which Herr von Schaper, at that time President of the Rhine Province, began to conduct with the *Rheinische Zeitung* à propos of the situation of the peasants in the Moselle area, and lastly debates on free trade and the imposition of protective tariffs—these were what first occasioned my concern for, and study of, economic problems."

The deliberations of the *Rheinische Landtag* regarding the theft of wood formed the subject of a lengthy article he serialized in the *Rheinische Zeitung* during October/November 1842. Characteristically enough, he mentions only this article as being the first step on the road of his economic and political studies, ignoring the two which preceded it. The first of them deals with the freedom of the press and sharply criticizes the reactionary Prussian censorship. "A censored press is always a bad thing, even if the fruits of it are good . . . a free press is always a good thing, even if its fruits are bad . . . A castrato is a poor sort of a man, even if he does have a good voice. Nature is good, even though it may produce abortions. The very essence of a free press is the characterful, rational, moral essence of freedom. The character of a censored press is the character*less* non-essence of unfreedom, it is a civilized monster, a sweet-smelling abortion." The article ends by arraigning the *Rheinische Landtag* for stifling the freedom of the press by its half-hearted attitude, wavering between "the deliberate obduracy of privilege and the natural impotence of a quasi-liberalism".

The second article was banned by the censor; and the manuscript has been lost. It concerned what were known as the "ecclesiastical troubles" or "Cologne troubles" (i.e. riots), a protracted conflict between the Prussian government and the Catholic Church regarding the children of mixed marriages. It ended with the government capitulating. "Prussia has kissed the pope's slipper while the whole world looks on," was Marx's comment, in a letter to Ruge. He characterizes the article as providing evidence that "the protagonists of the state have taken an ecclesiastical standpoint, the Church's champions a political one."

Compared with these two articles, breathing as they do the spirit of a radical liberalism, the third one (which analyses the laws enacted against wood-stealing and the debates on this subject in the *Rheinische Landtag*) is indeed a turning-point. Since Marx himself described this crucial change as a first step on the road of his politico-economic studies and the article in question as the first occasion he had to concern himself with economic issues, it provides precious material evidence for getting at what Marx understood by "economic problems" and what his approach to political economy was. As we shall see, this article also contains, and sets within a very concrete context, the principal elements out of which he was to build his *Critique of Hegel's Philosophy of Law* in the next two years. Because of all this, we are justified in discussing the article in some detail.

In point of fact, it originally had a broader purpose, embracing, in addition to the legislation against wood-stealing, the question of the distribution of land-holdings. Marx was able to execute only half this plan; for shortly before publication he was appointed editor of the *Rheinische Zeitung* and so never had time to finish the article. This deprived it, in a sense, of its climactic element, which should have consisted of an extensive analysis of the whole background to the problem of wood-stealing. The truth is that it involved a profound and ruthless conflict between the law of custom, stemming from the Middle Ages, which stood for communal ownership of the land, and the rise of capitalism. On the one hand, the peasants' right to parcel out the land among themselves was being threatened; while, on the other hand, legal action on an enormous scale was being instituted against the "theft" (as it was called) of wood, something the people regarded as a centuries-old inalienable communal right. The Prussian government had drafted a number of laws about this and had laid them before the *Rheinische Landtag*. This body consisted exclusively of land-owners; and the manner in which it employed its legislative powers to bolster the private interests of its members prompted Marx to take pen in hand.

He begins by noting the difference from the two earlier articles on the freedom of the press and the church troubles. The question of the distribution of land-holdings he calls "a life-size version of the real, earthly problem"; and the article in question is set *auf ebener Erde*, at ground level. These turns of phrase are, of course, an allusion to the fact that while the immediate problems may relate to the ownership of land, behind it all there lies an antithesis which in years to come Marx will present in the context of his *Critique of Hegel's Philosophy of Law*: namely, the contrast between a "critique of heaven" and a "critique of earth". If his critical analysis of the politico-legal problem of the freedom of the press and that of the church–state relationship came within the former category, now at last he has manifestly reached the level of the "critique of earth". From this we may infer that in the contrast between the two levels a great deal more is entailed than the mere opposition of the ideal and the material, or the antithesis between religion and law, theology and politics. For the two earlier articles are dealing in whole or in part with purely political issues. In contrast, it is clear from the way Marx handles what he calls this "down-to-earth" problem of the right to possession of land that the "critique of heaven" has an essential role to play in it.

This indissoluble link is apparent from the first pages, where

Marx is commenting on the discussions in the *Landtag* as to precisely what is signified by the term "wood-stealing". After some debate, the deputies were agreed that misappropriating dead wood, even just picking it up, comes under the heading of theft and deserves to be punished just as much as the misappropriation of living, green wood which has not yet been cut down. It was argued, in support of this, that all too often young trees were damaged with a chopper so that the wood would die and could later on be treated as dead wood. Marx observes that a more elegant, simpler way could scarcely be conceived of subordinating the rights of human beings to those of young trees. "On the one hand there is the necessary consequence of cutting off a whole lot of human beings, quite undisposed to crime, from the green tree of moral conduct and consigning them like so much dead wood to the hell of criminality, evil and wretchedness. On the other hand is the possibility that a few young trees will be maltreated. It need hardly be pointed out that the gods of wood carry the day, and down go the human sacrifices!"

This frontal attack, touching the very core of the whole juridical question, forms the introduction to an argument about the nature of property and ownership. There is a cardinal distinction between living wood and dead wood. To appropriate the former, one is obliged to separate it from its organic context by a violent encroachment. But in the case of dead wood there is no deprivation of proprietory rights involved, because that has already taken place. The person who gathers dead wood is simply executing a judgment pronounced by the nature of the property itself; after all, you simply own the tree, but the tree no longer itself possesses any branches. That is why woodgathering is essentially different from wood-stealing. The law is not absolved from the universal obligation to tell the truth. Indeed, the law actually has a twofold obligation; for it makes universal and authentic pronouncements as to the true nature of things. The true nature of things, therefore, cannot be regulated by the law, but the law must be regulated by the true nature of things. Should the law insist on calling an action that is hardly an offence committed against the wood "wood-stealing", then the law is lying, and the poor person is sacrificed to a legal fiction. As Montesquieu said, there are two sorts of corruption. One consists in the people disobeying the laws, the other in their being depraved by the laws. This latter ill is irremediable; for the remedy is itself contaminated.

This juridical untruth, Marx goes on to argue, has the further consequence of bringing the law as a whole into discredit. By misusing the category "theft" in this way, it makes real theft something admissible in the popular view. Indeed, the consequences are even more far-reaching; for the whole bottom is knocked from under the category "property" in this manner. If every infringement of property is to be equated without distinction and without more particular definition with theft, then is not all private property and ownership theft? Am I not perhaps through my private ownership of property depriving someone else of this property? May it not be that I am thereby infringing his right to ownership?

So Marx gets to the heart of the problem: namely, the question of what constitutes the title to property of those many people who own no property at all. He begins his argument with an attack on the scholarly and all-too-ready serviceability of those who pass for historians, who claim to have discovered the philosophers' stone, enabling them to convert every gross appropriation into the pure gold of justice and of law. In other words, the field of battle is the history of the law of property. Against the host of historians, who on historical grounds champion the rights of the property-owners, he enters the arena on behalf of the poor, politically and socially dispossessed masses. "In behalf of poverty we assert and lay claim to the *law of custom*, and that not as something merely local but as the law of custom proper to poverty in every land. We would go further and assert that the law of custom is naturally the law of these undermost, dispossessed and elementary masses and of them alone."

Once again Marx imports an apparently foreign element into the area of juridical argument. The first time, it was his cry about people being offered in sacrifice to the gods of wood which appeared to go beyond the merely legal context. This time, it is his introduction of so apparently opaque and obscure a factor as the law of custom. Yet his whole line of argument hinges fundamentally on those two things, or pivots around them. The first lies in the plane of the "critique of heaven", the

37

second touches the "critique of earth". Although on a different level and in opposite directions, the two pivots are continuous with each other; and the door which hinges on them both constitutes a single, coherent train of ideas. Both pivots are indispensable; if one is not there, the door comes off its hinges.

For this reason, we are going to take a closer look at the passage about the law of custom. Marx is very well aware that his importing this element threatens to reduce the system of jurisprudence to chaos and that his own weapons could be turned against him. Does he not himself leap to the defence of the truth and integrity of the judicial system and legislature? And so he hastens to explain that there is a very big difference between one law of custom and another law of custom. There is, after all, a customary law of privilege, of the privileged classes: their customs, so called, are usages in conflict with law and justice. Their "customs" date from the earliest period of man's history, when it was still a part of natural history. Actually, that was the bestial period of human history. The gods concealed themselves under the guise of animals and, just as in the animal kingdom, mankind was divided into a number of mutually hostile and divergent types. It is the period of basic inequality and serfdom. The period of serfdom requires laws of serfdom. Whilst the law of men is the very being of freedom, the animal law is the being of bondage, of unfreedom. Feudalism, in the broadest sense of the word, is the "animal kingdom" of the mind and spirit, the world of a divided and separated mankind, contrasted with the world of a humanity which *qua* humanity is distinguished from the animal kingdom, a humanity whose inequality is nothing other than the spectrum of colours presented by the rainbow of equality. Just as in the animal kingdom of nature the drones are put to death by the worker bees, conversely in the "animal kingdom" of the spirit, that is, feudalism, the workers are mortified by the drones.

The conclusion is obvious: when the privileged try to defeat justice as determined by the law and appeal to their customary rights, instead of any human content, they are insisting upon a law in animal or bestial guise, a form that is now reduced to the unreality of an animal mask.

We must linger for a moment over this last observation; for it

38

enshrines a subtle historical dialectic. The distinction between the "animal form or aspect" and an "animal mask" is the distinction between the animal period of man's history, in which the gods disguised themselves as animals, that is, in real animal guises, and modern times, in which the spirit of that animal period still hovers around, although its reality and substance have disappeared. Anyone who today, in a secularized world, still tries to make use of the thought-forms of a bygone phase of human history is at best continuing to wear a mask. It is the distinction between real, living religion and ideology. The former must take its historic course and pass away; the latter can and must be "un-masked".

Just as the period of feudalism, of the spirit's "animal kingdom", belongs to the past, so too the chief laws of custom cannot persist; for what they import runs counter to the form of universal law. That is not to deny that what is a right of custom may become a general law of the land. A reasonable right of custom in the period of general laws is nothing other than the habitual practice of that right as embodied in the law; for a right does not cease to be a "custom" because it has assumed the status of law—it has only ceased to be *simply and solely* a customary right. The right itself no longer depends on whether the custom happens to be reasonable or not; but the custom is rendered reasonable because the right becomes law, because the custom has become "a custom of the state".

Thus far Marx's argument accords closely with the thinking of the Enlightenment, based as that was on the universal validity of natural law. The privileged classes cannot lay claim to privileges that fail to accord with the universal rights of men. But his argument is a two-edged sword; and it is with the *other* edge that he delivers the decisive thrust. He had in fact launched his argument by postulating that the dispossessed masses have no other law at their disposal than the law or right of custom.

On closer examination we can see that the law of custom, even where grounded on reason, cannot be subsumed completely within the law of the land. There is an indivisible remainder; or to put it another way, the right of custom (or "common law") as a *distinct and separate area* alongside the law as defined in statutes only accords with reason as a right

39

existing *alongside* and *outside* the *law*, since the custom or usage is the *anticipation* of a statutory right. In the case of the privileged classes, there can be no question of any such anticipation, for they have got not only their reasonable rights recognized in law but even their unreasonable privileges which they have quite arbitrarily appropriated to themselves. If, therefore, these eminent rights of custom are in conflict with the notion of a reasonable right, the converse is true of the customary rights of poverty: they are rights in opposition to the customary practice of positive law. Their substance is not opposed to the form of the law but rather to their own formlessness. The form of the law is not in conflict with the substance of the customary rights of poverty, but their substance has simply not as yet got as far as assuming the form of statutory law.

For supporting evidence, Marx appeals to the history of the Old-Germanic legal system, the so-called *leges barbarorum*, laws which came into existence between the fifth and ninth centuries and, for the most part, are the customary laws of the various Germanic tribes, formulated and set down in writing. The description "laws of the barbarians" distinguishes this body of Germanic law from the *leges Romanorum*, which applied to the Roman population among the German tribes. It is not difficult to see that the enlightened legislation of modern times is decidedly partial in its use of this Germanic law of custom. Indeed, that law constitutes a principal source of the customary rights of the poor.

The most liberal legislation has confined itself, where civil law is concerned, to formulating the rights taken over from the past and to giving them a general validity. Where the legislature found no rights, none were conceded. It discontinued purely private usages, but in so doing overlooked an essential point. The fact is that whilst class injustice took the form of wilful and arbitrary appropriation, the rights of those who had no social standing at all amounted only to incidental concessions. The practice of liberal legislation was proper enough *vis-à-vis* those who enjoyed customary rights beyond the law, but it was quite improper when it came to those who had such rights "without the law". If it changed arbitrarily acquired privileges, in so far as a reasonable element of justice was to be found in them, into legal entitlements, such legislation ought

40

also to have changed the fortuitous concessions made to the dispossessed into obligatory concessions.

This line of argument becomes clearer if one considers the example provided by the monasteries. They are abolished, their assets are secularized; and it is right that this should happen. But people omitted to turn the incidental relief that the poor obtained in the monasteries into some other positive source of possession. Whilst the assets of the monasteries were turned over to private ownership and in one way or another the monasteries were compensated for this, no one took care to compensate the poor who lived off the monasteries. Instead, a new limitation was imposed on them; and they found themselves cut off from an ancient right. The same thing happened in every case where what had been privileges were made into (statutory) rights. Of course, this relief given to the poor was an ill circumstance in so far as one of their rights had been turned into a fortuitous concession; but the positive aspect was that they were enjoying some relief. Liberal legislation did put an end to a bad state of affairs; yet the positive side of it was not counterbalanced by transforming what had been a happy accident into an obligation, but by abstracting from the contingency.

The term "abstracting" (*abstrahieren*) has a central function in Marx's thinking. In the first set of lectures we saw it was of fundamental importance in the "critique of heaven". It is doubly significant, therefore, that we now encounter the term again in the context of a "critique of earth" and, more specifically, of a "critique of law". The significance of the term becomes even more telling when we consider that Marx has deliberately chosen as the subject of his critique in this passage the history of the secularization of the monasteries.

In our day, the term "secularization" is used so generally to describe the secularizing process which in modern culture has been occurring over the whole field of things religious and ecclesiastical that we tend to forget that the origin of the term is a material one, namely, the appropriation by the secular arm of church property. In the history of the term, the "critique of earth" precedes the "critique of heaven". Marx takes us back to the origin of the term but at the same time provides the historical development with a critical commentary. What actually concerns him is not the material spoliation of the monasteries, the appropriation of their assets, but simply and solely the legal form given to this "secularization". Here he puts his finger on an aspect of modern legal justice linked very closely with the principle of universality and obligation. To the extent that legislation has abolished privileges fortuitously and arbitrarily acquired, and has turned the reasonable law of custom into generally applicable positive law, it has indeed abstracted from the chance circumstance which in times past, in "the animal kingdom of the spirit", had been elevated to the status of a legal right; but at the same time it enshrined universal rights in positive law. That is to say, the principle of universality, instead of remaining an abstraction, was concreted in positive, enforceable law. But this concretizing process was incomplete, was in fact very one-sided; for no steps were taken to procure legal rights, in the form of concretized, positive law, for those who had previously enjoyed no privileges at all. Men simply "abstracted" from the total deprivation or absence of rights which was the lot of the poor; and the sheer concrete nature of poverty was simply overlooked. Through this method of abstracting, secularization became a very one-sided affair—one-sided, that is, in the way the abstraction of universality and reasonable obligation was concretized in favour of those who enjoy the privilege of having property. The victims of the abstraction were the property-less people, the dispossessed, who in the feudal period had enjoyed very concrete, albeit arbitrary and fortuitous, concessions.

But Marx goes further than that. He shows that this remarkable omission in modern law-making is not a historical accident or a legislative defect but is fundamentally and indissolubly bound up with the very nature of abstract private law. The one-sided character of such liberal legislation was inevitable, because all the customary rights of the poor were based on the fact that a particular kind of property-ownership was indeterminate in character: it was neither expressly private nor expressly public. This mixture of private and public rights is something we encounter in all medieval institutions. The faculty which liberal legislation brought to bear on such ambiguous forms was that of good sense or judgment. Now this is not only one-sided—this faculty of judgment or intelligence—it is its essential function actually to make the world a

thoroughly one-sided business—a great and admirable enterprise; for it is this one-sidedness that alone can give form to the
particular and distinct, wresting it, as it were, out of the
inorganic slime of the (undifferentiated) whole. The character
of things *per se* is a product of "judgment" or understanding.
Each thing must isolate itself and be isolated, in order to be
something. Whilst the understanding channels every part of
the world's content in an enduring exactness and, as it were,
solidifies the fluid essence of things, it brings out the multi-
tudinousness of the world; for the world would not be many-
sided, were it not for its many one-sidednesses.

The term "judgment", which Marx introduces here, has to
be interpreted in the context of the contrast that has been
treated as self-evident in German idealist philosophy since
Kant: the contrast between *Verstand* and *Vernunft*, between
judgment and reason. That is likewise clear from the account
Marx gives of the typical function of our "judgment". The
German language offers a peculiar difficulty here, in that there
is no adjective from the noun *Verstand* that adequately represents the contrast with *Vernunft*. The adjective *verständlich* means
"intelligible" and does not express what relates to judgment as
opposed to reason. In the preceding argument Marx makes
repeated use of the term *vernünftiges Recht*, whereas it now
appears from his argument that what he really means is "that
which evinces understanding", at any rate in those instances
where he has liberal legislation in view. There is an ambiguity,
however, in his use of the term *vernünftiges Recht*, in so far as the
essential grounds of his argument do indeed require this to refer
to the *Vernunft* that transcends *Verstand*. The truth is that on
this concept depends his central thesis that customary rights as
a distinct area next the rights that are determined in law are
alone "reasonable", "grounded in reason", *vernünftig*, where the
rights in question exist *beside* and *outside* the statutory law, and
where the custom is the *anticipation* of a legal right. That is the
customary right of poverty, the only right to which those who
have no rights can appeal. Poverty must appeal to a law of
custom; and at the same time it anticipates an as yet non-
existent law which cannot be comprehended by the enlightened,
liberal *Verstand* and by the legislation that is a product of it.

We might at this juncture be inclined to draw the

conclusion: the law of the poor is the law of *Vernunft*, of reason. Marx's line of argument must surely seem to lead to that conclusion. So it is the more significant that Marx does not in fact formulate this logical conclusion. We simply do not find the term *Vernunft* included anywhere in his argument; and the omission is certainly not accidental; on the contrary, it is of a piece with the peculiar structure of his critique. Precisely where we would expect the apotheosis of his argument in an appeal to *Vernunft*, we find the very last term we would have looked for, "instinct". Instead of ascending above judgment and understanding to the sphere of *Vernunft*, of Reason, in the manner of idealist philosophy, he appears to drop down to the bottom rung, where the human realm still touches that of the animals, that is, to the faculty of instinct.

But we want to follow in the wake of his argument, not to anticipate it. The faculty of understanding has performed a major and essential task by terminating the ambiguous and indeterminate formations of ownership, especially through its application of the categories of abstract private law, the pattern of which it was able to take over ready-made from Roman law. This legislative "know-how" saw itself as entitled to do away with the obligations towards the poorer class of people that went along with this indeterminate form of ownership, all the more justly where such ownership was also relieved of its political privileges. However, in doing all this the legislators overlooked a cardinal point: they forgot that even from the standpoint purely of private law, what was involved here was a two-sided affair: the rights under private law of the owner and the parallel rights of the non-owner. Furthermore, one has to remember that nowhere has legislation annulled the privileges of property-owning in constitutional law, but has merely stripped them of their hit-or-miss character and made them officially respectable. When, however, the faculty of judgment quite rightly enforced its principle of unity against the duplicity and incongruity of medieval law, it missed the fact that there are objects of ownership which in the nature of things can never acquire the character of having been marked out for private ownership. They are those objects that, by virtue of their elementary nature and their contingent existence, come under the heading of the right to occupation, that is, the right of the class which is excluded from all other ownership by that very same occupation-right and has the same position in civil society as those objects have in nature.

Thus there turns out to be a remarkable *harmonia prestabilita*, a pre-established harmony, between a category of objects which by their very nature fall outside every definition of private property and a category of subjects which, because of the nature of civil society, falls outside every form of private law. The faculty by which those subjects grasp the pre-established harmony is instinct. We shall now pursue Marx's argument further still in the ensuing passage.

It will be noted that the customs, which are those of the impoverished class as a whole, manage with infallible instinct to grasp ownership in its unresolved aspect; it will not just be noted that this class feels an urge to satisfy a natural need, but equally that it feels the need to satisfy an urge to justice, an instinct for justice. The dead wood may serve as an example here. It has no more organic relation to the living tree than the shed skin has to the snake. In the dry twigs and branches that have been snapped off and detached from organic life, in contrast to the sap-filled trunks and trees which organically assimilate air, light, water and soil to their own distinctive form and individual life, nature portrays, as it were, the contrast between poverty and riches. Human poverty senses this kinship and from this sense of affinity infers its right to possession; seeing the physical-cum-organic wealth marked out for the proprietor, it cites physical poverty as constituting the necessity and the accident of circumstance pertaining to it. In this random activity on the part of elementary forces, it descries a not unfriendly power, more humane than that of man himself. Instead of the fortuitous caprice of privilege there comes the chance play of the elements that snatch away from private ownership what it will no longer cede of its own accord. Just as the alms tossed on to the pavement are not destined for the rich, neither are these charitable gifts of nature. But even in her activity, poverty finds a kind of justice. In the very process of gathering, the elementary class of human society chooses a regulative position *vis-à-vis* the elementary power of nature. The same is true of the products which, growing wild, are a purely accidental and marginal aspect of property, and because

45

of their very triviality do not form an object of activity on the part of the real owner. It is just the same with gleaning during harvest, and customary rights of that sort.

Thus, in these customs of the poor is reflected an instinctive sense of justice. Their roots are positive and legitimate; and the form assumed by the customary right accords that much the more closely with nature here, because the very existence of an impoverished class is to this extent simply a "custom" or usage of civil society, a custom which within the orbit of considered, political organization has not so far found an adequate place.

With this conclusion the circle of Marx's argumentation, which began with an appeal to the law of custom, is completed. I have made a point of presenting the argument as literally as possible; but the German text contains an amount of subtle word-play that is in danger of being lost in translation. Moreover, the argument itself is of such fundamental importance to the structure and method of Marx's critique of law that it is well worth while recapitulating its main elements.

In the first place, we should take note of his distinctive use of the concept of "nature". It is not difficult to show from other writings of the young Marx as well that he bases himself on the theory of natural law or natural right that had filtered through from the legal and political thinking of the philosophy of the Enlightenment. I shall come back to this later on in a different connection. For the moment we are concerned simply with the interpretation of natural law in the context of the argument we have just been following. We have already encountered the expression "rightful nature of things": "The rightful nature of things cannot be assimilated to the law, but the law must adjust itself to the rightful nature of things." The law must speak truth, because the law is "the universal and authentic spokesman on the rightful nature of things". In point of fact, the term "rightful nature of things" is the literal converse and correlate of the concept "natural right" or "natural law". Just as there is a *lex naturalis*, so too is there a *natura legitima*. Nature itself figures human law; and for that very reason human law can and must reflect nature. Man and nature are attuned to each other and marked out for each other. To the naturalism of natural law there corresponds the humanism of the "rightful nature of things".

46

Although both these—natural law and the "rightful nature of things"—are natural and self-evidencing, that does not in the least imply that they are immediately apparent or lie ready to hand. On the contrary, it takes some hard work to allow expression to what is "in the nature of things" and to catch the voice of nature and human nature. This exacting task also goes on as a historical process throughout the course of man's history. When we look more closely, we find the idea of "nature" present in Marx's argument at three different levels which are likewise historical phases.

The lowest level is that of "natural history" (*Naturgeschichte*). On this level the history of mankind was unfolding during that long run of centuries when human society was no more than a "spiritually and mentally animal kingdom" (*geistiges Tierreich*).

The second, more elevated and qualitatively different level is that of "reasoned justice" (*vernünftiges Recht*), a level first attained in human history with the period of civil society and the philosophy of the Enlightenment. Modern, positive law is a product of "legislative judgment" (*gesetzgebende Verstand*), but not simply that: the character of things is itself a product of judgment, of intelligence (*der Charakter der Dinge ist ein Produkt des Verstandes*). The word "character" here has a pregnant meaning that contrasts directly with the term "nature". The understanding, the intelligence, sets its stamp on reality, it gives reality "character"; and only then does reality become comprehensible, graspable, manageable. It is only through the activity of the intelligence that any such thing as a distinct multiplicity of "things" comes to exist. Everything must isolate itself and be isolated in order to be something (*jedes Ding muss sich isolieren und isoliert werden, um etwas zu sein*). Things "are something or other", they have *Dasein*, existence, *that*-ness, only through being distinguished, separated from the whole, through being set apart. We are reminded of Spinoza's words, *omnis determinatio est negatio*, every determination is also a denial. Man's understanding, his intelligence, creates out of the primeval chaos of undifferentiated totality by segregating "things". As it creates, it separates. What we have here, in fact, is the idea of *Verdinglichung* or "reification", which in the writings of subsequent years was to play such a major role in the thinking of the young Marx.

47

However, the inevitable one-sidedness of the activity of the intelligence, entailing as it does an invaluable gain, is at the same time a loss. Not so much because the separating and distinguishing intelligence cannot possibly grasp the whole but because there are "things" on which that intelligence cannot leave any kind of impress: things which differ qualitatively from the "character" of the things defined by the intelligence. Nonetheless, they are most certainly "things", in the sense of real, palpable and perceptible objects, equally as real as the "things" registered by the intelligence. Note that Marx is not alluding here to any mystical realities that are somehow beyond the reach of the intellective faculty. He is not intent on ascending from earth to loftier spheres, but is concerned with material, earthly things. Their qualitative difference from the things perceived by the reasoning intelligence does not lie, therefore, in one or another mystical attribute; but this distinction is a necessary consequence of the intellective faculty's own activity. Whilst man's intelligence creates "things", at the same time, and involuntarily, it gives rise to their opposites. Every determination is at the same time a denial. At the very moment when the intelligence distinguishes a thing, it sets a boundary. And boundaries have the peculiar property of fencing off and separating an "inside" from an "outside". Along with the definition of what it "is", the "thing" is furnished with a determination of what it is *not*. This is implied, actually, in the term "private law"; for the Latin verb *privare* means "to deprive" or "to dispossess", whilst the technical expression for the negative prefix "a-" in words like "a-moral" and "a-theist" is *alpha privans*. Private law, which defines, demarcates, fences off and gives the force of law to private ownership and property, isolates a private territory from the publicly accessible area, strips away the public and communal character of this particular, segregated terrain. Thus all private law is really a *privilegium*, a *pri*vilege. This had already prompted Marx, when faced with a totally undiscriminating approach to the appropriation of any kind of wood in whatever form, to raise the question whether, on the contrary, all private ownership is not in fact theft, because the owner is thereby depriving everyone else of their rights to ownership. During the years that followed, in his critical examination of Proudhon, Marx was to probe yet further into this question.

He turns now to deal with the assertion that all private rights constitute a two-edged sword and have a dual character. Besides the private rights of the owner, there are private rights of the non-owner. That looks like a contradiction in terms, in so far as private rights in law are generally interpreted as being exclusively rights of the owner. Indeed, liberal legislation has not so much abolished the constitutional privileges of the Middle Ages as impressed upon them a bourgeois character, that is, transformed them into *privilegium* in the modern, individualistic sense of modern private law. Certainly that is how the one-sided intellective faculty is bound to envisage it. But, precisely because of its essential one-sidedness, that faculty is blind to the other side of the case. It fails to perceive that there are objects of ownership which by their very nature can never acquire the character of property intended for private ownership (*dass es Gegenstände des Eigentums gibt, die ihrer Natur nach nie den Charakter des vorherbestimmten Privateigentums erlangen können*).

Here we find the concept "nature" used in direct contrast to the concept "character". The intelligence can only comprehend the "character" which it has itself impressed on reality; but it is in no position to recognize the dual nature of its own activity. If the private law of civil society is the positive application of natural law, then the intelligence is blind to the inevitably negative implications of its positive operation. The two-sidedness of natural law contains a paradox, which is bound *per se* to remain hidden and obscured from the intelligence. Nature stands over against nature. Over against the nature that has become "thing", that has acquired a "character", there stands another nature, as it were, the back side or reverse side of nature. Just as we cannot get a back view of ourselves, nor for that matter observe things simultaneously at front and back, so it is impossible for us to see both sides of nature at one and the same time. In order to do so, we have, as it were, to turn nature on its back, see it in reverse.

This puts us on to the third rung of a three-tiered concept of nature that passes through its first phase in the natural history of the "animal kingdom of the spirit" and through its second in a natural law on which the intelligence has set the impress of civil, private law. This third phase presents us with the really distinctive thing, consisting really in a double negation. First, the faculty of intelligence itself negates the natural history of the animal kingdom of the spirit. Now the intelligence is negated in its turn or, better, the involuntary and unconscious negation implied in the activity of the intelligence is offset and converted into a positive factor. It is particularly difficult, however, for the positive element to find expression, since language has already taken its "character" from the intelligence. Therefore we have either to content ourselves with a double negation or we fall back on the terminology which really belongs with the first phase, the phase of natural history and the animal kingdom of the spirit.

This makes intelligible the terms to which Marx has recourse in order to give a positive content to the specific "nature" of the objects of ownership which by definition fall outside the area of private property. These objects have an "elementary being" and an "accidental existence", and for that very reason come under another kind of rights, the "rights of occupation" (*die durch ihr elementarisches Wesen und ihr zufälliges Dasein dem Okkupationsrecht anheimfallen*).

The term "right of occupation" comprises the fundamental contradiction of modern private law. The fact is that a right of occupation is a contradiction in terms. Occupation is arbitrary appropriation, assuming possession of. In principle it is a capricious act which belongs to the category of irresistible power—exerted by a blind fatality. Where occupation becomes a (legal) right, there prevails the maxim that "might is right", there prevails the law of the "animal kingdom of the spirit": "animal" in that might has the force of law; "of the spirit" in that might is elevated to the status of right.

Yet this term is a coin with two faces; and it is the reverse side that brings to light the full range of problems inherent in the obverse. When might comes to be right, in consequence there is a right accruing to powerlessness. The private rights of the owner entail the private rights of the non-owner. It is an inverted right of occupation, namely, the right of the class excluded by the right of occupation from all other ownership (*also dem Okkupationsrecht der Klasse anheimfallen, welche eben durch das Okkupationsrecht von allem andern Eigentum ausgeschlossen ist*).

Does not introducing the "right of occupation" in fact knock the bottom out of justice as such? If *summa ius*, the highest justice, is simply *summa iniuria*, the culmination of injustice, is there then any law in human society other than the law of the jungle? No; this conclusion conflicts with the specific character of Marx's dialectical mode of thinking and misses the whole point of it. For in the first place it is precisely the activity of the intelligence, whereby reality gets its character *qua* "things" impressed upon it, that Marx is here recognizing to be totally necessary. The intellective faculty has a necessary creative function in the humanizing of reality, whether it be that of nature or of human society. In that sense the second rung of the concept of "nature", that of reasoned justice, is really a phase of natural law, in the twofold meaning of "nature" and of "law".

No; Marx does not nullify the rights of reasoning intelligence, judgment (*Verstand*) and the law based on judgment; he simply exposes the unavoidable and essential one-sidedness of intellective activity and of reasoned justice. It is that basic one-sidedness through which alone the intelligence is able to be creatively operative that sets a definitive boundary to it. The intelligence cannot accomplish everything. It can, of course, cast its net over the whole of reality, but there are holes in the net. Reality is essentially a more comprehensive affair than the intelligence can ever grasp, describe or perceive. There will only be an *adequatio rei et intellectus* if we understand by *res* the "thing" with the stamp of the intelligence upon it, and if we reduce *intellectus* to "intelligence", "understanding", "judgment". There is, however, an aspect of reality which eludes that understanding. Marx does not try to make out his case for this in the "heavenly" plane—he does not need to resort to mystical and religious arguments—but he observes simply and exactly what actually happens in nature. If the law of the jungle does prevail in nature, that is by no means the end of it. There is an aspect of the jungle which so far from falling below the level of reasoned justice goes above and beyond it. Thus we encounter the jungle, not only on the first rung of the nature-concept, but also on the third, the highest rung. In the goings-on of the elementary forces there is a friendly power, more humane than man is himself (*in diesem Treiben der elementarischen*

51

Mächte eine befreundete Macht, die humaner ist als die menschliche).
Evidently, not all power is inhumane. There is in nature a
power at work which reasoned justice, in its one-sided effort to
humanize nature and society, passes over. The dead and fallen
wood is a case in point. The storm rips it from the tree with
which it had an organic connection. The play of natural forces
brings about a remarkable sifting process. Whilst the living tree
comes under the private rights, or right of occupation, of the
owner, the torn-off, dead branches accrue to the private rights,
or right of occupation, of the non-owner. In that sense the
right to these dry sticks is wholly a part of natural law, it
simply answers to the provisions of nature, which has provided
this wood especially for gathering. Indeed, the humanity of the
forces of nature is even such that it, as it were, corrects the
inhumane consequences of a humanizing, reasoned justice. The
"chance play of the elements" steps in on behalf of the dispossessed, where the "arbitrary will of the privileged" seeks to
withhold from them an elementary right, a natural right (*An
die Stelle der zufälligen Willkür der Privilegierten ist der Zufall der
Elemente getreten, die von dem Privateigentum abreissen, was es nicht
mehr von sich ablässt*).

How, amid all the capriciousness of the jungle, do we set
about detecting this humanity on nature's part? Can man
develop a special organ for this purpose, a sixth sense? Have we
here, at the third stage of the concept of nature, at last arrived
at the corresponding third stage of humanity, at which man
ascends beyond the intellective level and rises into the sphere of
the Idea? Do we see here at last what is signified by the feeling
for religion; does man possess a latent organ for "higher"
things, a special mystical sense? Are we now penetrating to the
hidden core of the religious *a priori*?

No; nothing of all that. There is no organ whatever, which
man might be thought to possess, that would enable him to
perceive this humane aspect of nature. What does exist, on the
other hand, is a special category of people, the class of those
without property. What also exists is a particular correspondence between this special category of *people* and a special
category of *objects*. The correspondence consists in the fact that
this special class of people occupies in civil society the same
position as this special category of objects does in nature

(welche in der bürgerlichen Gesellschaft dieselbe Stellung einnimmt wie jene Gegenstände in der Natur).

By analogy with the proposition of an *adequatio rei et intellectus* one might express Marx's proposition as an *adequatio naturae et paupertatis*, a correspondence between nature and poverty. Of course, he does mention a special faculty which in man is designed to register this correspondence with nature, namely, instinct. Yet this instinct is not a universal human faculty, as the intelligence would claim to be; it is not a human "capacity" which is inherent in man and which he can "possess", nor a sixth sense alongside the other senses. We must pay close attention to the particular expressions Marx chooses to employ when defining this instinct. In the first place, he does not say that human beings possess this instinct; but he talks about the customs of the impoverished class, which are able to fasten with infallible instinct upon the unresolved aspect of property and ownership (*dass die Gewohnheiten, welche Gewohnheiten der ganzen armen Klasse sind, mit sicheren Instinkt das Eigentum an seiner unentschiedenen Seite zu fassen wissen*). In the second place, when he comes to speak about people themselves, he envisages this instinct not as a faculty or attribute that one has, but precisely as the reflection of a *non*-proprietor, of a non-possessor, of a lack, a deficiency. We "have" this instinct in the way that we "have" a deficiency.

Marx's use of language points straight to this remarkable *adequatio naturae et paupertatis*. The term *Trieb*, which might quite simply be translated as "urge" or "instinct", in his terminology has a radically different function from that of indicating merely an animal instinct, such as the predatory instinct or sexual impulse. In its specific meaning the term *Trieb* may be described under three aspects. The first is that of *Bedürfnis*, of want—but in the elementary sense of poverty, that is to say, of that lack of *everything*, which is altogether a situation of want. That is radically different from an instinct that one tries to satisfy in perfection of an already favourable and assured position. The second aspect makes the radical difference from an animal instinct even clearer; this need is an "urge to justice". That is something specifically human. The predatory instinct and sexual impulse man shares with the animals; but the "urge to justice" is typically human. The situation with the class of poor people is not only *dass diese Klasse den Trieb fühlt, ein natürliches Bedürfnis, sondern ebensosehr, dass sie das Bedürfnis fühlt, einen rechtlichen Trieb zu befriedigen.* The term "urge to justice" seems to present the same sort of contradiction as the term "right of occupation"; indeed the two notions correspond to each other.

To the third aspect to the term "urge" or "instinct", only the German language can do full justice. Dead wood is a product of the *Treiben* (drive, motion) of elementary forces. The fortuitous and arbitrary play which natural forces "carry on" with the wood carries the dead wood into the arms of the non-owning class, the dispossessed. Through this they receive their elementary right, which is "carried" to them, as it were, along *with* the dead wood. Now with this *Treiben* (drive or motion) of natural forces there corresponds the urge to justice (*rechtliche Trieb*) naturally felt by the poor as a class.

We are completely in the grip of accident and caprice here. The impoverished class, which has become the victim of the "chance" wilfulness of the privileged and of the bourgeois private law they have produced, encounters in the accident and caprice of natural forces a fundamentally humane power with a corrective function. It is an "elementary" power, that is, the power of the elements; and it is the "elementary" class, the class of the poor, that corresponds to this elementary natural order. Just as the private rights of those with property correspond to a physical abundance, the living tree, so do the private rights of the property-less correspond to the dead wood, to physical deprivation. And just as the poor class feel this elementary correspondence as an urge to justice, so too is its practice of a specific kind, in so far as it creates a specific order. The gathering of dead wood is the work of the elementary class in human society, whereby it adopts a regulative position towards what is produced by the elementary power of nature. It is a gathering together (*Sammeln*) of what nature has scattered here, there and everywhere. And what is true of dead wood applies also to everything that grows wild and is therefore a "fortuitous accidence of property" (*ein ganz zufälliges Akzidenz des Besitzes*). With gleaning during harvest, the position is the same.

It is the epitome of insignificance, a negligible remainder, a postlude following the symphony of civil society, of private law, of wealth, of organic nature, when that symphony is already completed. But let us make no mistake! In this accidental play of caprice and accident a *law* is being created; this passive class of human society is creating an *order*. Beneath the palimpsest of the law based upon reasoned judgment, another text, as yet illegible but nonetheless in writing recognizably human, emerges, which with the greatest effort Marx is bent upon deciphering, word for word. It is the text of a natural law other than that laid down in civil law, the natural law of the third stage. For the time being this new natural law still lies concealed in an old-German law of custom which had appeared to be exploded definitively by the *leges Romanorum* and in particular by the modern civil law, based on Roman law. This new natural law is at present still only to be detected in the instinctive sense of justice of the impoverished class. For the time being this new law is still unformed, it has as yet received no "character" of its own, it is still purely a law of custom, just as up to this point the existence of the poor as a class is no more than a custom of civil society, having so far found no adequate place in the framework of the conscious organization of the state. Thus the form of the customary law is for the time being fully in accord with the nature of this new law (*die Form des Gewohnheitsrecht is hier um so naturgemässer, als das Dasein der armen Klasse selbst bisher eine blosse Gewohnheit der bürgerlichen Gesellschaft ist, die in dem Kreis der bewussten Staatsgliederung noch keine angemessene Stelle gefunden hat*).

So the customary law of the poor anticipates a new form of society and of political organization. It is the existence of the poor class as pure fact—a fact which no form of civil law whatever can annul, though it may seek to ignore it—which lays the dynamite under modern private law and is the seed of a new social order. The building has still to rise and the contours are as yet shown only in outline; but the corner-stone is already laid.

Yet it is not Marx's concern in this article to appear as the architect of a coming society. As journalist and observer, he is purely and simply the critic. Nor is he concerned with civil private law as such, not even in the first instance with legislation; for as he hastens to say in the introduction, he just is not familiar with the full text of the proposed law against wood-stealing, he knows it only from the debates on the proposals in the *Rheinische Landtag*. The complete text was known only to the deputies. The core of his criticism, therefore, is political, not juridical. In other words, in his critique of civil private law, he is getting at the structure of civil society and of the constitutional system and law that go with it.

In the subsequent pages the article shows, through a razor-keen analysis of the debates held in the *Landtag*, that, as representatives of the dignity of the official constitutional law, the deputies let the matter go completely by default and lowered themselves to become busybodies intent on furthering the interests of private ownership. What he envisaged those interests to be he makes clear from an example. To an urban delegate's defence of the customary right of the poor to pick fruit growing wild, like bilberries and bearberries, another deputy replied that in his neighbourhood these fruits were already commercial articles and were exported in bulging crates to Holland. Marx's commentary fastens on to this, and he notes that things have gone so far that the customary right of the poor has been made a monopoly of the rich. Evidence is offered that it is possible to monopolize a communal possession; and so the logical conclusion is that it must *be* monopolized. The nature of the object calls for the monopoly, because the interest of private ownership has invented it. (*Die Natur des Gegenstandes verlangt das Monopol, weil das Interesse des Privateigentums es erfunden hat*). The modern whim of a number of commercial dealers bent on financial gain becomes irrefutable, directly it supplies residue for the early-Teutonic concern with land and soil (*Der moderne Einfall einiger geldfuchsender Handelskrämer wird unwiderleglich, sobald er Abfälle dem urteutonischen Interesse von Grund und Boden liefert*). The target of Marx's criticism is not so much the rising tide of capitalism in Germany as the manner in which an economic development quite literally prescribes the law to the state and the force of law is given to naked violence.

This is a glaring example of a development which also underlies the legislation against wood-stealing. The early-Teutonic *Interesse* of the landholders is quickly transformed into the modern *Interesse* of the capitalist. The term *Interesse*, which we encounter here for the first time, is to develop in Marx's thinking into one of the central categories of his ideological critique. We find the material for its construction already present in this article. The "interest" of private ownership is the true counterpart of the "urge to justice" of the impoverished class. The puny, wooden, mindless and self-seeking soul of "interest" sees only a single point, that is, the point at which it is injured, just as a chicken will fly into the passer-by who happens to get in its way. The "chicken eyes" of interest turn the least misdemeanour into a capital crime. Moreover, private interest is pusillanimous, because its heart, its soul, is an external object that can always be stolen and damaged; and who does not quail before the danger of losing heart and soul? No wonder that a state which becomes the servant of private interest proves an inhumane source of legislation; for its highest nature is an alien and material one.

The real force of Marx's argument is that, faced with the inhumanity of private interest, he recalls the state to its imperishable duty to protect humanity. Private interest makes the one sphere in which a person's dealings are antagonistic the sphere within which that person conducts his life. It turns the law into a rat-catcher who sets out to exterminate vermin; for private interest does not study nature and therefore sees rats as no more than verminous. The state, however, must see more in the wood-stealer than the "forest enemy". Is the citizen not linked to it by a thousand nerve fibres; and is the state entitled to sever all those nerves because that citizen has of his own initiative cut just one nerve? No; the state will see in the wood-stealer a man; for the state mutilates itself whenever it turns a citizen into a criminal. Above all, the *moral* legislator will shrink from placing an act which in the past has been considered blameless within the category of criminal activities.

The state has the means of safeguarding the rights of the citizen brought before a court in a way that accords with reason, the principle of generality and dignity residing in the state as well as with the rights, life and claim to proprietorship of the said citizen. If private ownership is too petty and small-minded to rise to the level of the state, the state is not thereby obliged to so demean itself as to adopt the arguments of private ownership which are at variance with reason and justice.

Every modern state, however hard it may be to recognize in it the idea of the state, as soon as there is any attempt to turn it into an instrument of private interests, must surely exclaim, "Your ways are not my ways, nor your thoughts my thoughts!"

At a climax in his argument, when Marx wants the exalted character of the state to shine forth in its full lustre, he turns for help to a quotation from the Old Testament. This quotation from Isaiah 55, verse 8, fits so naturally and inevitably into the course of the argument that only a familiarity with the biblical text will serve to remind the reader that what confronts him here is a typical Old Testament prophecy. The inevitableness of it drives home the close kinship with the spirit of the Torah which is palpably evident throughout the article. So far, I have resisted the temptation to point to signs of this intrinsic affinity, even where the text itself prompts a comparison with some passage in the Bible. The fact is that the force of Marx's argument lies in the *absence* of any explicit reference to the Bible. It is not only that he does not need this; but an appeal to the Bible is put out of his reach by the sophistry of those he is attacking for the way they hitch the Christian religion to the wagon of their private interests. We would be enervating his argument, therefore, were we to insist on coaxing him back on to the path of his opponents, a path he had already abandoned.

Yet for that very reason this quotation from Isaiah, at this point, is all the more telling. The prophetic adjunct, "Hear the word of the Lord", is naturally left out. The word of the Lord becomes the word of the state—and of the state speaking and acting at the level which "is appropriate as well to its reason, generality and dignity as to the rights, life and property of the citizen on trial". It is the word of the state that stands so far above the objectionable level of private interest that it is fully operative in support of the rights of the oppressed person who has no rights. "The watchmen are blind," we read in an apposite passage from Isaiah (Isaiah 56:10 f.), "they are all without knowledge, they are all dumb dogs, they cannot bark; dreaming, lying down, loving to slumber. And these dogs are greedy, they can never have enough; they are shepherds that cannot attend, they have all turned to their own way, each to his gain, without exception." The spirit of this prophetic judgment is something we can recognize in Marx's analysis of the

Sophistik des Interesses to which the *Rheinische Landtag,* despite its vocation to guard and protect the dignity of the state and the law, had fallen victim.

The *Landtag* deployed some astounding pieces of sophistry in the argumentation of the legal procedure in cases of wood-stealing, particularly in upholding the central position assigned therein to the forester. The new legislation not only allowed this employee of the landowners to bring a charge of wood-stealing, but also gave him the right to compute the value of the stolen wood. It would have been difficult to choose a worse valuer; for the person of the forester is the very embodiment of the tutelary spirit of wood (*der personifizierte Schutzgenius des Holzes*). The forester and the wood grow together, as it were. The wood is everything to him, it is bound to be of absolute value in his view: and in his assessment-return he will assess not only the value of the stolen wood but his *own value* as well, which is, in fact, the value of his activity as a forester. Do you really believe that this man will not leap to defend the *value* of his object every bit as much as its *substance*?

A propos of this question of the valuation of stolen wood, Marx introduces the term "surplus value" (*Mehrwert*). As the concepts "value" and "surplus value" are to become key concepts in Marx's later work, *Das Kapital*, it is important to see how the term makes its first appearance in his writings. The issue here concerns the penalties, embodied in the legislation, to which the wood-stealer is subject—penalties that can involve, besides some years of corrective punishment, restitution in the form of forced labour for the benefit of the wood owner. In this way, Marx contends, the wood-stealer becomes an item of capital for the owner of the forest, and the theft itself is converted into a form of interest. Indeed, the surplus value of the wood, that economic bigotry, is changed by the theft into something of substance (*sogar der Mehrwert des Holzes, die ökonomische Schwärmerei, verwandelt sich durch den Diebstahl in eine Substanz*). A moment ago we came across the term "substance" as the absolute value that the forester assigns to the wood because he identifies the wood's value with his own. He puts his heart and soul into the wood, as it were, and then, like the forester he is, he watches over his own heart and soul; or to put it another way, the substance of the wood has become *his* substance, he has acquired a "wooden soul". Now the term "substance" returns as the "surplus value" the wood acquires when the theft is converted into capital for the wood owner. The "surplus" in "surplus value", the surplus over and above the exact "value", comes about through the metamorphosis of an *object*, wood, into the *person* of its owner. In that metamorphosis, the exact value is transposed into an in principle unlimited *surplus* value; in principle unlimited, because the surplus value fundamentally represents the absolute value of the person of the wood owner.

Marx calls this an "economic chimera" or a piece of "economic bigotry" (*ökonomische Schwärmerei*). It stands in radical contrast to the exact valuation of the wood that would be carried out by an impartial assessor. He confronts the stolen wood in a spirit of sceptical distrust, sizes it up with a very prosaic glance and using a profane measure (*er misst es mit scharfem prosaischem Auge an einem profanen Mass*), and tells you down to the last cent how much it is worth.

"Sceptical distrust", "prosaic glance" and "profane measure" are the critical points of reference that mercilessly expose every form of "economic bigotry", treat an object with objective judgment as an object and prevent a person from being transformed into an object or an object into a person. Objective assessment treats the value of an object as objective value and resists any attempt to turn it into a subjective value that would make the value a surplus value and, in principle, absolute value. Just as objectivizing the subject nullifies the absolute value of the subject and makes it, in principle, value-less, so *vice versa*, subjectivizing the object lends it a surplus value, an absolute value, which does not belong to it. "Value" becomes "substance".

We have here before us, in essence, the critique which Marx is to elaborate later on in the *Kritik der politischen Ökonomie*. That is why it is of cardinal importance to see straightaway, at the outset of this critique, that the "critique of law" is at bottom a "critique of religion". Where injustice has assumed the mask, the religious mask, of justice, a critique of law cannot be other than at the same time a critique of religion.

Indeed, the term *ökonomische Schwärmerei*—economic bigotry —is a striking expression of the essential unity of Marx's critique of law, of economics and of religion. For *Schwärmerei* is a typical term from the critique of religion. It recurs in Marx's analysis of the sophistical spirit of private interest (*sophistischen Geist des Privatinteresses*). Private interest possesses two sorts of measure and weight, with which it weighs and measures human beings, two kinds of viewpoint on the world, two pairs of spectacles, one of which produces black and the other variegated colours. If it is a question of exposing other people to its manipulations, or of glossing over dubious means and resources, then private interest dons its multi-colour spectacles, enabling it to see its manipulations and means steeped in fantastic glory; then private interest assumes the role of virtuoso conjurer and mesmerizes itself and others with the unpractical and sweet chimeras of a generous and trusting soul (*da gaukelt er sich und andere in die unpraktischen und lieblichen Schwärmereien einer zarten und vertrauensvollen Seele ein*). But the moment the question of self-advantage arises, ownership puts on its worldly-wise, dark spectacles, the practical ones. Then it is a matter—behind the scenes where the illusions of the stage fade away—of submitting the tools and resources to the hard test of usefulness.

There is nothing more fearsome than the logic of self-interest (*die Logik des Eigennutzes*). That logic, which transforms the wood owner's employee into a state official, also converts the authority of the state into an employee of the wood owner, whose interest turns out to be the moving spirit of the entire mechanism. All the organs of the state become so many ears, eyes, arms, legs, with which the interest of the wood owner hears, watches, assesses, protects, grasps and walks. And this predominating soul of the mechanism becomes, in the romantic conception of the legislator-cum-wood owner, in the hazy notion of his own personal superiority, in a poetic ecstasy, magically transmuted into the true guarantor meting out justice to the wood-stealer.

Terms like *nebelhafte Vorstellung, poetische Selbstentzückung, romanhafte Vorstellung* might function without more ado in the critique of religion; but we are concerned here with the critique of law. Once the term "ideology" is introduced, actually in connection with the expression "free will of private persons" (*freie Wille der Privaten*), employed by one of the deputies. Marx explains this as a "sudden, rebellious entrance of ideology"; for "when it comes to the ideas, we have before us simply and solely the followers of Napoleon". The sophistry of interests has so manipulated "free will" that it is precisely covered by the arbitrary conduct of privileged private persons.

This sophistry has manipulated the law in so masterly a fashion that we are landed by the period of public law in the period of a tribal and dynastic law returning with twice its former strength. Those who own ancestral estates use modern advances to arrogate to themselves both the private punishment typical of a barbarian outlook and the public punishment that belongs with a modern world view. Wood possesses the remarkable property, directly it is stolen, of acquiring for its owner capacities of a public nature which he did not possess before. If, beside a private right, the wood owner possesses a constitutional right *vis-à-vis* the wood-stealer as well, then it would seem that he has been robbed not only of the wood but of the state too; and so the state has become a private asset of his. Evidently, the thief has been a second Christopher, carrying in the stolen logs the state itself upon his back.

Once again Marx has recourse at a climactic point of his critical analysis to a directly theological conclusion. Having first, in a passage quoted from Isaiah, made the state a mouthpiece of the Word of God, he now compares the state with Christ. His purpose is the same, namely, to illuminate the exalted character of the state and to show how impossible it is that the state should ever come to be an item of private property. His case is argued with great subtlety: it is not the private landowner, the usurper who claims the state as his private property, who is equated with Christopher, but the wood-stealer. The image is a striking one: the wood-stealer, carrying the stolen logs on his back, turns under the manipulations of private ownership into a second Christopher. He carries "in the stolen logs the state itself upon his back". First the wood is raised to the status of a divinity, acquires an absolute value; and then, *via* an absolutized private law, even the law of the state is turned into a private asset. But, Marx would imply, even were the wood to allow of this metamorphosis, when it comes to the state, it is really quite absurd. Just as Christopher collapsed beneath the load of Christ so the burden of constitutional law is too heavy for any private person. The analogy is so subtle that it unites in a single focus the critique of law with the critique of economics and of religion.

The sophistry of private interest is compared on several occasions with that of Shylock in Shakespeare's *Merchant of Venice*. Eventually it gets to the point where the forest owner acquires, instead of a chunk of wood, a "one-time human being" (*an die Stelle des Holzblockes einen ehemaligen Menschen*). Woe to the state that sells itself to interest of this kind. The state is bound to say, I guarantee justice against all the vagaries of chance and accident; but the state cannot say, a private interest is guaranteed against all the whims of accident, is immortal. The state is powerless against the nature of things; it cannot make something that is finite immune from the conditions of finitude, from fortuity (*Der Staat kann nicht angegen die Natur der Dinge, er kann das Endliche nicht gegen die Bedingungen des Endlichen, nich gegen den Zufall stichfest machen*). If the woodstealer is too poor to make restitution, all that means is that every legitimate way of obtaining compensation is closed. The world is not for that reason out of joint, nor does the state thereupon forsake the celestial path of its justice and authority; and you know by experience the transitory nature of earthly things—an experience that can scarcely strike your deep-rooted, religious sensibility as an intriguing novelty or as more strange than storm or fire or pestilence. If the state is supposed to turn the thief into a temporary serf, then it would be sacrificing the imperishable nature of justice to your private interest. You want the state to relinquish its sacred authority so that your hunk of wood may be avenged.

One of the representatives of the landed nobility observed that a lot of thefts involving wood were committed in order to obtain board and lodging in gaol; for which reason he argued for putting the prisoners on a bread-and-water diet. This remark drew from Marx's pen the ironical query whether the real remedy for thieving might not rather be to *elicit a livelier sense of religion*. He had heard the *Landtag* speak so often and so affectingly of this. Who could have suspected then that bread and water are the true means of grace? What a handsome parade of words there had been then, with a view to procuring for the people of the Rhineland a seat in heaven; and how prodigal they are with words now, with a view to lashing a whole class of the population into hard labour on bread and water, a scheme which even a Dutch planter can scarcely permit himself to apply to his black workers. What does all this signify? That it is easy to be holy when one has no thought of being human.

So Marx reaches his conclusion: *interest has scored over justice* (*das Interesse hat das Recht überstimmt*). Interest is of its very nature blind, immoderate, partial, in brief, a lawless natural instinct. And can there be such a thing as lawless laws? Whereas the Rhinelander should carry the day in the *Landtag* over the privileged class, and the person *qua* person should count for more than the forest owner, the *Landtag* has on the contrary become *a class assembly, a gathering of private interests* (*Ständeversammlung der Sonderinteressen*). In contrast to what some authors think they discover as an ideal romanticism, an unfathomable depth of feeling and fruitful source of morality in the representation of private interests, the reality is that it serves to abolish every natural and intellectual distinction. In its place is enthroned the amoral, injudicious and unfeeling abstraction of a given matter and a given consciousness which is the slave of that abstraction.

Wood is as much wood in Siberia as it is in France; forested estate is forested estate in Kamtshatka as much as in the Rhineland. If then wood and those who own it are *ipso facto* the law-makers, there is nothing to differentiate between those laws, unless it be their geographical location and the language in which they are expressed. This reprobate materialism (*verworfene Materialismus*), this sin against the holy spirit of whole peoples and of mankind itself, is a direct consequence of the doctrine which the *Preussische Staats-Zeitung* urges upon the legislature: namely, when the matter in hand is a law concerning wood, to think exclusively in terms of wood and woodland, without seeking to resolve the special material problem in political terms, that is to say, within the total context of the rational and moral character of the state (*Staatsvernunft und Staatssittlichkeit*).

"The savages of Cuba took gold to be the *fetish of the Spaniards*. They held a solemn celebration with song and dance,

64

and then threw it into the sea. If the Cuban savages had attended the session of the *Rheinischen Landstände,* would they not have taken *wood* to be *the Rhinelanders' fetish?* However, a subsequent session would have taught them that fetishism is bound up with animal-worship; and the savages of Cuba would have tossed the *hares* into the sea in order to save the *people."*

This final passage is an allusion to the draft legislation denying the peasants the right even to hunt hares on their own land.

3

Contradictions in the material order of living

As Marxism has developed into a more or less rounded system, the terms "material" and "materialism" have assumed a central function which, precisely because of that, has become a source of the most intractable, widespread and curious misconceptions. These have been and are certainly not only and not even primarily nurtured by the opponents of Marxism, but are closely bound up with its historical evolution. They come not just from outside, but more especially from within. That is one of the reasons calling for a detailed analysis of Marx's development in the years 1842 and 1843, which he himself considered to be crucial to his career and the formation of his thinking.

In 1859, from the standpoint of his *Kritik der politischen Ökonomie*, he describes his activities of seventeen years before, when he was editor of the *Rheinische Zeitung*, as his first confrontation with "so called material interests". Next, as a result of the critical analysis of Hegel's philosophy of law, which he carried out in 1843 and 1844, he formulates the notion that legal relations (*Rechtsverhältnisse*) and constitutional forms (*Staatsformen*) are rooted "in the material circumstances of life" (*in den materiellen Lebensverhältnissen wurzeln*), and proceeds further to define this rooting as "ideological forms" (*ideologische Formen*), in which people become conscious of the "contradictions in the material order of living" (*Widersprüche des materiellen Lebens*).

What is formulated here is the basic idea of "historical materialism", so called. Marx accounts for the emergence of

66

this insight as being expressly the result of his study of Hegel's philosophy of law. Even so, the term "materialism", where we encounter it in the first confrontation with "so called material interests", has a significance almost the opposite of the term as it has acquired a settled position in the compound phrase "historical materialism". It is interesting to check the closing passage of the article on legislation against wood-stealing (which I reproduced almost word for word at the end of the previous lecture) against the use of the terms "matter", "materialism" and "material".

What is said there about the "so-called material interests" is that they annul every natural and intellectual distinction (*alle natürlichen und geistigen Unterschiede*) and enthrone instead the amoral, uncomprehending and unfeeling abstraction of a particular matter and of a particular consciousness which is their slave (*die unsittliche, unverständige und gemütlose Abstraktion einer bestimmten Materie und eines bestimmten, ihr sklavisch unterworfenen Bewusstseins*). If we dissect the sentence, it would appear to involve two things. In the first place, the allegation that what is being enthroned is an *abstraction*, endowed with a kingly authority. An abstraction becomes sovereign ruler. The *Rheinische Landtag*'s claim to represent the Rhine province is exposed as being a representation solely of private interests (*Sonderinteressen*). Whilst an awareness of "right" and of "law" is the Rhinelanders most considerable provincialism, private interest as such knows neither province nor homeland; it is indifferent to the general as to the local good (*dass das Sonderinteresse, wie kein Vaterland, so keine Provinz, wie nicht den allgemeinen, so nicht den heimischen Geist kennt*). Private interest admits only of the abstraction in which every natural and mental distinction is obliterated.

In the second place, that abstraction has a dual character: it is the abstraction of a particular *matter* and the abstraction of a particular *consciousness*. But in this twofold character the abstraction is one and indivisible; for the consciousness is a slave of the matter. Enthroned along with the abstraction of the matter is the lackey of this royal master, its obedient servant, "consciousness". And in this twofold unity of master and servant this abstraction is the complete negation of morality, understanding and feeling.

Mark well that the complaint is not levelled at consciousness for being a sovereign ruler, nor at the imbalance usually referred to as "idealism"; nor again is the reproach aimed at the philosophy generally characterized as "materialism", which elevates matter into a controlling principle. No; the critique concentrates exclusively on the abstraction's being made into an absolute monarch. One might see in this an attack of "idealism"; for the abstraction would seem to be a typical product of idealizing activity. Even that conclusion is wrong, because what is at issue in the first instance is the abstraction of a particular *matter*. It is the matter which has the initiative, the consciousness following blindly after; the matter is active, the consciousness passive. Indeed, contained in the grammatical construction is a double meaning which would appear to be deliberately calculated, and in any case expresses an essential ambiguity. The phrase "abstraction of a particular matter and of a particular . . . consciousness" can mean that matter and consciousness are the object, or that they are both the subject, of abstraction. In other words, one can read it as meaning that a process of abstracting from matter and consciousness is taking place, or alternatively that matter and consciousness themselves produce the abstraction. In point of fact, one might suppose that the first interpretation would obviously apply in the case of the matter, whereas the second would seem to fit very well with consciousness. After all, we naturally tend to think, matter must be the object and consciousness the subject: matter is that which is abstracted from *by* consciousness. This way of thinking conflicts with the explicit statement that matter plays the active role and consciousness passively follows after. Thus the ambiguity applies to matter and consciousness in *this* hierarchy and in *this* reciprocal relation. There is abstraction from consciousness in so far as, and because, it is the slave of a matter which is the object of abstraction and which drags the consciousness along with it, so to speak, in the wake of the abstraction-process. Similarly, when it is the consciousness that produces the abstraction, this only occurs in the wake of the abstraction-producing matter.

Yet we must not push the contrast to extremes; for the distinction between the predominance of matter and the slavish position of consciousness is continued by their unity. When consciousness becomes the slave of matter, is subjected by and subjects itself to matter (*ihr sklavisch unterworfen* can mean both), it then brings with it all that it possesses and all its capacities, and matter assumes command over the complete arsenal of consciousness. It therefore conflicts with the grammatical construction to pose the question whether matter is at times able to play an active role and of its own accord produce abstraction; for matter and consciousness are bracketed together. Equally meaningless is the question whether, in the process of abstracting, consciousness does not play the leading role; for the abstraction-process includes the two together: matter *and* consciousness.

We must single out yet another feature of this cardinal passage. It says of abstraction that it is the negation of morality, understanding and feeling (*unsittliche, unverständige und gemütlose*). What this means is that where there is abstraction *by* matter and consciousness together, and where there is abstraction *from* matter and consciousness together, at the same time—and by definition—there is a process of abstraction from morality, understanding and feeling. The abstraction takes the place of "every natural and mental distinction"; for all differences are obliterated, every distinction is done away with. In the expression "natural and mental" is enshrined a twofold unity of nature and mind, a twofold unity that is embodied in morality, understanding and feeling. They are "natural and mental" functions which for that very reason reflect the diversity contained in nature and mind. This harmony of "nature and mind" is nullified by an abstraction-process in which consciousness becomes the slave of matter. And the rich diversity of "nature and mind" is destroyed in a process in which matter and consciousness are turned into a colourless and soulless abstraction, in which nature and mind are both eliminated; in which morality, understanding and feeling are obliterated. Where the abstraction from matter begins to predominate, the reality of nature, united in harmony with mind, is lost. Where the abstraction from consciousness collaborates in this dictatorship, the reality of mind, united in harmony with nature, is belied.

This Marx now judges to be "reprobate materialism"

(*verworfene Materialismus*). In the adjective "reprobate", is expressed total condemnation, the absolute negation of the *beatus*, the "blessed", in the beatitudes. "Reprobate", cast away, is the situation of those condemned to hell. Again, this "reprobate materialism" is described as "this sin against the holy spirit". Once more, as on several earlier occasions, in looking for the superlative that will transcend all relative judgments, Marx reaches for a biblical expression. Just as previously he had described the inviolable and exalted character of the state, the guarantor of justice and humanity, by a comparison with God and Christ, so now he defines its total opposite as the "sin against the holy spirit". It is, after all, that sin which Jesus said is unforgivable—and is so in distinction from all other sins (Mark 3:29).

Here again, however, there is no trace of any explicit appeal to the Bible. Just as in both the earlier cases the concern was not with God and Christ but with the exalted character of the humane, constitutional state, so now it is not the doctrine of the holy spirit which is under discussion, but the "sense of right and of law" which is the most considerable provincialism of the Rhinelanders. The matter at issue is the "urge to justice", the "instinct for justice", which is a natural possession of the impoverished class. That is the "holy spirit of the peoples and of human kind". This elementary justice and this elementary sense of justice have continued to be preserved in the law of custom, whether in Siberia or in France, in Kamtshatka or in the Rhine province. It is something provincial because it is elementary and concretely human; and so it is universal. It is the holy spirit "of the peoples and of humanity".

Materialism is the unforgivable desecration and total denial of this spirit in two respects. In the first place, it is a direct consequence of the doctrine that, in the case of a law concerning wood, it behoves the legislator to consider nothing but wood and woodland (*bei einem Holzgesetz nur an Holz und Wald zu denken*). The sting of this materialism lies in the "nothing but", in the absolute concentration on this one point, to the exclusion of all other aspects and in disregard of all the connecting lines which intersect at this point. This absolutizing, this abstracting, isolating, is *the* sin of sins. It is the "abstraction of a particular matter": wood remains wood as much in Siberia as

70

in France. And the "abstraction of a particular consciousness", which has become a slave to this particular matter; forested estates are still forested estates in Kamtshatka as in the Rhine province. Such total disregard of every mental and natural distinction, that is the unforgivable sin of materialism, the idolatrous worship of abstraction, a worship which reduces "a particular matter", a concrete reality, linked by a thousand nerve fibres with the whole of nature and of mind, to an abstraction: wood = matter.

In the second place, materialism is a violation of justice; for it teaches the lawmaker that he has no business to resolve the special material problem on a *political* basis, that is, within the total context of the rationality and morality of the state. Whilst consciousness becomes a slave to the *abstraction* of a particular matter, the legislature becomes a slave to the *abstraction* of a special material problem, a special material task (*die einzelne materielle Aufgabe*). For the third time in this passage we have the concept of "matter", on this occasion as an adjective. Wood is indeed matter; and so the problem to be resolved is of a material nature. It has to do, not with wood in general, but with the forests of the Rhineland, which is why it is a specific issue. Furthermore, for the legislator, wood and forest are not simply objects; he is confronted with the problem (*Aufgabe*) of the particular relation of *this* concrete wood and of *these* concrete forests to the concrete *people* who live in the Rhineland. Those people form a society, a community, which in its turn is organized in the context of a state; and this state makes laws, procures justice. Therefore the lawmaker has a directly *political* task, namely, the proper ordering of society as a whole. For that reason he must resolve this special material problem within the total context of the rationality and morality of the state (*im Zusammenhang mit der ganzen Staatsvernunft und Staatssittlichkeit*). If, on the other hand, the legislator isolates a single aspect, if he abstracts the one factor, "private ownership", from all other factors that have a bearing on the case, he is then deposing justice and is instead kneeling before the abstraction of a concrete matter and the abstraction of a concrete problem.

It must by now be evident that the term "materialism" in this cardinal passage, which represents the first confrontation with "so-called material interests", belongs to the terminology of Marx's *critique*. It is pre-eminently a *critical* term; and in this term the unity of Marx's critique is once again expressed. The critique of religion: materialism is fetish-worship, adoration of the wood-god, the absolutizing of abstract "matter"; it is a sin against the holy spirit. The critique of law: materialism is a total disregard of the rights of the human being, which are sacrificed to a juridical abstraction: ownership. The critique of politics: materialism is the repudiation of the duty assigned to the state of serving the whole of society—a repudiation on behalf of private interest. The critique of economics: materialism attributes to wood, which has an exact, profane, relative value, the surplus value of its owner's individuality; it gives to a relative piece of matter the absolute value of the person.

Hence the adjective in *verworfene Materialismus*. Materialism is something reprobate, it falls under the judgment, it is the target of criticism. Whatever aspects in Marx's later development may be added and whatever the metamorphoses that may follow in the course of Marxism's further evolution, from now on this basic *critical* note is always to be sounded in the term "materialism". Indeed, the persistent sounding of this basic note will enable us to gauge the extent to which the term "materialism" is still connected with the central core of Marx's philosophy. Even in that sense the term is an essentially *critical* category.

Actually, this passage is not the only one in which the critical implications of the term become evident. In an article dating from the same period entitled, *Uber die ständischen Ausschüsse in Preussen*, there occurs a passage that expresses a closely parallel train of thought. The *ständische Ausschüsse* had very recently been set up by King Frederick William IV. They were provincial advisory bodies, elected from the provincial diets to represent the different "estates" of the realm. Following up his articles on the meeting of the *Rheinische Landtag*, Marx subjected the composition of these advisory bodies to a critical analysis. He demonstrates how fictive they are in character, in that they are supposed to advise the king even on affairs of state. They were brought together for that purpose in a central advisory body which met in Berlin. What *new* element is it, Marx enquires, that quite suddenly changes those who represent provincial interests into the representatives of state interests, and gives their *special* activity the character of a *general* one? It might seem that this new element is simply and solely the *common place* of meeting. Is purely abstract space, however, able to give a man of character a new character and to bring about a chemical dissolution of his mental and spiritual being? One would be kow-towing to a crudely material mechanism if one were to ascribe an organizing soul purely and simply to a spatial area (*man würde dem materiellsten Mechanismus huldigen, wollte man dem blossen Raume eine solche organisierende Seele zumuten*). Here then a *material mechanism*, which ascribes to the *abstract* unity of *space* a unifying capacity, is contrasted with the essential nature of the state as a living organism that can be held together only by an "organizing soul".

This contrast runs like a conspicuous thread through the entire analysis. Marx starts by exposing the contradiction inherent in what was stipulated in respect of these advisory bodies. One condition of membership was that one should have been a landowner for at least ten years consecutively and that one should belong to a Christian church. The two conditions are in conflict anyway; for one would then have to posit a "Christian landholding" besides a "Jewish landholding"—and that is absurd. More serious is the fact that the general stipulation of land ownership clashes with the principle that these bodies are to represent the various classes; for it is only in the case of the peasant farmer that landholding is an essential attribute of his class.

That brings Marx to the central core of his analysis, namely, to the contention that the whole principle of representation on the basis of class distinction is in conflict with the essential nature of the state. With this in view, he appeals to the basic notion of an analogy between the structure of the state and the natural order. Anyone who studies the life of organic nature must perceive there the spirit of a vital unity. Even the elements do not remain separate but are incessantly merging into one another, so that in the living organism every trace of the varying elements completely disappears. Differentiation no longer consists in the discrete existence of the various elements but in the vital activity of the several functions, all infused with one

73

and the same life; so that their distinctness is not something already *there*, preceding life, but is rather something continuously emerging from life, and likewise continuously vanishing and being merged back into it. Now just as nature does not draw the line at the existing elements, but even on the bottom rung of natural life, in the metereological process, shows this diversity to be a merely sensory phenomenon with no intellectual truth in it, no more can or should the state, this natural kingdom of the mind (*dieses natürliche Geisterreich*), seek and find its true nature in a given sensory phenomenon. It argues superficiality, therefore, if we seek to explain distinctions of class in terms of a "divine providence".

The apologetic that would defend representation on the basis of class distinction miscomprehends the nature of the state as a living organism; it is aware only of a number of heterogeneous parts existing side by side and held together by the state in a superficial and mechanical fashion. Anyone who examines the actual character of the Prussian state will discover the actual areas into which the organization of the state is compartmented and within which the whole life and activity of the state are carried on. They are districts, municipalities, provincial governments, military departments and so on, and not the four categories of classes or estates that exist only in the fictitious world of legal instruments and registers. The real differences, which through their intrinsic nature are at every moment being absorbed into the unity of the whole, are free creations, springing from the genius of the Prussian state, and not raw elements imposed on the present by the blind necessity of nature and by the disintegration of a past age.

As the whole principle of representation on the basis of class distinctions is wrong, Marx also attacks the proposal from the liberal side that besides land ownership "intellect" (*die Intelligenz*) be recognized as a category of representation. That is absurd; for not only is "intellect" or "intelligence" not a *special* element of representation, but it is no *element* at all; intelligence is a *principle* which cannot form part of any *composition* of elements, but is only able to produce out of itself an *organic, articulated structure* (*Gliederung*). We can never speak of intelligence as of an integral part, but only as being, as it were, the organizing soul (*organisierenden Seele*). Where the political

74

intelligence is concerned, it will control land ownership by the principles of the state instead of letting the law be prescribed by the private egoism of land ownership. Similarly, the clock-maker sets the movement of a timepiece according to the sun, and not the other way round. For the intelligence nothing outward exists; for it is the soul, which defines everything from the inside out. For land ownership, on the contrary, everything is external that exists outside itself.

If a representation of intelligence is to have any meaning, therefore, it must spring from a desire for the intentional representation of the national intelligence, that is to say, of the intelligence which does not seek to uphold special needs over against the state, but whose deepest need it is to validate and make effective the state itself—as its own act, as its own state. To be represented is in the very nature of the case a passive thing: only what is material, spiritless, dependent, threatened, needs a representation; but no element of the state should be material, spiritless, dependent, threatened. The representation should not be envisaged as a representation of this thing or that thing, which is not the nation itself; but it is in point of fact *self-representation*, state-action, on the part of other forms in which the life of the state expresses itself, only distinguished by the universality of its content. The representation is not to be regarded as a concession to defenceless weakness, to powerlessness, but rather as the conscious vitality of the very peak of energy and strength. In an authentic state there is no landed interest, no industry, no material thing that as a raw, basic element could make a deal with the state. No; in any true state there exist mental and spiritual powers alone; and only in their political resurrection, in their political rebirth, are natural forces, as it were, enfranchised in the state. The state imbues the whole of nature with spiritual and mental nerves; and at every point it must appear that what is in control is not matter but form, not nature minus the state but the state-as-nature, not the *unfree object* but the *free human being*.

The term *dominieren*, which serves to express the absolute sovereignty of form over matter, of mind over nature, of the free subject over the unfree object, of the state as the natural realm of the spirit over sensory nature, is bracketed by Marx with the term *kritisieren*. Thus he declares that it is not for the landed interest to "criticize and control" (*kritisieren und beherrschen*) the political intelligence, but *vice versa*. Thus the *critique* is that transformation in which the natural forces undergo their "political resurrection" (*staatlichen Auferstehung*), their "political rebirth" (*politischen Wiedergeburt*). Therefore he vigorously defends the freedom of the *critical* press as the most powerful leverage for culture and the spiritual nurture of the people; a critical press converts the material struggle into an ideal struggle, the struggle of flesh and blood into a battle of minds, and that of need, of desire, of empiricism into one of theory, of intelligence, of form.

Once again the trend of Marx's thinking and his terminology —in particular the central position of the ideas of "resurrection" and "rebirth"—remind us naturally enough of biblical theology; and once more the point is made that the state occupies a theological position as the realm of freedom. More specifically there is an inescapable analogy with the dialectic of the natural and the spiritual, as developed by Paul in his First Letter to the Corinthians, chapter 15—a dialectic pivoted around the resurrection. It is significant in this context that, in his article on the *Rheinische Landtag* debates on the freedom of the press, Marx describes the statute book or legal code as "a nation's bible of freedom" (*die Freiheitsbibel eines Volkes*). Laws are the positive, light, universal norms within which freedom has acquired an impersonal, theoretical existence, independent of individual caprice. That is why preventive laws, especially all legal forms of censorship, conflict with freedom as that is embodied in the law. There are no effectively preventive laws. The law is only preventive as injunction. It begins to operate in fact only when it is infringed; for it is only *true* law if it incorporates the unconscious natural law of freedom as the considered law of the state (*das bewusstlose Naturgesetz der Freiheit bewusstes Staatsgesetz geworden ist*). Where the law is real law, that is, the being of freedom, it is man's real existence in freedom. For that reason the laws cannot obviate, cannot pre-vent (*prävenieren*), a man's actions; for they are, after all, the laws governing man's inner life, the laws of human activity as such, the considered and reflected images of human living. Thus the law retires before the life of man as a life of freedom; and only at the moment when his actual conduct has shown that a man has ceased to obey the natural law of freedom does the law as state law compel him to be free; just as physical laws only confront me as an alien force if and when my life has ceased to be the life of these laws, in other words, when it has become sick. Censorship is based on the view that disease is the normal situation or that the normal situation, freedom, is a disease.

In the law of the state, therefore, unconscious matter acquires a conscious form, and the unconscious natural law of freedom is brought to consciousness; it is the conscious reflection of man's mode of life. That is why Marx resists every attempt to subjugate this essential principle of freedom intrinsic to the nature of the state, more especially to one or another religious principle. Every given sphere of freedom is the freedom of this or that particular sphere, just as any given mode of life is that of a particular nature. How perverse would it be of the lion to insist on conducting himself by the laws of life proper to the polyp? How wrong would I be about the cohesion and unity of the physical organism, were I to conclude that because the arms and legs are active in their way, therefore the eye and ear —those organs which wrest from a human being his individuality and make him a reflection and echo of the universe —must have an even greater right to activity, to an activity in which the activity of arms and legs is raised to a higher power (*potenziert*)? Just as in the cosmic system each separate planet simply revolves around the sun, whilst at the same time turning on its own axis, so in the system of freedom each of its worlds revolves only about the central sun of freedom, whilst at the same time circling around itself.

Elsewhere (*Der Leitende Artikel in Nr. 179 der Kölnische Zeitung*, summer of 1842) Marx deploys this idea as a weapon against meddling by religion in matters of state, and to combat the idea of a Christian state. The state cannot be a construct of religion, but can only be constructed on the basis of the rationality of freedom (*aus der Vernunft der Freiheit*). That is the task of philosophy. Philosophy, after all, has done nothing in the realm of politics that physics, medicine, each and every science, has not done in its own sphere. Francis Bacon declared theological physics to be a vestal virgin, barren and unfruitful. He emancipated physics from theology, and lo! it bore fruit.

Just as you do not ask the doctor whether he believes, no more do you have to ask the politician. Round about the time of Copernicus' great discovery of the real solar system, the law of gravity governing the state was discovered as well; its gravity was found to be in itself. Just as the various governments of Europe, with the prime casualness of accepted practice, tried to apply this result to the balance-of-power system between states, so had Machiavelli and Campanella earlier, and later Hobbes, Spinoza, Hugo Grotius and others up to Rousseau, Fichte and Hegel, begun to develop the state from reason (*Vernunft*) and experience, not from theology; as Copernicus declined to take seriously the idea that Joshua stopped the sun at Gideon and the moon in the valley of Ajalon. The latest philosophy had only continued to build on what had already been begun by Heraclitus and Aristotle. For that matter, we have to remember that the Prussian system of law was a product of the philosophy of the Enlightenment and the Napoleonic Code, not of the Old Testament but of the school of Voltaire, Rousseau, Condorcet, Mirabeau, Montesquieu and of the French Revolution.

However, for earlier thinkers in the area of constitutional law, the state was a construction based on the human passions, on ambition or the need for sociability; in so far as they constructed the state from reason (*Vernunft*), it was the reason of the individual and not that of society. The more ideally orientated and more fundamental notion provided by the most recent philosophy, on the other hand, construed the state in terms of the idea of the whole (*aus der Idee des Ganzen*). It envisages the state as the mighty organism in which juridical, moral and political freedom has to be realized, and in which the individual citizen, in obeying the laws of the state, is merely obeying the natural laws of his own reason, of human reason.

The analogy between the state and nature and the idea of the state order as a spiritual order within the natural realm, is likewise to be found in Marx's critique of the proposals for a new divorce law. This project the Prussian government kept strictly secret—which did not prevent the *Rheinische Zeitung* from publishing it in the autumn of 1842. The editors' refusal to name the person who had handed them the text of the draft legislation was one of the reasons which in the following year led to the banning of that paper. The publication of the proposals touched off a lengthy public discussion in which Marx as the editor involved himself by contributing several articles.

True to his method, he subjected both the proposed legislation itself and the criticism of it voiced by its opponents to a critique of his own, and tried to push through from empiricism to theory, from the outer surface to the inner logic of the issue. His critique is based primarily on two objections. The first one concerns the half-heartedness of this attempt at reform, which in fact turns out to be an obscure and dissembling revision: the Prussian Domestic Code of 1794, dominated as it is by a feudal structure, is left unaffected and still functions as the basis. It may well be true that no legislation can decree moral behaviour; but still less can it legalize immorality. The Prussian Domestic Code rests on an intellective abstraction (*Verstandsabstraktion*) which, having no substance in itself, took over a natural, juridical and moral susbtance as so much external and in itself lawless matter (*aüsserliche, in sich selbst gesetzlose Materie*) and then tried to mould this spiritless and lawless matter (*geist- und gesetzlose Materie*) to an extrinsic goal. This antiquated legal system treats the objective world not on the basis of the laws inherent in it but of certain capricious, subjective considerations and of a plan that has no essential relation with the business at all.

The second fundamental objection that Marx adduces against the proposed divorce law has to do with the failure to understand the *secular* character of marriage. The proposals treat of marriage, not as a moral, but as a *religious* and *ecclesial* institution. The critics are indeed opposed to the way in which the scheme involves religion in the affairs of the law; but they themselves halt between two opinions and omit to say whether the essential nature of marriage is religious or not. In a sense the legislature is logically consistent; for it subjects marriage to the authority of the church. In point of fact, it sees the essence of marriage not as human morality but as spiritual sanctity. It sets the power of a higher authority in the place of autonomy; a supernatural sanction in the place of a natural hallowing from within; a passive obedience to commands that stand over and above the nature of the marriage relationship in the place of a loyal conformity to the nature of that relationship. Is it not

self-evident, then, that the legislature is putting secular
marriage beneath the supreme control of the religious
authorities?

The critics, on the other hand, are trammelled with a
divided viewpoint. In it, conscience is divorced from the sense
of justice, the world of law from the world of the mind and
spirit, so that a gap is created between law and spirit, between
jurisprudence and philosophy. They adopt a eudaemonistic
standpoint, having in view only the happiness of the two
partners to marriage, which they regard as being threatened by
the legal indissolubility of marriage. As opposed to that, Marx
bases his critique on the standpoint of the philosophy of law.
Marriage is not just a matter between two people but of the
whole family; and every divorce is at the same time a division
of families. The philosophy of law looks not only to the individual intention of two private persons and does not permit
the arbitrary will of the marriage partners to prescribe the law;
but it takes as a yardstick the *intention of marriage*, the moral
substance of this relationship. The law-maker has to regard
himself as a student of nature. He does not *make* the laws, he
does not invent the laws, but simply formulates them, makes it
possible for the intrinsic laws of spiritual relationships to come
to expression in conscious, positive laws (*er spricht die innern
Gesetze geistiger Verhältnisse in bewussten positiven Gesetzen aus*).

Nobody is obliged to enter into marriage; but anyone, as
soon as he has done so, must be obliged to pledge himself to
obedience to the laws of marriage. The person who gets married
does not *make* marriage, does not *invent* it, any more than a
swimmer invents the nature and the laws of water and of
gravity. Marriage cannot be centred, therefore, in his caprice,
but his caprice has to adapt itself to marriage. Whoever
arbitrarily abrogates marriage is saying in effect: the arbitrary,
the lawless, is the law of marriage; for no reasonable person
(*Vernünftiger*) will presume to regard his own actions as
privileged actions, as actions permitted to him alone; he will
rather declare those actions that *are permitted to all* to be legal
actions.

With this, Marx comes to a crucial point of his critical
analysis, nay, to a critical point of his whole philosophy of law.
At this critical point he finds himself in conflict, therefore, with

Hegel's philosophy of law. In the *Grundliniën der Philosophie des Rechts* Hegel says: marriage is in essence indissoluble, but only in so far as it is viewed in terms of the pure concept of marriage, its essential nature (*An sich, dem Begriffe nach, sie die Ehe untrennbar, aber nur an sich, d.h. nur ihrem Begriffe nach*). Marx does not try to counter this proposition; but he shows on the contrary just how platitudinous Hegel's utterance is. Indeed, it does not say anything specific about marriage at all. All moral relations are *in essence* (*ihrem Begriffe nach*) indestructible. A *true* state, a *true* marriage, a *true* friendship are indestructible; but no marriage, state, or friendship corresponds entirely to its essential character. Just as an actual friendship even within the family, and an actual state in world history, is destructible, so is an actual marriage in the state. No moral *existence* whatever tallies with its *essence*, at any rate not as of necessity.

Now, just as in nature destruction and death appear as a matter of course wherever an existence has altogether ceased to answer to its destined purpose, and just as world history decides whether a state has become so much the opposite of the idea of the state that it has no further claim to continued existence, so does the state decide under what conditions an *existing* marriage has ceased to be a marriage. The divorce is nothing other than a declaration that this or that marriage is a *deceased* marriage, the existence of which is a mere fraud and delusion. It speaks for itself that neither the arbitrary will of the legislature nor that of private persons, but only the *essential nature of the thing itself* can determine whether a marriage has died or not; for it is common knowledge that a *certificate of death* is based on the fact and not on the desires of the interested parties. If, however, in the case of *physical* death one looks for totally convincing proofs, must it not then be required of the legislature that it register the occurrence of a *moral* death only as a result of the most unmistakable symptoms, since it is not merely its right but also its duty—the duty, that is, of self-preservation—to guard and protect the life of moral relationships.

There can be no guarantee that the conditions under which the *existence* of a moral relationship ceases to tally with its *essence* have been accurately established at the level of science and of the general understanding and not in accordance with this or that prejudice unless the law is the considered expression of the popular will, in other words, has been brought about with and through that popular will. The law is then the expression of a deliberate submission to moral-cum-natural powers—the opposite of the contemptuous material posture whose only concern is with the caprice of the marriage partners, the opposite too of that disdainful idealism which recognizes only a mindless obedience to an authority above morality and nature.

Thus Marx's critique of the divorce legislation, based on the philosophy of law, steers a true course between the Scylla of materialism and the Charybdis of idealism. The key idea in it is the term "moral existence" (*sittliche Existenz*). In its moral *essence* marriage is indissoluble, but in its moral existence it is dissoluble. The contradiction between *essence* and *existence* is death. We have already been able to follow the trail to this crucial idea in Marx's reflections on the nature of freedom as the spiritual order of the state organism and of unfreedom as a symptom of disease, whereby the organism no longer responds to its true nature. This train of thought is now radicalized into the absolute contrast between an existence and its essence, a contrast that manifests itself as death.

The analogy between the order of nature and the spiritual order of the state is still preserved; but now a third concept, a middle term, is inserted between them: world history. The true state and true marriage are imperishable, because the idea is eternal; but the actual state and the actual marriage exist in time, they exist in history. The point at which nature and history meet is death, the fact of death. Death is not a fact of nature, in so far as it is in conflict with the idea of the natural order as a living organism. Even at the natural level, therefore, death is the expression of an inner contradiction, that is, of the contrariety existing between existence and essence, between existence (*Existenz*) and relevance to a destined purpose. In nature, death simply occurs as a manifestation of this contradiction; but, at the mental and spiritual level, death is the consequence of a considered decision. World history determines whether the actual existence of the state still answers to its essential nature; and the state is dissolved, disintegrated, the moment there is nothing of that correspondence left. Just as world history records the death of a state and issues a death certificate, so does the state determine whether a marriage has died and is in fact therefore already dissolved. The conditions are laid down in the law; and the guarantee that these conditions are really being met is then present, if the law is the considered expression of the popular will. Even *that*, however, is impermanent; for the state is in turn a mortal organism, whose death is declared and certified by world history.

Marx's critique of the Prussian state is really rather like the critical diagnosis made by the doctor who declares from the symptoms of disease and, if they are present, from the unmistakable symptoms of death, that the actual existence of the organism under scrutiny no longer answers to its essential nature and purpose as a living organism. The question of who gives the doctor the authority to utter such a diagnosis or, to put it even more basically, the question who is really doctor and who is patient, Marx answers by appealing to the onward-going course of history. His basic argument for the complete freedom of the press is founded on the perception that there is no body, no court of appeal, competent to authorize this, and that precisely for that reason freedom of criticism ought to exist. He reminds us of the lessons to be learnt from church history and from the history of science and philosophy. Thus Kant would never have allowed that Fichte had a claim to be a philosopher, Ptolemy that Copernicus was an astronomer, Bernard of Clairvaux that Luther had any title to be called a theologian. Every scholar sees his critics as being so many *"unqualified writers"*. Or must it be left to the unlearned to decide who is a competent scholar? We are bound, apparently, to leave the verdict to unqualified writers; for those who are qualified can hardly be judged in their own cause. Or should competency and authority be linked to a particular class? The shoemaker, Jacob Boehme, was a great philosopher. Many a philosopher of reputation is no more than a big shoemaker.

The progressive, critical process whereby history is continually subjecting itself to criticism and registering the contradiction between factual existence and idea involves the need to make new laws for regulating situations not provided for in the existing laws. That is the *truly historical* notion of things, as opposed to the imaginary one, which silences the reason manifesting itself in history (*Vernunft der Geschichte*) in order to devote to its bones the worship properly given to the relics of history.

On January 19, 1843, silence was imposed on Marx's critical activities by the Prussian government's decree banning the *Rheinische Zeitung* as from April 1, and for the interim period putting the paper under very stringent censorship. The shareholders addressed a long-winded apology to king and government. To the allegations expressed in the governmental decree, Marx appended some marginal comments of his own. Once again he makes an appeal to the critical progress of history. A given trend is not immediately reprehensible because the government has declared it to be so. The *astronomical system of Copernicus* was not only declared to be disreputable but was actually repudiated by the highest authority of the time. The imputation that the *Rheinische Zeitung* had been intending to launch a deliberate attack, and a fundamental attack, on the Prussian constitution Marx rebuts by recalling that as regards the foundation of the constitution there was a very great diversity of viewpoint. In his own lifetime Hegel believed he had laid down the basis of the Prussian constitution in his *Philosophy of Law*, and the government and the German public believed so too. The government demonstrated this, for instance, through the official propagation of Hegel's writings; the public, conversely, by accusing Hegel of having become the philosopher of the Prussian state. What at one time Hegel had believed is nowadays the belief of the philosopher of law, Friedrich Julius Stahl. In 1831, the year of his death, Hegel lectured in the philosophy of law by special command of the government. In 1830 the official *Gazette* declared Prussia to be a monarchy surrounded by republican institutions. It now pronounced Prussia to be a monarchy surrounded by Christian institutions. With such a great diversity of opinion regarding the Prussian constitution and its basis, it would seem no more than natural that the *Rheinische Zeitung* should have *its* opinion too: one that admittedly may differ from the interpretation favoured by the government at the moment, but that can nonetheless adduce as highly authoritative both Prussian history and many elements now current in the life of the state.

The charge of undermining the principle of monarchy Marx

counters with the remark that the *Rheinische Zeitung* has never shown any predilection for a particular form of state. Its only starting-point was a *moral and rational commonwealth (sittliches und vernünftiges Gemeinwesen)*; and it set store by the monarchy only in so far as that is the embodiment of principles which ought to be realized under any form of state.

The accusation that his paper was bent on stirring up dissatisfaction with the existing state of affairs in the field of legislation Marx parries by pointing out that the government shows its own discontent by, for example, pressing for the revision of the divorce laws. Any development in the legislative field is impossible without development of the laws; a development of the laws is not possible without criticism of the laws; any criticism of the laws must engender some discord between the laws as they exist and the heart and mind of the citizen; this discord will present itself as dissatisfaction. The logical conclusion is that loyal participation by the press in the growth of the state is not feasible unless the press is permitted to arouse dissatisfaction with the existing state of affairs.

Finally, as regards religion, so runs Marx's sarcastic comment, his paper has acted in complete conformity with the censorship law of 1819, by opposing a fanaticism that carries the verities of religion into politics and so gives rise to confused thinking; in other words, by opposing precisely those actions which the censorship is meant to combat.

Marx said in a letter to Ruge that he saw the banning of the *Rheinische Zeitung* as an *advance* of political awareness. Moreover, he had found the atmosphere becoming stuffy and unbearable, and had had enough of slaving away, even on behalf of freedom, and of being obliged to fight with needles instead of rifle-butts. "So the government has restored me to freedom . . . I can do nothing more in Germany. People here are self-deceived."

When the shareholders' meeting began to make efforts, by softening the hostile tack, to have the ban lifted, Marx decided not to wait for the crucial date; and some weeks before that, in the middle of March, he resigned.

In the 1859 preface to the *Kritik der politischen Ökonomie* he says of his voluntary resignation that the shareholders' illusion that they might be able to get the death-sentence on the paper rescinded gave him a welcome opportunity to withdraw from the public scene to the quiet of his study. "The first task," he goes on, "which I undertook in order to offset the doubts that assailed me was a revision of Hegel's *Philosophy of Law*; and the Introduction to that was published in the *Deutsch-Französische Jahrbüchern*, brought out in Paris in 1844. My studies led me to the conclusion that like forms of state legal relations (*Rechtsverhältnisse*) are neither self-explanatory nor to be understood in terms of the so called universal development of the human mind, but rather are rooted in the material circumstances of life (*materiellen Lebensverhältnissen*), the totality of which, in the wake of the English and French thinkers of the eighteenth century, Hegel sums up in the phrase 'civil society' (*bürgerliche Gesellschaft*); but that the anatomy of civil society has to be looked for in political economy."

We shall have to return to this passage yet more frequently; for it sums up in a single sentence the successive stages of Marx's route to the *Critique of Political Economy*. Now we are concerned only with the first part of the passage. It expresses first of all a negative conclusion: namely, that legal relations and forms of state are not self-explanatory and cannot be understood, either, in terms of the so-called universal development of the human mind. The positive conclusion connects up with that: these relations and forms are rooted rather in the material circumstances of life which are defined as "civil society".

For an understanding of this negative-positive conclusion we do best to refer back to three passages already discussed. We take as our starting-point the passage where Marx comes into line with the most recent philosophy of constitutional law, which regards the state as the main organism in which juridical, moral and political freedom ought to be realized and in which the individual citizen, in obeying the laws of the state, is merely obeying the natural laws of his own human reason. The problems raised by this way of putting it revolve around the terms "organism" and "be realized" (*Verwirklichung erhalten*). After all, if this philosophical view did indeed correspond to reality, and the state were indeed such an organism, then legal relations and forms of state would certainly "be self-explanatory". The development of Marx's thinking, which we

86

have been following in his articles of 1842 and early 1843, involves no break at all with this constitutional philosophy. On the contrary, the basic idea of an analogy between natural order and state order is also the basis of his critique of religion on the one hand and of "reprobate materialism" and "eudaemonism" on the other; for both run counter to nature. Religion disrupts the spiritual-cum-natural order of the state with supernatural factors; materialism upsets its spiritual character through a blind empiricism, consciousless matter. The turning-point in Marx's development does not lie, therefore, in any departure from this philosophy of constitutional law but in a confrontation with the problem of its "realization" (*Verwirklichung*). Marx has discovered that there is a yawning gulf between the idea of this state-organism and the ideal of the realization of freedom; and the doubts that assail him arise from the question if and how that gulf can be bridged. As a journalist he is brought rudely face to face with this problem by the conflict with the Prussian state, which has eventually persuaded him that there would seem to be simply no place in Germany for his critique. The substance of that critique is enshrined in two passages.

The first forms part of the critique of the legislation against wood-stealing. The existence (*Dasein*) of the poor as a class is up to this point simply a custom of civil society, which has not so far found an adequate place in the framework of the conscious organization of the state (*Staatsgliederung*). This expression "has not so far found an adequate place" (*noch keine angemessene Stelle gefunden hat*), is a weak formulation of the earlier statement that this class "occupies the same place in civil society as does the dead and fallen wood in the living nature of the forest". The poor as a class are so much dead wood. Within the "large organism" of the state there is no place for this dead wood, it simply falls outside it. Between the two yawns the gulf which in nature separates living material from dead. The stark fact of the *existence* of the impoverished class has confronted Marx with the so far unbridgeable contrast between the idea of the state as an all-embracing organism and the ideal of its realization. Just as in natural science a crisis regarding basic assumptions arises the moment research comes up against observed evidence which can have "no adequate place" within the model of nature being used for the investigation, so is Marx's thinking overwhelmed by fundamental doubt now that he is up against a category of people which fits not at all into the model of the state organism.

The second passage indicates how by a quite different route Marx comes to stand before precisely the same gulf. Analysing a draft divorce law, he concludes that all moral relations are indeed indissoluble in essence and in truth (*ihrem Begriffe nach*), but that both the actual state in world history and actual marriage in the state are most certainly dissoluble. This is another way of stating the conclusion that legal relations and forms of state are not "self-explanatory" (*aus sich selbst zu begreifen*). The point at which the "concept" (*Begriff*) is no longer adequate to make these relations and these forms "explanatory", conceivable (*zu begreifen*) is the moment at which "an existence (*Dasein*) has ceased altogether to answer to its destined purpose" (*seiner Bestimmung durchaus nicht mehr entspricht*). In nature, that is death: the dead branches that the storm has wrenched off or that have been hacked from the felled tree and thrown away as useless. In civil society, that point is the "existence of the poor class as such" (*das Dasein der armen Klasse selbst*): it no longer answers to its purpose, it is dead wood, severed from the living organism. In the state, that point is the dissolution (*Auflösung*) of marriage: a "severed" marriage is contradictory of the "idea", the "concept" of marriage, it is the negation of a relation which as a legal relation is "conceivable", comprehensible "in and of itself". It is the same in the end with the forms of state that belong to the past and whose existence is in conflict with their "idea": like dead wood and poverty they are a dead existence; like a dissolved marriage they have become the negation of their "idea", their "concept", and are therefore no longer "conceivable", comprehensible "in terms of themselves". Their moral existence has died.

Thus death, whether natural or moral, is the crucial contradiction that prevents us from comprehending natural and moral existence from its "idea", from its essence and its truth, "in terms of itself". Death brings the definitive separation between truth and reality; it is the point at which reality has become untrue and truth unreal. A deceased marriage is a

88

marriage "whose existence is a mere fraud and delusion" (*deren Existenz nur Schein und Trug ist*). Similarly, the impoverished class form a category of citizens whose citizenship is mere fraud and delusion. Likewise, a state which in its reality is the negation of its truth is just a sham state: "I can do nothing more in Germany. People here are self-deceived."

We have now been able to explain the negative conclusion to which Marx had come in rather more detail, using his own words. That also applies to the addition that legal relations and forms of state are not to be comprehended "in terms of the so called universal development of the human mind" (*aus der sogenannten allgemeinen Entwicklung des menschlichen Geistes*). Death, after all, is the definitive end of development; death makes it manifest that an existence is separated from its allotted purpose, that it has ceased to develop in the direction of its intended goal; in death an existence resolves itself, is dissolved (*aufgelöst*). Nature changes from living organism into dead, passive, mechanistic matter which cannot be understood at all in terms of the "idea" of the organism. The spiritual organism of the state ceases to develop further in accordance with the general purpose and end of the human mind, evolution has become devolution, the dead form of the state is an item of spiritless matter, now totally incomprehensible in terms of the "idea" of the spiritual organism. But it applies also to world history as an expression of "the universal development of the human mind". A deceased form of state lies under the judgment of world history, sentence of death has been pronounced upon it; its dead existence is no longer comprehensible in the least from the living development of world history.

Now that we have managed to account for Marx's negative conclusion, can we likewise explain its positive complement? Legal relations and forms of state are *not* comprehensible in terms of themselves, that is to say, the fact of their dissolution, of their negation, is *not* to be understood by this means. How then are they to be understood? Apparently, at any rate, in a way not accordant with their "idea". They have to be understood by reference to something else, something foreign to their nature. To put it another way: because they can themselves be the negation of their nature, because "no moral existence *necessarily* corresponds to its essential nature" (*keine sittliche*

Existenz entspricht, oder muss wenigstens nicht ihrem Wesen ent-sprechen), therefore they have to be interpreted in terms of the negation of their nature.

Now we must attend closely to Marx's choice of expression. The positive part of his conclusion does *not* say that legal relations and forms of state can *of course* be understood on the basis of the material circumstances of life; he says only that they *are rooted* therein (*vielmehr in den materiellen Lebensverhält-nissen wurzeln*). Let us first analyse the phrase "material circumstances of life". We have already become familiar with the term "material" in the context of Marx's various writings of this period; and without exception the term turned out to have a negative implication *vis-à-vis* organic nature as well as the spiritual organism. Matter is unconscious, mindless, passive, mechanistic. Purely "material" is the *dead* organism which has disintegrated into lifeless elements, has become a simply material substance. Even so, Marx speaks quite explicitly of "material circumstances of *life*". Here we seem to encounter a contradiction in terms. Indeed, we must go one step further and ask ourselves whether perhaps this terminological contra-diction adequately expresses a real contradiction. The con-tradiction is the fact of *death*. The actual fact that dead legal relations and deceased forms of state do exist is not to be under-stood in terms of the "idea" of life; but it is essentially bound up with the further reality that there are "material circumstances of life", that is, circumstances of life that have come to be "matter", that are deceased. This interrelation is a *hidden* one; for what is visible is the "fraud and delusion" of the dead existence which still persists as a living organism, whilst in reality it is already a living corpse. This hidden connection is expressed in the phrase "are rooted" (*wurzeln*). The root of a tree or plant eludes the eye, one sees only the trunk or stem, the leaves and the fruit. One cannot examine the root, either; for to do that one would have to dig it up and so destroy the living organism. If the root is diseased, then the plant may still flourish for a time; but it is a kind of sham life. If we want to prove that the plant is doomed to death, however, we shall have to expose the root, unless we wait quietly for the leaves to die off and so reveal what in concealment was already a fact.

Now Marx does not assert that legal relations and forms of

state are to be understood by reference to the material circumstances of life that together go by the name of "civil society". He says only that those relations and forms *are rooted* therein.

Does this mean that one must abandon any form of "notion", of "idea"? No; the sentence is not yet finished, it moves straight on into a third clause which starts with a "however". This third part stands in contrast to the second: "however, the anatomy of civil society must be looked for in political economy" (*dass aber die Anatomie der bürgerlichen Gesellschaft in der politischen Ökonomie zu suchen sei*). Anatomy is, literally, cutting asunder, cutting into the constituent pieces, analysing, splitting into atoms, resolving. The anatomist's dissecting knife really does the same thing that is achieved by the process of dissolution set going by death. The perfect anatomy of the living organism is the pathological anatomy, the autopsy, the postmortem. Anatomy can be applied adequately only to the dead organism. In order to be able to dissect the root one has to put paid to the life.

The third clause, then, looks back to the first one, which posits the incomprehensible character of legal relations and forms of state on the basis of their "idea". The second clause explains that the *root* of these incomprehensible relations and forms lies in the material circumstances of life of civil society. The third clause answers the question how this hidden interconnection can ever be brought to light: by anatomy. It is the scalpel of the critique of political economy that penetrates to the root and determines accurately whether the living organism (the "circumstances of life") of civil society is really alive or whether it is only leading a sham life, a life marked off for death. Only exposure of the root makes it possible to provide exact evidence. How difficult and protracted a task this anatomy entails is expressed in the verbal phrase "must be looked for" (*zu suchen sei*).

The critical exploration that awaited him and was to be his life's work was at the same time the long and arduous road to self-liberation from the doubt that had assailed him. A critical revision of Hegel's *Philosophy of Law* was the first step in that direction. The doubt that had affected him from his first encounter with Hegel's thought is whipped up into a storm. We have to interpret the word "doubt" in its original sense of a duality, an inner dividedness, a being at variance with oneself. Indeed the remarkable ambivalence that we noticed earlier is a striking feature of the articles belonging to this period. On the one hand, Hegel is complimented as the great philosopher of constitutional law, in the tradition that runs from Machiavelli *via* Hugo Grotius and Rousseau to the nineteenth century; the upholder of true philosophy which has emancipated itself from theology, has discovered the "law of gravity" of the state, contemplates the state with a human vision and unfolds the natural laws of the state from reason and experience. On the other hand, Hegel is subjected to a radical critique. He is reproached with having wanted to subsume concrete problems of morality and law under universal concepts, which admittedly define the truth, but contribute nothing to an understanding of concrete reality. If that would appear to be a purely philosophical criticism, a second charge is of a far more serious nature, not least because of the context in which it is set. The remark, inserted almost *en passant*, that in 1831 Hegel taught the philosophy of law by special behest of the government, forms part of Marx's last act as editor of the *Rheinische Zeitung*, his critical analysis of the ban imposed by the government, appended to an official letter to that government. To the philosophical doubt felt by the disciple concerning the master a political misgiving is added also; and the barb pierces deep into the flesh. The parting with a journalistic career, the parting with Germany, the parting with the Prussian state, is at the same time a parting with Hegel. The special mention of the date, 1831, acquires an extra and peculiar value in the light of the situation. It was the year of Hegel's death. We may recall how Marx drew an analogy between natural death and moral death. In nature, death is the manifestation of the contradiction between existence and appropriate end or use; but a similar contradiction also becomes manifest in moral death. By special command of the government Hegel taught the philosophy of law in the year of his death. Was it also the year when his philosophy died; and was the governmental instruction which enthroned him as the state philosopher actually a sentence of death passed upon his philosophy of state law? Eleven years afterwards, by special order of the government, silence was imposed on Marx's *critique* and the death sentence of the

Rheinische Zeitung was signed. Yet what the government regarded as a finale the victim felt to be a step forward in political awareness. In the light of this conflicting analogy the critical revision of Hegel's *Philosophy of Law*, in pursuit of which he had withdrawn from the public stage into the seclusion of the study, assumes a singular perspective. Only a radical critique and a fundamental revision are able to resurrect Hegel's philosophy from a philosophical death.

4

Hegel's accommodation of civil society to the state

ANYONE who one and a half centuries later examines
Hegel's lectures on the *Philosophy of Law* and, with a
sharp eye for the text, sets Marx's critical commentary
side by side with them, must surely realize the distance that
separates him from Hegel and Marx alike. Hegel ran lecture
courses on the *Philosophy of Law* in the period between 1821 and
1825; Marx wrote his *Critique* in 1842 and in the summer of
1843, and the Introduction to his *Critique* in the following year.
That is, the master was followed by his critical disciple at a
distance of scarcely twenty years. In 1831, the year of Hegel's
death, Marx was thirteen years old. He only just missed
sitting among Hegel's audience in the Berlin lecture-room.
Everything that Marx has written about Hegel exudes the
feeling of an immediate relationship, as direct and profound as
the bond between father and son. For Marx, Hegel was not as
yet a figure relegated to the past. Whilst Marx's writings are
indeed rich in historical reflection, one looks to them in vain for
any historical and biographical consideration of the course of
Hegel's development. That is all the more remarkable in that,
as I pointed out in my first series of lectures, Marx examined
very critically indeed the development of the philosopher,
Schelling, for example, and set out to demonstrate the decadence of the older Schelling from a comparison with the work
he did as a young man.

Admittedly, we have to allow for the fact that Hegel's dis-
tinctively youthful work was unknown to Marx; but the works

he *did* know would have provided more than enough material in themselves for a genetic analysis of Hegel's thinking. The road that leads from the *Phänomenologie des Geistes* (1807) by way of the *Logik* (1812–16) to the *Rechtsphilosophie* (1821–25) marks the successive stages of Hegel's development. Although Marx made a profound study of each of these major works, one can find no trace in his commentaries of a historical comparison. He sees not a progress, a career, with its landmarks but a philosophical whole, undifferentiated even in its parts. For historical reflection a degree of mental and intellectual distance is necessary. In Marx's relationship to Hegel this indispensable distance is lacking; his reflection is different from that of an onlooker or of a man gazing out from a lofty vantage-point. He stands plumb in the middle of the philosophical thinking he is criticizing; indeed, he quite deliberately chooses that position. Although his *Critique* is rooted in the conscious awareness that he is living in the post-Hegelian period, at the same time it is the knife of self-reflection that probes down into the roots and analyses the basic interrelation. The postulate of physical science embodied in the definition *post non propter*—a temporal sequence does not of itself entail any casual connection—does not meet the requirements of critical, philosophical reflection, it casts about for the essential relation that links Hegel's thought with the post-Hegelian consciousness. In the preliminary studies for the dissertation Marx put it like this: that the task is to construe Hegel's basic form of consciousness and in so doing to transcend it. This approach he sees as the only productive way of sizing up the progressive adaptation of Hegel to the ruling political powers. He is no more ready to consider that phenomenon, of which he is as fully aware as his young Hegelian colleagues, from a moral standpoint than he is interested in a historical or biographical explication. His reflecting is done from the inside, it is not any kind of external observation.

The modern reader of Marx's *Critique* of Hegel can come nowhere near the immediacy of his critical reflection, the more so when one takes into consideration our critical remoteness from Marx's thought. We are cut off by a historical gulf, and we see Hegel and Marx standing together, as it were, on the farther side. This loss of immediacy can only be made good by a gain in historical awareness which we owe in particular to the fact that meanwhile insight into Hegel's development has grown considerably and a careful study has been made of his early works. That achievement belongs to the twentieth century. Where we are concerned, the aim that Marx set himself—that of construing Hegel's basic form of consciousness—can only be approached indirectly, through a biographical analysis of his philosophical thinking. Marx envisaged this "construction" in a critical, indeed, a negative sense, as a means of clarifying the essential connection between Hegel's growing political conservatism and the fundamental defects of his philosophical system. The fact that our historical insight has grown permits us nowadays a critical construction which is also positive and would appear to be the hidden reverse side of Marx's negative *Critique*.

At first sight, it is a surprising discovery to find already figured out in Hegel's youthful work the critical reflection of which the young Marx made himself the interpreter. But as one weighs the matter further, initial astonishment turns to insight into the method Marx had proposed to himself. His construction of Hegel's essential form of consciousness turns out to be based on analysis of Hegel's inwardly divided state, which we recognize in a biographical perspective. Indeed, to the practised eye it is quite possible to uncover the inner contradictions even in the *Rechtsphilosophie*, the work of the more mature Hegel; but if one checks with the early work, they are already evident at first reading. It will be enough for the purpose of illustration to cite a document which Hegel wrote at the age of twenty-eight.

In 1798 he wrote a critical study on "the most recent internal circumstances of Württemberg and in particular on the defects of the constitution". Here Hegel shows himself, even in the concrete analysis of the German situation, to be a supporter of the ideas of the French Revolution. He gives voice to the generally widespread and deep-rooted feeling that the existing state fabric was on the point of collapse. There was universal anxiety and fear of such a breakdown; but people preferred to let things slide to the point where an ineluctable fate would sweep everything away with it as it fell than deliberately to bring down the fabric, so long as there was still time to decide what was untenable and what might remain standing. What obtuseness to think that institutions which had ceased to meet the needs of human beings and laws from which all the spirit had departed would yet be able to survive. Justice is the only true yardstick; for the task now is, open-eyed, to submit everything, item by item, to examination. Those who suffer injustice must demand an end to that injustice; and those who have wrongfully seized property must freely surrender it.

In the heart and mind of the older Hegel, indeed, the flame of this apocalyptic awareness that lifeless institutions are destined to die, does seem to have been wellnigh smothered under a covering of contemplative thinking. Shocked by the July Revolution and forced on to the defensive by the charges against him of slavish subjection to church and state, he complains in the year before his death, at the end of 1830, of the totally paramount political preoccupation which presently leaves room for nothing else—a crisis in which everything that had been operative and effectual before seems now to have become problematical. Shortly before his death he concludes the Foreword to the second edition of his *Logik* by voicing the fear that in this politically turbulent age there is no place any more for the unimpassioned calm of purely contemplative knowledge.

The distance separating the young Hegel from the old is so impressive that it may threaten to distort our view of Hegel as a whole. Although the course of development from the youthful champion of the French Revolution, *via* the glorification of Napoleon, to the state philosopher of the Prussian monarchy may be explicable in biographical and psychological terms and may also be understandable and acceptable, at any rate by political conservatism, that does not help to clarify our picture of Hegel but rather obscures it. To the construction of Hegel's basic form of consciousness, such a descriptive account of a career, based on external observation, can make no contribution, let alone be a springboard for transcending the defects of his form of consciousness. Since that was precisely what Marx was after, this notion of Hegel cannot be the mirror in which his *Critique* of Hegel's *Rechtsphilosofie* is justly and truly represented.

Perhaps the best introduction to Hegel's *Rechtsphilosofie* is the one he wrote himself, the Foreword to the *Grundliniën der Philosophie des Rechts (Outline of the Philosophy of Law),* of 1821. On occasion the actual Introduction *(Einleitung)* with which the work begins may shed some light.

Hegel starts by showing the connection between this *Philosophy of Law* and his *Logik,* written several years previously. His *Philosophy of Law* differs from an ordinary compendium by reason of the speculative method, which develops its subject step by step in the manner of scientific demonstration. The speculative method lets the notion develop independently and does no more than follow closely the immanent self-unfolding of the notion and the unfurling of its various aspects. The driving principle behind the movement of the notion is such that the particular is not just resolved into the universal but, *vice versa,* at the same time is engendered in its particularization out of the universal. This principle bears the special name of *dialectic.* Not the negative dialectic which one finds so often in Plato, but the positive dialectic of the notion. This dialectic is not an external activity of subjective thinking, but the very soul of the matter, putting forth its branches and fruit organically. This development of the Idea as the proper activity of its rationality *(Vernunft)* is merely observed by subjective thinking as by an onlooker, without its adding anything to that development. To consider a thing rationally *(vernünftig)* means not to bring reason *(Vernunft)* to bear on the object from the outside and so to tamper with it, but to find that the object is rational on its own account *(ist für sich selbst vernünftig).* Here it is mind in its freedom, the culmination of self-conscious reason, which gives itself actuality and engenders itself as an existing world. The sole task of philosophic science is to bring into consciousness this proper work of the reason of the thing itself *(Vernunft der Sache).*

The speculative method is as much opposed to a kind of scientific reasoning based on an external knowledge acquired by the understanding as it also differs radically from any attempt to derive truth from inner feeling, imagination or fantasy. The truth about law, morality and the state has been long established and been made common knowledge in public laws, as well as being common property in the morality of everyday life and in religion. Free speculative thinking, however, does not unquestioningly accept whatever is given, whether it be based on the external, positive authority of the state or public opinion, or is supported by the authority of inward feeling and emotion and by the "witness of the spirit", which directly concurs with it. No; speculative thinking insists upon grasping what is given; it will not rest until it has brought the content of what is given, which is already inherently rational, into the *form* of rationality; for the identity of form and content is the philosophical Idea.

At this point Hegel immediately adds the warning that freedom of thought is something quite different from the thinking up of novelties which diverge from truths publicly recognized. The speculative philosophy of state and church, in particular, is opposed to the idea that theory is bound to start all over again from the beginning, as though a state or a constitution had never before existed. Of course, it is taken for granted that philosophy alone can bring nature as it is within its ken: in other words, that nature is inherently rational (*vernünftig*) and that what human knowledge has to investigate and grasp in concepts is this actual reason (*Vernunft*), present in nature—not the superficial phenomena and coincidences but the eternal harmony which is the law and essence immanent in nature. On the other hand, this insight is not applied when what is in question is the ethical world, the state. On the contrary, the universe of mind is left to the mercy of chance and caprice, it has to be God-forsaken, so that in virtue of the atheism of the ethical world, truth is inevitably to be found outside it.

The phrase "atheism of the ethical world" Hegel intends as a parallel to the atheism of the natural world. In that context he directs his attack more especially against Epicurean philosophy. Just as, according to Epicurus, the "world in general" is governed by accident, so according to this atheism of the world of ethics this last should be given over to the subjective accident of opinion and caprice. Hegel does not use the term "atheism", however, in the customary sense; for he at once goes on to say that a conception of this kind, which is based entirely on subjective feeling, may also assume the guise of a piety that relies on saintliness and on the Bible. Whether in an atheistic or religious form, there is opposition to true philosophy, to speculative philosophy. Its substance is the inclusive knowledge of God and of physical and mental nature, the knowledge of the truth.

This brings Hegel to his main theme: the relation of philosophy to the actual world. Philosophy is the exploration of the rational (*Vernünftigen*), that is to say, the apprehension of the present (*Gegenwärtigen*) and the actual, not the erection of a beyond (*Jenseitigen*) supposed to exist, God knows where, or rather which exists, and we can perfectly well say where, namely, in the error of a one-sided, empty ratiocination.

By way of an example he reminds us of Plato's *Republic*. In an important passage in the chapter on "civil society" Hegel will return to this; and I shall be going further into his thinking in that context. Anticipating that, he here sums up his argument in an analysis of the inner contradiction in Plato's philosophy of the state. The current view of Plato's *Republic* sees it as an empty ideal. That is a misconception; for in essence Plato's *Republic* is nothing but an interpretation of the nature of Greek ethical life. But at the same time Plato was conscious of a deeper principle breaking into that life, which at first sight was bound to appear in it only as a longing still unsatisfied, and so only as something pernicious. Plato was all too conscious of this deeper, unsatisfied longing and felt himself obliged to seek for help in order to combat it; but this help, which would have had to come from on high, he could only seek in the first instance in a particular external form of that same Greek ethical life. By that means he thought he could master the baneful influence of this invading principle; but in fact the outcome was that he did fatal injury to the deeper impulse which underlay it, namely, free infinite personality. Still, his genius is proved by the fact that the principle on which the distinctive character of his Idea of the state turns is precisely the pivot on which the impending world revolution turned at that time.

What is rational is actual and what is actual is rational (*vernünftig*). On this conviction the plain man takes his stand, as indeed does philosophy; and from it philosophy starts in its study of the universe of mind as well as of nature. If reflection, feeling or whatever form subjective consciousness may take, looks upon the present (*Gegenwart*) as something vacuous and looks beyond it with the eyes of superior wisdom, it finds itself in a vacuum, because there is actuality only in the present

(*Gegenwart*). If, on the other hand, the Idea is held to be "an idea and nothing more", something represented as being true, philosophy rejects that and comes up with the view that nothing is real, is actual, except the Idea. The thing then is to recognize in the show of the temporal and transient the substance which is immanent and the eternal which is present (*gegenwärtig*). For the rational (*Vernünftige*), which is synonymous with the Idea, enters upon external existence simultaneously with its actualization and so emerges with an infinite wealth of forms, shapes and appearances. Around its kernel it throws a motley outer lining within which consciousness is initially at home—a covering layer which the concept has first to penetrate before it can find the inward pulse and feel it still beating in the outward forms.

However, this infinite wealth of forms and circumstances, developed in the realm of outward appearance, is not the subject-matter of philosophy. Hegel sees his philosophy of state and law purely and simply as an endeavour to apprehend and portray the state as something inherently rational (*ein in sich Vernünftiges*). As a piece of philosophical writing his work must put as far away as it possibly can the idea that it is somehow called upon to construct a state as it ought to be (*wie er sein soll*). It is not the task of philosophy to teach the state what it should be; but rather are we to learn from philosophy how the state, that is, the universe of mind, is to be understood.

Hic Rhodus, hic saltus.

To comprehend what is, this is the task of philosophy, because what is, is reason (*Vernunft*). Every individual is a child of his time; so philosophy too is its own time apprehended in thoughts. It is just as foolish to nurse the delusion that a philosophy can ever transcend its contemporary world as to suppose that an individual can overleap his own age, can jump over Rhodes. If his theory really goes beyond the world as it is and builds an ideal one as it ought to be, that world exists indeed, but only in his opinion—an unsubstantial element where anything you please may, in fancy, be built.

The expression *Hic Rhodus, hic saltus* is seized upon by Hegel as the starting-point for an argument that penetrates to the religious core of his philosophy. The passage which now follows, is of the greatest importance to see the connection between Hegel's philosophy of state and law and the religious core of his speculative thinking. Only on a basis of insight into the connection as we find it in Hegel's work is it possible to understand the intrinsic cohesion of Marx's critique of heaven and earth.

Hegel picks up the phrase *Hic Rhodus, hic saltus*; but as with the modulation of a theme in a musical composition, he now starts from a play on words: The "here is Rhodes, here the leap" gets modulated into:

Hier is die Rose, hier tanze—Here is the rose, dance thou here.

This punning alludes to the image which Luther chose as his device: a black cross at the centre of a heart surrounded with roses. But Hegel gave this emblem a unique modulation. The point is, so his argument runs, to apprehend reason (*Vernunft*) in the cross of the present (*im Kreuze der Gegenwart*) and thereby to enjoy the present. This rational insight reconciles us to the actual, the reconciliation which philosophy affords to those in whom there has once arisen an inner voice bidding them to comprehend. For it is a matter not only of sustaining subjective freedom in substantive actuality but also of taking a stand with subjective freedom, not in anything particular and accidental but in the actuality of the Idea (*in dem, was an und für sich ist*). On the other hand, what lies between reason as self-conscious mind and reason (*Vernunft*) as an actual world before our eyes, what separates the former from the latter, is the fetter of some abstraction or other which has not been liberated into the concept. The philosophical Idea is the conscious identity of form and content. Form in its most concrete signification is reason (*Vernunft*) as speculative knowing, and content is reason (*Vernunft*) as the substantial essence of actuality, whether ethical or natural.

It now becomes clear in what sense Hegel set out to modulate the image of the rose and cross in Luther's device and make it useful to speculative philosophy. True philosophy completes the work of faith. Characteristic of the modern age is the obstinate refusal to recognize in conviction anything not ratified by thought; moreover, this is the specific principle of Protestantism. What Luther initiated as faith in feeling and in the witness of the spirit, is precisely what spirit, since it became more mature, has striven to apprehend in the concept, so as to free itself into the present (*Gegenwart*) and so re-discover itself in the world of today.

It looks as though Hegel has tacitly shifted over from the field of the philosophy of law to that of the philosophy of religion. That mistaken idea, however, can only spring from a failure to grasp the essential connection between the two parts of his speculative philosophy. In fact, Hegel's argument has done no more than prepare the ground for the conclusion on which his *Philosophy of Law* is based. The completion of the work of faith by speculative thought he now proceeds to sum up as the relation between half philosophy and "true philosophy". Whilst "a half-philosophy leads away from God", true philosophy on the other hand leads to God—and the same is true of the state. A half philosophy locates knowledge in an approximation to truth. This lukewarmness is every bit as paltry as the cold despair that would settle for a compromise with the actual world because you really cannot expect too much of this time-bound existence. There is less chill in the peace with reality which true knowledge supplies.

Hegel is still talking, let it be remembered, about the actual nature of the state. The content of true philosophy, after all, is the speculative knowledge of God and of physical and mental nature, a knowledge of the truth. The state is mental nature, the ethical universe. Knowledge of the truth is knowledge of reality, it is knowledge of God and of physical and of mental nature.

To end with, he tops his argument that philosophy is a way of grasping present actuality with an indirect demonstration. Returning to the claim, rejected earlier on, that we have to teach the state what it ought to be, he shows once more how absurd that is; but he now approaches the problem from the opposite side. There again, philosophy cannot entertain the idea of having to instruct the world in what it ought to be (*wie sie sein soll*), because philosophy in any case always comes on the scene too late for that. The fact is that, as the thought of the world, it appears only when actuality is already there, cut and dried, after its process of formation has been completed. History too shows that it is only when actuality is mature that the ideal first appears over against the real; only then does the ideal build up for itself this same world, apprehended in its substance, into the shape of an intellectual realm. When philosophy paints its grey in grey, then a form of life has grown old, and by this grey in grey it cannot be rejuvenated but only understood; the owl of Minerva spreads its wings only as twilight descends.

With this image Hegel concludes the Preface to his *Philosophy of Law*. It may seem at first sight that the owl, who sets about her task when the sun is already declining, is going to set her stamp on the whole work; but that is a delusion and rests on a fundamental misconception. From start to finish, Hegel's argument is designed to show that true philosophy is nothing other than the recognition of present actuality. Starting from this basic thought, he resolutely rejects every view that pretends to a different relation to reality, whether it be the founding of knowledge on an inner sentiment or on an opinion, or the striving to ascend above and beyond present actuality into an ideal realm to whose norms reality ought to conform. He does not deny that an ideal construction of this kind may have a relation to the actual world; on the contrary, he expressly defends Plato's *Republic* against the prevailing view that it represents no more than an empty ideal. Plato's *Republic* is indeed the expression of the nature of Greek ethical life, it certainly does have a philosophical relation to present actuality, that is, to the actual world of Plato's time. For himself, Plato did indeed grasp his world in its substance and did build that world up for himself in the guise of an intellectual realm. Hegel does not believe, however, that such a philosophical relation to present actuality is feasible in any other way than as a reflection of a process of maturation that has already reached its culminating point. This reflection is only real wisdom as being the self-contemplation of the greybeard who has completed his life's course and is preparing himself for the end; it is the self-contemplation of the ripened fruit, now on the point of bursting open; it is a final glance at the world, which is very close to departing, a glance at the world which in effect has already become a glance backward into the past. In the possibility of looking ahead, the anticipation of a coming world, the reaching forward to grasp a reality still hidden in the womb of the present, actual world, in this Hegel would appear to have no belief at all. Every construction of an ideal realm in contrast to present actuality, which is supposed to conform itself to the design of the ideal construction, is to him an empty ideal, pure abstraction.

It says a great deal, therefore, that at the end of his Preface Hegel refers back to Plato. He had already on an earlier occasion explained the inner contradiction of Plato's philosophy of the state in terms of Plato's awareness that a new principle was starting to gain ground in the ancient world, an intuitive sense of an impending revolution in the world. Against this new principle Plato took the firmest possible stand. Indeed, Plato's genius is like the movements of Minerva's owl, movements that presage the onset of night. Hegel, on the other hand, takes this new principle as his starting-point. His philosophy of law would be inconceivable without that revolution which Plato had seen approaching and against which he had tried to protect himself in his intellectual realm. This new principle is that of free and infinite personality. Whereas the *Vorrede*, the Preface, ends with the owl of Minerva, announcing the approach of night, the work itself begins straightaway with this new principle, the corner-stone of Hegel's philosophy of state and law.

This perspective also reveals in a different light the assertion that what is reasonable is real, and what is real is reasonable. This statement follows immediately on the passage showing how great was Plato's genius from the fact of the presentiment in his philosophy regarding the breakthrough of this new principle and of the revolutionary change coming upon the world. The rationality that Hegel has in view is the rationality of this new principle, and the reality is that of the revolutionized world.

The central problem of Hegel's philosophy of law is the question of how the dilemma on which Plato's philosophy of the state foundered can be resolved for our own time. Plato felt the breaking through of the new principle of free and infinite personality to be the forced entry of an alien intruder who had to be warded off at all costs. The best he could do was to man the battlements of Greek morality as it then was, or in other words to entrench himself in an external form. The modern epoch, on the other hand, takes this very principle as its point of departure; and so the problem presented by the philosophy of state and law today is in a sense the reverse of the one that Plato was confronted with. The question nowadays is how, starting as we do from the principle of free, infinite personality, we can arrive by a reasonable route at the idea of an extrinsic morality, of a universe of mind, the state, and do so in such a way that both factors, the inner principle and the external order, can exist in perfect harmony with each other, nay, can be apprehended as identical the one with the other.

This whole nexus of problems likewise governs the structure of Hegel's *Philosophy of Right*. It comprises three parts: abstract right (*das abstrakte Recht*); morality (*die Moralität*); ethical life (*die Sittlichkeit*).

The starting-point of "right" in this context is the free will, that is to say, that freedom is the substance of the will, and the system of right is the realm of actualized freedom, so that the world of mind is, as it were, the will's second nature. Before this starting-point becomes a complete reality, the free will has to undergo a process of development. It begins with the stage of abstract right, based on the principle of personality, which is aware of itself as something infinite, universal and free. Not until the human subject attains consciousness of itself as a completely abstract "I" does the subject start to become a personality. Thus, personality is the foundation of an abstract, purely formal right, summed up in the imperative: be a person and respect others as persons. To the abstract notion of personality there corresponds an abstract matter: property. The first section begins, therefore, with a consideration of the right to property.

The next stage of development of the free will is morality (*Moralität*). Hegel draws a sharp distinction between morality (*Moralität*) and "ethical life" (*Sittlichkeit*). Morality is the standpoint on which the free will attains to interior reflection and takes a position as subjective individuality over against the universal. At this stage therefore a division appears. The right of the subjective will is opposed to the right of the world and the right of the objective idea of freedom, which is not as yet rooted in the subjective consciousness. An inner intention, wellbeing, is still unreconciled with the external reality of the existing world.

The third and highest stage of development of the free will is the ethical system or "ethical life" (*Sittlichkeit*). In this stage the opposition, the contrast, unbridgeable in the stage of morality, is overcome. The ethical system unites in itself both aspects of the idea of the good, the inner aspect of morality and the outward aspect of the world in which the good assumes a shape. In the stage of "ethical life" (*Sittlichkeit*) freedom becomes an identity of objective and subjective freedom, a unity of substance and subjective will.

The substance of "ethical life" is subdivided into three elements, the very number constituting the process of development of the free will which in this third and highest stage is on the way to its completion. These three elements are: the family (*die Familie*); civil society (*die bürgerliche Gesellschaft*); the state (*der Staat*). The family represents the element of natural mind (*Natürlicher Geist*). The principle of free, infinite personality, however, resolves the natural family relationship into a multiplicity of persons who encounter each other in an external context: civil society. To the extent that this relation, this bond, represents only an external cohesion it is the outside of the substance of the ethical system. Moreover, at this level the natural family-unit is dissolved, divided up into self-dependent persons. That is why Hegel defines civil society as the stage attained by the substance of ethical life in its disruption (*Entzweiung*) and "appearance" (*Erscheinung*).

The level constituted by civil society, therefore, cannot possibly be the final point of the developmental process; for division strives after reunification, the outward manifestation has not so far disclosed its essence. In the last phase of the process the sphere of civil society is transmuted into the state. Whilst in the sequence imposed by speculative thought the state looks like a result of the whole development, this shows it in fact to be the very foundation of the process. Actually, the state is the true ground, outside which the family and civil society could not take shape; and it is the idea of the state itself that disrupts into these two elements. The state is the ethical idea, now actualized; it is ethical mind *qua* the substantial will manifest and evident to itself, knowing itself and thinking itself, accomplishing what it knows, as far as its knowledge may extend. The state is absolutely rational (*das an und für sich Vernünftige*) inasmuch as it is the actuality of the substantial will. It is an absolute and unmoved end in itself, in which freedom attains to its supreme right, just as this final end has a supreme right *vis-à-vis* individuals, whose highest duty is to be members of the state.

The chapter on the state is divided into three sections: constitutional law (*das innere Staatsrecht*); international law (*das aüssere Staatsrecht*); world history (*die Weltgeschichte*). This three-fold division discloses the three successive elements of the developing process of the ethical substance at this highest level.

In the free self-subsistence of the particular subjective will the state is at the same time universal, objective freedom. That is the actual and organic mind which is realized, in the first instance as the mind of a single nation (constitutional or internal polity), *via* the interrelation of particular national minds (international law), in world history, and thus reveals itself as the universal world-mind whose right is supreme. The history of the world is the world's court of judgment. If, in the chapter on the state, one could suppose for a moment that the state as the ethical universe is the absolute and final end of the process, then this ethical universe is in its turn placed at the mercy of the supremely dynamic play of world history—the ocean into which the fortunes of each particular state run out. In the end the autonomy of states, as Hegel puts it, is exposed to contingency (*ist der Zufälligkeit ausgesetzt*). The dialectic of the finitude and limitation of particular states gives rise to the universal, unlimited mind of world history, just as, conversely, they fall under the judgment of world history, whose right is supreme.

Thus, in conclusion, we see how very much Hegel's philosophy of state and right is fundamentally bound up with his philosophy of history. This cohesion is also expressed in the structure of his system of philosophy, constructed as it is on the threefold division into logic (as pure science), the philosophy of nature and the philosophy of spirit (the two sciences of reality, *realen Wissenschaften*). The philosophy of spirit is in its turn sub-divided into subjective spirit, objective spirit and absolute spirit. In this middle part, of objective spirit, the philosophy of state and right is set beside the philosophy of history.

On closer inspection we discover this dialectic of history,

108

whereby the seemingly static, self-subsistent universe of the state is placed at the mercy of an even higher, extremely dynamic right, in the structure of the philosophy of law. Between the natural cell of the ethical organism, the family, and the totality of the ethical organism, the state, Hegel has driven the wedge of an unquiet, disquieting element, alien, negative, and, in relation to family and state inorganic, civil society. This element succeeds, in the process by which the free will develops, the element of the family, just as finally the element of the state is succeeded by that of world history. Within the philosophy of law as a whole, civil society is the historical element *par excellence*, the intrusion of history into an organic whole aspiring to self-sufficiency and an absolute status.

In point of fact, the dual title of Hegel's philosophy of law in itself enshrines the range of historical problems which it is an attempt to master. The title "Elements of the Philosophy of Right" (*Grundlinien der Philosophie des Rechts*) is accompanied by a subtitle, "Natural Law and Political Science" (*Naturrecht und Staatswissenschaft*). This duality expresses the fact that when natural law, on the one hand, and political science, on the other, are united, what emerges is the philosophy of right. In this, Hegel's philosophy of law expressly differs from the modern theory of natural law as that had developed in the sixteenth and seventeenth centuries; and it is no less emphatically remote from classical political science. His speculative philosophy of right is aimed at overcoming the one-sidedness of both, so as to develop and integrate them into a higher unity. In the Introduction (*Einleitung*) to the *Philosophy of Law* he argues that philosophy is stranger to the contrast between subjective inclination and the objective reality of positive law. No more can philosophy accept the authority of "the sentiments of the heart" as the ultimate authority of positive law; for in both these the dominating element is that of accident and caprice. Law from the philosophical viewpoint is to be distinguished from positive law; on the other hand, we must not turn the distinction into an opposition, for the philosophy of law is meant to be nothing other than speculative thinking about present reality as it has developed in the actual history of law. In this context Hegel uses the expression: "natural law or law

from the philosophical viewpoint (*das philosophische Recht*)".
This might give the impression that he simply identified the
two—philosophical and natural law—as distinct from positive
law. That this is a misconception seems clear from the series of
lectures on the *Philosophy of Law* which he gave during the
winter semester of 1822/23, that is to say, in the year after the
publication of the *Grundlinien der Philosophie des Rechts*. In
them he distinguishes very sharply between natural law and the
philosophy of law. In nature a law is validated in the final
instance purely because of the fact that it is there; in the sphere
of right, on the other hand, the laws are subject to a distinctive
criterion. Right is a product solely of mind; for nature has no
rights. Freedom cannot be thought of in the form of nature
but must be conceived in the form of the notion in which freedom is mediated, is reconciled with itself and with nature in a
higher unity. The term "natural law" in fact needs an overhaul
at this point; for what is presupposed in this term is a perfect
harmony of law and nature.

Hegel's uncertainty about the relation between nature and
law may be told from the development of his thinking through
various periods. At the same time, there is reflected in the
course of Hegel's development the whole question of the
development of natural law in the various phases of the history
of European thought. In a historical-cum-critical analysis of
the theory of natural law, written almost twenty years before
the *Philosophy of Law* (i.e. in 1802/3), Hegel sets over against
each other two methods of scientific procedure, the "empirical"
approach of the seventeenth, and the "formal" approach of the
eighteenth century at its close. Both, however, have a common
basis in the division between moral law (*lex moralis sive
naturalis*) and empirical nature. Thus the empirical approach,
as counterpart to positive empiricism, constructs a purely
negative concept of nature, whether it be a "state of nature" or
"human nature". As opposed to this negative notion, which he
sees as a product of the idealist philosophy of Kant and Fichte,
the young Hegel tries to establish a positive notion, that of an
"ethical nature". But his use of the "nature" concept is
ambiguous. On the one hand, he admits a connection with
Spinoza's concept of "nature" as a divine totality (*deus sive
natura*). On the other, he uses it in the formal sense of the term

"by nature", the Greek *phusei*. Hegel's notion of an "ethical nature" therefore conceals both a metaphysical notion of totality and Aristotle's definition that the whole "by nature" precedes the parts. In this ambiguity he secures himself a double justification for the idea of an "ethical universe" which enjoys absolute priority over the morality of the individual. The picture that Hegel has in his mind's eye is of the totality of the Greek *polis*, where the individual citizen derives his subjective morality or ethical life from the ethical substance of the political entity.

However, a few years later Hegel abandoned this line of thought and put the whole emphasis on the priority of the ethical subject, the individual, free personality. Starting from Hobbes' proposition that man is called upon to forsake the state of nature (*exeundum e statu naturae*), he adopts the line running from Rousseau to the idealist philosophy of Kant and Fichte. The philosophy of right cannot possibly have its point of departure in nature, for "by nature" man has neither rights nor obligations. Only *qua* person is man the subject of right; and he becomes a person only in the notion of freedom, which entails a break with the state of nature. Hegel grounds natural law no longer in the "ethical nature" of the whole but in that of freedom, which the subject himself produces.

Thus we see Hegel's thought, throughout the various phases of its development, following a typical oscillating motion between the whole and the parts; between the priority of the ethical universe and the capacity to originate of the ethical subject. An oscillation which one can follow in the ambiguities and shifting interpretations of the concept of nature. A similar nexus of problems encumbers the other element his *Philosophy of Law* attempts to assimilate: political science.

A dominant feature of Hegel's work, even in his youth, is his admiration for the living, substantial unity of the *polis*, which made Greek antiquity stand out so impressively from the impending disintegration and the demise of inherited religion that Hegel observed in his own age. It is not hard to discover in his *Philosophy of Law*, particularly in the chapter on the state, the influence of the *polis* idea, just as the term "political science" in the subtitle to this work connects with a tradition going back to classical antiquity. The distinctive thing about

Hegel's *Philosophy of Law*, however, is that besides political science he pursues another line as well: that of "civil society" (*bürgerliche Gesellschaft*). The term does not occur in the subtitle; but in the structure of the *Philosophy of Law* it in fact assumes a crucial position. That in itself tells us how difficult Hegel himself found it to give formal endorsement to the real importance which the notion of civil society was beginning to assume in his thinking. This is bound up with the various historical problems attendant on the development of the concepts "state" and "civil society".

Right through the Middle Ages as far as the modern period political science in Europe has continued to build on a terminology taken over from Aristotle. That terminology made no distinction between the notions of "state" and "civil society". The Greek word for "society" or "community", *koinonia*, like the Latin terms, *societas* and *communitas*, means simply combination, association. Yet these are the basic classical conceptual tools for defining the ancient *polis*, the state as *koinonia politikè* (Latin *societas civilis*). Aristotle simply equated this term with the term *polis*. The Latin tradition of European political science continues this and speaks without any distinction or differentiation of *civitas sive societas civilis sive res publica*. In this respect there is an uninterrupted line running from Thomas Aquinas and Albertus Magnus *via* Bodin, Hobbes and Locke to Immanuel Kant.

So strong was this tradition that even Rousseau could not resist its authority. In fact, he regards the state projected in his *Contrat social* as identifiable with civil society (*société civile*, Latin *societas civilis*). At the same time, the problems begin to manifest themselves in Rousseau, of which Hegel was to be the first to become so clearly conscious that he was able to express them in a sharp terminological distinction. Rousseau's problems turn around the contrast between human being and citizen, between natural order and civil order. One has to choose between the two; for the *société civile*, the civil society or state, cannot be built on a foundation of the initial human state of nature. The wretchedness of his time he sees as residing in the fact that people are being tossed to and fro between the two, that they are neither *homme* (man) nor *citoyen* (citizen). They are merely *bourgeois*, a hybrid mixture, in fact, nothing. Rousseau's design for a *société civile*, in which a man is in the full sense a citizen, *citoyen*, is based, on the one hand, on the modern theory of natural law as the reasonable freedom of the self-conscious subject, and, on the other hand, has in view the example of the classical *polis*.

The transition from Rousseau to Hegel is marked by an obvious shift in terminology. Rousseau's thinking helped to pave the way for the French Revolution; and Hegel's philosophy is speculative reflection upon the fact of the Revolution and its consequences, especially the emancipation of civil society from the classical political tradition. That is why Hegel's critique of Rousseau is also his critique of the French Revolution. He recognizes the major significance of Rousseau's break with traditional natural law, by grounding law (or "right") in the rational freedom of the human will, by which man is distinguished from animal. But Rousseau mistakenly wanted to derive the *société civile* of the state from the freedom of the individual. He was unable to resolve the discrepancy between the *volonté de tous* (the will of all) and the *volonté générale* (the general will), since he could only envisage free will as the individual will. The universal will he takes to be, not the inherently rational principle of the will, but only the "general" element which arises as a conscious product of the individual will. As a result, he reduces the association of individuals in the state to a contract (*contrat social*), based on their caprice, opinion and express approval, given according to whim. As an automatic consequence of this faulty construction, Hegel sees the destruction of the absolutely divine (principle of the state), of its absolute authority and majesty (*das an und für sich seiende Göttliche und dessen absolute Autorität und Majestät zerstörenden Konsequenzen*). The course taken by the French Revolution is for him the decisive proof of this consequence. In both the *Philosophy of Law* and the *Philosophy of History* (*Philosophie der Geschichte*) he exposes the positive and negative side of the French Revolution as the essential problem. He was teaching the philosophy of history, which is very closely related in his system to the philosophy of law, in the same period (from 1822); and the final chapter of the *Philosophy of Law*, dealing with world's history, is a *résumé* of the scheme to be developed in greater detail in the philosophy of history.

The French Revolution forms the crown and climax of Hegel's *Philosophy of History*, which ends by illuminating the importance of this upheaval for world history. He glorifies the unique act of the Revolution, which was this: that all at once the conception, the idea of right was made the foundation of a form of government. Never since the sun had stood in the firmament and the planets revolved around it, had it been shown that man's existence centres in his head, that is to say, in thought, on the basis of which he builds reality. Anaxagoras was the first to say that *nous*, mind, governs the world; but now man has reached the point of recognizing that thought must govern spiritual or mental reality. All thinking beings rejoiced in the arrival of this epoch. Lofty emotions took control of men at that time, a spiritual enthusiasm thrilled the world, a conviction that now at last a true reconciliation of the divine and the terrestrial had come.

He then outlines the course of post-revolutionary history *via* Robespierre and Napoleon to the restoration of the constitutional monarchy. For him, this development is proof of the unresolved dilemma of the Revolution, threatened from outside by the "catholic principle" bent on destroying the Revolution, undermined from within by the erroneous starting-point of the subjective will. He then goes further into this range of internal problems. In the final instance, the main imbalance consists in the fact that the ideal general will is also construed as the empirically general will; that is to say, that individuals as such should rule or share the task of government. Liberalism takes as the basis of everything the atomistic principle, the principle of the individual will. But it is impossible to establish a firm organizational structure on the quicksand of formal freedom, of this abstraction. The particular decrees of a government meet at once with opposition from the side of liberty; for those decrees are not general but are expressions of a particular will, that is, of arbitrary power. The will of the many brings down the government and the opposition takes its place, to be opposed in turn, as the government, by the many. Thus agitation and unrest are perpetuated. This collision, this nodus, this problem, Hegel concludes, is the point at which history now stands; and it is this problem that it will have to solve in times to come.

So Hegel's *Philosophy of History* ends up with the crucial dilemma of the French Revolution. He does not himself provide a solution; but he passes on the problem as the principal task confronting the future and the generations to come.

In the *Philosophy of Law*, too, he analyses the dilemma. The false starting-point of wanting to build the state with the bricks of individual acts of will has led, on the one side, to a revolution in world history that set out to create an entirely new basis for history in pure thought. This thought, however, was an empty abstraction, without the real content of the idea, of reason (*Vernunft*). Thus the revolution was perverted into its opposite and ended in a display of naked force and frightfulness.

Hegel had already stated in the Preface, that everything situated in the no-man's-land between reason as subjective mind and reason as objective reality is an unconceptualized abstraction. He now refers back to this. As over against the principle of the individual will he reminds us of the basic conception that the objective will is inherently rational, is the idea of the will, whether it be endorsed and recognized by individuals or not; on the other hand, the subjective will is only the one side, and thus a one-sided aspect of the idea of the rational will which unites in itself objective and subjective elements.

It is this idea of the rational will that is actualized in the state. The state is both the objectively and the subjectively rational (*das an und für sich Vernünftige*); for it is the actuality of the substantial will; in the state the particular self-consciousness is raised to universality.

It looks here as though Hegel does in fact see in the state the solution to the dilemma constituted by the contrast between the whole and the parts, between objective reality and subjective consciousness. Starting from the priority of the whole over the component parts, in other words, from the proposition that the whole is more than the sum of the parts, one may indeed find an embodiment for the idea of an ethical universe in the state, but at the expense of the original freedom of the individual citizens. If, conversely, one takes as one's starting-point the primary rationality of the subjective will, then one can certainly construct a state order built up out of individual parts. But that order may collapse at any moment, should a number of the individual parts decline to keep their place within the whole construction; for such a state order is no more than the sum of particular volitional acts. In fact, it looks as though the final chapter on the state presents us with the highest stage of the development of the free will, the speculative synthesis in which the thesis of the objective whole and the antithesis of the subjective part are reconciled and so become an absolute unity.

Moreover, as a vehicle for this speculative synthesis Hegel had available an appropriate terminology which had been handed down unaltered from classical antiquity right up to Rousseau. After all, in the traditional terminology, which equates *civitas* (Greek *polis*) with *societas civilis* (Greek *koinonia politikè*) and also with *res publica*, the dilemma does seem to be resolved. The term *civitas* expresses the priority of the whole over the parts, while, on the other hand, the term *societas civilis* envisages the whole as a combination or unification of the parts. The function of the term *res publica* could then be to express the synthesis.

But just at this point there breaks through in Hegel's philosophy, aiming as it does at an all-embracing synthesis, the inner conflict of present reality, which his thinking was intended to render comprehensible. Curiously enough, it is because Rousseau clings so firmly to the classical terminology that Hegel is finally forced to part company with it. What emerges here is a dialectic typical of the clash of continuity and discontinuity in the historical tradition. At the end of the eighteenth century, modern political philosophy looked back to the example of the ancient *polis*, and in so doing became all the more acutely aware of the distance separating the modern period from classical antiquity. Hence Rousseau's proposal for simply dropping words like *citoyen* and *patrie* altogether from the spoken language. At the same time, Rousseau was so very much tied to the classical tradition still that for his modern construction of the state as a *contrat social* he retained the classical expression *société civile*. Hegel's critique of Rousseau's political theory and of the French Revolution forced him to criticize the classical terminology too. He was the first person in the history of political science to import a sharp distinction into the classical terminology. The term "state" (*polis*, *civitas*) became the expression for the ethical universe that has priority over the subjects who form part of it. In sharp opposition to that he made the other term, "civil society" (*koinonia politikè, societas civilis*), a one-sided and exclusive expression for the social actuality which is characterized by the independence of its individual members. This sharp division made it possible, in the sphere of "civil society", to do full justice to Rousseau's individualistic starting-point, which in the sphere of the state, where Rousseau had wanted to apply the principle, he had so sharply criticized. This bifurcation of the terminology, on the one hand put an end to the ambiguity inherent in Rousseau's attempt to unify ancient and modern thought in a single political construction, and, on the other hand gave Hegel's theory of the state all the room it needed to compass the speculative construction of the state as the universe of mind, undisrupted by the intrusion of modern society; whilst in the other direction it gave room for modern society to be presented and observed in the clearest possible profile, as it had never been before.

Thus the sharp terminological cleavage in Hegel's *Philosophy of Law* is made to express a separation between state and civil society, which he identified more sharply than any predecessor or contemporary had done. He comes down explicitly against any confusion of the two factors, apparently unconscious of the fact that such a "confusion" had been the hallmark of the whole tradition of European political science, a tradition which he had been the first to abandon. If the state is confused with civil society, he argues, and its end is defined as the security and protection of property and personal freedom, then the interest (*das Interesse*) of individuals as such is the ultimate goal that unites them; and so it is entirely up to a man himself whether he wants to be a member of the state or no. No; the state's relation to the individual is something quite different; since the state is mind objectified, the individual has objectivity, authenticity and an ethical life only to the extent that he is a member of the state.

Along with this terminological divide goes a second modification which distinguishes Hegel's terminology from that devised by Rousseau. The contrast between *homme* and *citoyen*, in addition to the term *bourgeois* to denote the hydrid abortion that is neither man nor citizen, the phenomenon of the modern "private person", taking away from the initial totality of nature without having attained as yet to the *ordre civile*—this tripartite terminology Hegel takes over from Rousseau; but its meaning undergoes a radical change. Hegel rejects Rousseau's concept of an original state of nature in which a man is simply and solely a man. Hegel's developmental philosophy recognizes no other definition of "man" than what is consonant with each successive phase of development. Thus the terminology varies as each successive chapter of the *Philosophy of Law* may require. At the level of abstract right we hear of the *person*, at the level of morality of the *subject*, at that of the family of the *member*; and in civil society as such we have the citizen (*Bürger*). To this Hegel adds, in brackets "(*qua bourgeois*)", thus deliberately picking up Rousseau's term. Here on the basis of wants (*Bedürfnisse*) we have before us the composite idea we call *man*; thus this is the first and indeed really the only time that *man* in this sense comes into it. He is actually alluding here to a definition he had provided a moment before, distinguishing man from animal. An animal's wants are limited in scope; and its ways and means of satisfying them are equally limited. In this respect, too, man evinces a capacity to transcend the general prevalence of this dependent state, first by the multiplication of wants and the means of satisfying them, and second by his ability to divide a concrete need into its separate components and to differentiate them in such a way that the several parts and aspects in their turn become different needs, particularized and so more abstract.

In Hegel's usage, therefore, Rousseau's *homme* simply merges into the *bourgeois*; together they constitute the *homo economicus* of modern economics, to which Hegel gives express prominence as the science of the "system of wants" (*System der Bedürfnisse*), the basis of modern civil society.

As a thinker of the French Revolution, Hegel had also become acutely aware of how important, historically, was the economic revolution which had given rise to modern civil society. That is especially clear from his critique of Plato's theory of the state. If, on the one hand, Rousseau's *Contrat Social* had become for him the critical boundary-line at which it becomes manifest that a one-sided, subjective starting-point is untenable, on the other hand, Plato's State was a red light duly warning him against the snares of an exclusively objective solution. I have already cited from the *Vorrede* of the *Philosophy of Right*, Hegel's critique of Plato's political philosophy, which was powerless in face of the impending world revolution. In the chapter on civil society, Hegel picks up this thread once more. Even down to the use of words, he draws a comparison between the downfall of ancient Greece, on the one hand, and the intrusion of modern civil society into the traditional structure of European society, on the other. Anyone who reads, in the last chapter of the *Philosophy of Right* on world history in the framework of the four successive world realms, the account of the Roman realm as successor to the Greek, is reminded almost word for word of the description Hegel had given earlier of modern civil society. In both, a disintegration occurs of the substantial unity of life, an endless tearing in pieces of the ethical life into the extremes of the private self-consciousness of persons and abstract universality. Plato had no defence against this beyond idealizing the substantial ethical life of the Greeks; for the ancient *polis* was not proof against the disintegration of a natural morality and the infinite reflection into itself of self-consciousness. There lies the fundamental difference between the world revolution in classical antiquity and the modern revolution constituted by modern society. For the principle of the freedom of the subject, which ancient Greece proved unable to assimilate, has come to be the foundation of modern civil society and has been taken up into the polity of the modern state.

Hegel sees the distinction between the ancient world and the modern period as located in the principle of the self-subsistent, inherently infinite personality of the individual, the principle of subjective freedom, which in an inward form is linked with the Christian religion and in an external form had arisen in the Roman world. In this dual provenance, from the civilization of Rome and from Christianity, there are reflected the problems that have dogged the Christian history of Europe; and at the same time it serves to bring out the ambivalence of Hegel's *Philosophy of Right*. Within the context of world history Hegel describes the problems entailed in the succession of the Roman realm by the Germanic realm. The Germanic realm is the history of Christian Europe, prepared for in the history of the

People of Israel, which has already suffered the infinite grief of the loss of a natural ethical life, which accompanied the collapse of the Roman realm. In this absolute nadir, in this extreme negativity, mind pressed back upon itself grasps the infinite positivity of its inward character, the principle of the unity of the divine nature and the human, the reconciliation of objective truth and freedom as the truth and freedom appearing within self-consciousness and subjectivity. It is this task of reconciliation that has been entrusted to the principle of the north (*nordischen Prinzip*), the principle of the Germanic peoples.

But this inward principle of reconciliation at first discloses its content in an opposition between a mundane realm still dominated by barbarous custom and by caprice, and a "world of beyond" (*jenseitige Welt*), an intellectual realm whose truth, the truth of the mind, is still veiled, in the barbarous imagery of a frightening, superior force.

Hegel here sums up in a single sentence Augustine's doctrine of the *civitas terrena* as opposed to the *civitas Dei*, and the whole story of Christianity in the Middle Ages. Then, in the closing section he gets to the reconciliation of these opposites, a task reserved for the modern period. In the stern struggle between the two realms, between the mundane realm and the "realm of mind", there is also a meeting of the two. The realm of mind lowers the place of its heaven to the earthly level of a common worldliness of fact and idea. Conversely, the mundane realm raises its abstract consciousness to the level of thought and of rational being and rational knowing, to the rational plane of right and law. In this mutual encounter the bottom drops out of what was to start with the opposition between the realm of the mind and the mundane realm. The world of the present has discarded its barbaric and tyrannical character, whilst the realm of truth has surrendered its "world of beyond" and its arbitrary force. Thus the reconciliation which is disclosed in the *state* as the image and actuality of reason is now something objective. In the state, self-consciousness finds in an organic development the actuality of its substantial knowing and willing, just as in *religion* it finds the feeling and ideal representation of its own truth, and in *science* the free, conceptualized knowledge of the same truth. So the *state, nature* and the *ideal world* are mutually complementary manifestations of a single truth and reality.

Hegel's *Philosophy of Right*, then, ends with the noble prospect of a reconciliation between heaven and earth, between religion and law, between theology and politics. Yet this prospect is attained through the depths of negation and extreme contrast and polarity; it stands like a rainbow above the Flood of our modern society. It is as though only with the end of the philosophy of right can the critique really and truly begin.

5

Critique of Hegel's Philosophy of Right

A "CRITICAL revision of Hegel's *Philosophy of Right*" is how Marx later described the study that occupied him in 1843 and 1844. The title could in fact be extended to the whole of Marx's activity as a thinker; indeed, as an embodiment of his thought it could be used to sum up his life's work. More careful examination will show that this work of revision keeps pace with the course of his development from his first acquaintance with Hegel's philosophy up to the final pages of *Das Kapital*. When we put Hegel's *Vorrede* (the Preface to his *Philosophy of Right*) beside Marx's studies in preparation for his dissertation, it is very much a familiar tune that we hear. I am thinking especially of the central theme, featuring as it does the unsatisfactory character of Plato's philosophy of the state *vis-à-vis* the dawning of subjective freedom and the impending revolution in the world. The subject of Marx's dissertation is directly related to Hegel's *Vorrede*, which took an open stand against Epicurus' philosophy of chance and accident. It is as though Marx was determined from the very start to resist the master to his face by deliberately setting Hegel's major opponent, Epicurus, on a pedestal.

Later on, it looks sometimes almost as if Marx is sticking systematically to the scheme of Hegel's *Philosophy of Right*. His first article on so-called material interests, the article on legislation against wood-stealing, one could regard as commentaries on the first page of Hegel's *Philosophy of Right*, which deals with abstract right, more especially the first chapter on the right to ownership. With proper regard to the order of sequence, the article on the divorce law, written not long after, not only links up in fact with the first chapter of the third part of Hegel's *Philosophy of Right* in which the family—to take marriage for a start—is treated as the main element of the ethical life, but in this article there is even a positive stand taken against the way Hegel deals with divorce.

Next, he appears to make a jump straight to the third chapter on the state; but this leap is really one made by Marx's *Critique*, which in point of fact reverses Hegel's order of sequence. First, he has to settle accounts with Hegel's political theory, before he can get down to the real work, the critical revision of Hegel's doctrine of civil society. But even in following this third chapter Marx seems to be going about it systematically. The first section, on constitutional law, is discussed in Marx's critique of Hegel's constitutional law; in this connection he takes extreme care to pay special attention to Hegel's views on the relationship of the state to religion (which had been passed over in the critique of Hegel's constitutional law), implicitly in the "Introduction" to that critique and explicitly in the article on "the Jewish question". Where the second section on international law is concerned, one need only glance at the list of articles Marx wrote during the eighteen-fifties for the New York *Daily Tribune* to see how radical and how assiduous was his concern with international politics; whilst the final section on world history is in a sense critically remodelled by Marx in his *Critique of Political Economy* (*Kritik der politischen Ökonomie*) and the philosophy of economic history unfolded there.

The second chapter of the third part of Hegel's *Philosophy of Right*, which deals with civil society, is what really continued to occupy Marx for the rest of his life. Once he had discovered in this chapter the central complex of problems raised by Hegel's philosophy of right, it became the lever of his critical philosophy. The article on the legislation against wood-stealing had already penetrated to the core of these problems. The problem of civil society is the real theme of Marx's critique of Hegel's constitutional law; but the philosophical-cum-economic manuscripts of 1844 are likewise impossible to understand without the background of Hegel's views. The same thing is true of the critique of Bauer, Stirner and Proudhon. But it is really from 1847 onward that Marx's life work, the *Critique of Political Economy*, can be summed up under the heading, "critical revision of Hegel's *Philosophy of Right*". The problems raised by civil society, as outlined by Hegel with unprecedented clarity, dominate *Das Kapital*. The deep irony of Marx's relation to Hegel leaps to the fore at the end of his life in one of the last chapters of *Das Kapital*. The theme of freedom in Hegel's *Philosophy of Right*—a note persistently heard in the dialectic of freedom and necessity—breaks through in the vista of the future which Marx outlines, the perspective that sees lying on the far side of the sphere of material production as such, beyond the horizon of the realm of necessity, the realm of freedom. But this vision is fractured by the critical irony of Marx's revision of Hegel's trinitarian speculation; this visionary passage forms part of the forty-eighth chapter of *Das Kapital*, which deals with "the trinitarian formula", that is to say, the *economic* trinity.

So, to the very end of his life, Marx remains preoccupied by this task of revision; and so he himself has summed up his life's work. I need only remind you of that one sentence from the *Foreword* of the *Critique of Political Economy* of 1859, which I have already analysed in part in an earlier lecture. In it, he sums up in a single breath his work of revision: his discovery of the roots of legal relations and forms of state in the material conditions of Hegel's "civil society", and the anatomy of those roots in political economy. He could not have made it more evident that the key to his life's work is to be found in the *Critique of Hegel's Philosophy of Right*.

Marx's account does indeed represent a remarkable abridgement of the historical perspective. Hegel's expression *bürgerliche Gesellschaft* (civil society) he traces back to the use of this term in the England and France of the eighteenth century. That is fair enough, in so far as Hegel identified with a tendency already present in modern natural law and in particular took over the term "bourgeois" from Rousseau. However, the radical separation of the terms "state" and "civil society" is Hegel's very own accomplishment; so much so, in fact, that his thinking had a long way to go and to develop before he was at last, in the 1821 *Philosophy of Right*, able to complete the terminological operation. An identification which from classical times had been handed down quite automatically in European thought was now cleft in two, split into two contrasting terms. Neither Marx nor Hegel himself saw the historical originality of this terminological operation in this far-reaching perspective. Marx did have an intuitive sense of the problem presented by the terminological tradition and by Hegel's break with it. In a letter to Arnold Ruge of March 5, 1842 Marx gets to speaking about his recently written article containing the critique of Hegel's natural law in its bearing on constitutional law. He has in view here what in a letter written some weeks later he calls the *Critique of Hegel's Philosophy of Right*, and in a letter dated in August he calls his article tilting at Hegel's theory of constitutional monarchy.

In a previous lecture (part I, chapter 10) I used these letters to show that what Marx did with this article in 1843 was in fact implementing something he had done already in the previous year; so I need not go any further into the history of the matter now. At the moment I am concerned with Marx's own description of his article. In the aforementioned letter of March 5, 1842 he writes: "The crucial thing is the refutation of constitutional monarchy as a hybrid affair, totally self-conflicting and self-eliminating." And then he adds: "*Res publica* cannot be translated into German." These two observations, taken together, touch the heart of the problems at issue.

I was talking in an earlier lecture about the Greek and Latin tradition regarding the terms "state" and "civil society". What emerged was a parallelism between the Latin terms *civitas* and *societas civilis* and the Greek *polis* and *koinonia politikè*, respectively; our terms being, respectively, "state" and "civil society". But as the Latin terminology is richer, the Greek pair is expanded and becomes the trio: *civitas sive societas civilis sive res publica*. I remarked that in this third term, *res publica*, we have the synthesis of the first two. A synthesis is what Hegel was after in his theory of the state. But precisely that theory is the storm-centre of Marx's *Critique*, which reveals Hegel's concept of constitutional monarchy to be a *Zwitterding*, that is, a hybrid, a bastard, a hermaphrodite; an absurdity, conflicting with itself and destroying itself. To this characterization he attaches his remark about the impossibility of translating *res publica*.

Marx has noticed, evidently, that there is some difficulty about this term. We have already seen what problem he is up against. The term is the third member of a trio, the first two of which have already been rendered as "state" and "civil society". Hegel was aiming at a synthesis for which he could find no better term than "state". Marx spots the structural fault in Hegel's construction. On the one hand, there is a duplicity about it; on the other, it fails to bring out the real point at issue: namely, the synthesis of state and civil society in a *res publica*. An untranslatable term! Untranslatable and therefore unmanageable or, conversely, the anticipation of a synthesis which has not so far materialized anywhere in any shape or form and so is lacking an adequate term. A certain state of affairs to which no name has yet been given in our modern languages.

In the context of this more far-reaching perspective, which Marx himself points to, Hegel's *Philosophy of Right* and Marx's *Critique* fall into a proper relation to the classical and European tradition, to the as yet unrealized potentialities of the future, and to each other. Time now to go on and follow in its main outlines Marx's *Critique* of Hegel's constitutional law. The first part of my lectures has already thrown some light, up to a point, on the aspect of the "critique of heaven". At issue now is the theme proper, which belongs to the domain of the critique of earth.

Marx's *Critique* does not extend beyond the first section of the chapter on "The State" (*Der Staat*), a section dealing with constitutional law (*das innere Staatsrecht*). This section is subdivided into two: the internal form of government or constitution (*innere Verfassung für sich*) and sovereignty *vis-à-vis* foreign states (*die Souveränität nach aussen*). Of these two, Marx deals here only with the first, the internal constitution. That is itself divided in turn into three sections, so that the scheme looks like this:

A. Constitutional law (*das innere Staatsrecht*) (par. 260 to 329)
   I The internal or domestic constitution (*innere Verfassung für sich* (par. 272 to 320)
     (a) the crown (*die fürstliche Gewalt*) (par. 275 to 286)
     (b) the executive (*die Regierungsgewalt*) (par. 287 to 297)
     (c) the legislature (*die gesetzgebende Gewalt*) (par. 298 to 320).

Marx's *Critique* covers sections 261 to 313. Thus his article stops short halfway or more through the part dealing with the legislature. Just before the section with which he starts there is one other which introduces the subject of constitutional law. In it Hegel summarizes the principle of modern states. The prodigious strength and depth of this principle lie in the fact that it engenders two contrasting but dialectically inter-related processes. On the one hand, in the womb of the modern state the principle of subjectivity is able to develop fully and to culminate in the self-subsistent extreme of personal par-ticularity; personal individuality and its special interests (*Interessen*) have the possibility of complete development and obtain recognition of its subjective right (in the system of family and of civil society). But at the same time, in the womb of the modern state the principle of subjectivity is brought back within the substantive unity, so that this unity is maintained in the principle of subjectivity itself. In this unity of opposites the state is the actuality of concrete freedom.

Marx probably started his *Critique* at this section; but the first page of the manuscript has been lost. On the second sheet, the first of the surviving manuscript, he summarizes the con-tent of this section quite briefly as the argument that concrete freedom consists in the identity of the system of particular interests (*Sonderinteresse*) (of the family and civil society) with the system of universal interests (*allgemeine Interesse*) (of the state). After the term "identity" he adds between brackets *sein sollenden, zwieschlächtigen*. By this, he means to say that the identity postulated by Hegel is not actual but an ideal, some-thing that ought to be but is not (as yet). And furthermore he characterizes this identity as hybrid, a similar appellation to *Zwitterding*, which we were talking about not long ago. Thus, in the very first sentences of his *Critique* Marx puts dynamite under Hegel's whole construction. For in the Preface to the *Philosophy of Right* Hegel expressly and positively takes his stand against every attempt to construct a state as it ought to be (*wie er sein soll*), and made his own philosophy diametrically opposed to it. At the same time, Hegel presents the speculative idea of the state as the conscious identity between subjective form and substantive content. Marx takes a bold and direct stand against both claims—and in such a way that by an apparently quite casual addition (in brackets!) he turns what Hegel actually meant upside down.

In the next section Hegel goes more deeply into the relation between family and civil society, on the one hand, and the state, on the other. There are two sides to that relation. As contrasted with the spheres of private rights and private welfare, the state is, on the one hand, an *external* necessity and a higher authority, to whose nature the laws as well as the interests (*Interessen*) of this private sphere are subordinate and on which they are dependent. But, on the other hand, the state is the *immanent* end of this private sphere and draws its strength from the unity of its own universal end and aim with the particular interest of individuals; individuals have obligations towards the state to the degree that they have rights as well.

Marx begins his *Critique* with an analysis of the relation between *external* necessity and *immanent* goal. Hegel classifies under external necessity both being subordinate to the state and being dependent on it. The former, the subordination of the private sphere, is obviously an external necessity. But about the condition of dependence Hegel is less clear. Hegel illustrates this by a specific reference to Montesquieu's notion that the parts—the laws concerning the rights of persons—are dependent on the whole, on the state. This reference to Montesquieu, however, relates to an *immanent* dependence. Even so, Hegel subsumes this immanent dependence at the same time under the relation of *external* necessity. Only so is it to be understood why in case of conflict the laws and interests of family and civil society must defer to the laws and interests of the state. It is not empirical conflicts, however, that Hegel has in view; what concerns him is a fundamental dependence in virtue of which the sphere of family and of civil society is subordinate to the state as a "higher authority". The union of the private sphere with the sphere of the universal, the state, is therefore an external, enforced union; the identity is a seeming identity, leading to internal discord. That is why Hegel describes this aspect as an *external* necessity; it is the aspect of alienation (*Entfremdung*) within the union.

Over against this, Hegel sets the other aspect, the state as the *immanent* end of the private sphere, in other words, as a union of the universal end and the particular interests of individuals, expressed in the unity of duties and rights. But in the opposition between the two aspects, between external necessity and immanent end, there lies an antinomy which Hegel is unable to resolve.

As Hegel envisages it, the state as the ethical universe, as the interpenetration of the substantive and the particular, is in itself the union of my obligation to the substantive and the embodiment of my particular freedom; in other words, the union of my duty and my rights.

In the next section (262), which as we shall see Marx treats as being of fundamental importance, Hegel explains things in more detail. The actual idea, that is, mind, divides itself in the plane of its finitude into two ideal spheres of its concept, family and civil society, in order that out of the ideality of these two spheres it can be for itself infinite, actual mind. To that end, the actual idea, *qua* mind, assigns to these spheres the material of this its finite actuality, that is, human beings *en masse*, so that the function assigned to the individual is visibly mediated (*vermittelt*) by circumstances, caprice and his own choice of his situation in life.

This section Marx translates into prose, as he ironically says, and then analyses. If it is indeed circumstances and individual caprice that form the state's point of contact with family and civil society, then evidently the reason (rationality) of the state (*Staatsvernunft*) has no bearing on this assigning of the material of the state to the spheres of family and civil society. The state simply emerges from these spheres in an unconscious and arbitrary fashion. Family and civil society appear as the dark element of nature whence the light of the state is kindled.

Hegel makes it look as though the actual idea, mind, sets to work in accordance with a definite plan, and divides up into finite spheres in order eventually to return into itself. Just at this point Marx puts his finger on Hegel's logical, pantheistic mysticism. What is in actuality the assigning of the material of the state by circumstances and caprice, is expressed by speculation as manifestation, as phenomenon, appearance. The actual mediation by circumstances and caprice is only the appearance of a mediation, which the actual idea performs with itself and which goes on behind the scenes. The actuality is not expressed as what it is in itself, but as a different actuality.

Common empiricism has not its own mind but an alien mind as its law, whilst conversely the actual idea has as its embodiment (*Dasein*) not an actuality developed out of itself but a common empiricism.

The idea is subjectivized; and the actual relation of family and civil society to the state is envisaged as the immanent, imaginary activity of the idea. Family and civil society are the presuppositions of the state; it is they who in a real sense are active. But in speculation it is the other way round. When the idea is subjectivized, then the actual subjects, such as family, civil society, circumstances, caprice and so forth, become unreal, objective elements of the idea, elements which signify something else.

The assigning of the "state material" to the individual *via* circumstances and caprice is not posited expressly and without qualification as what is true, necessary, rightful and reasonable; yet, on the other hand, this does happen, only in such a way that the mediation through circumstances and caprice is presented as an apparent mediation, so that these factors remain what they are and at the same time acquire the significance of an aspect of the idea, are elevated into result and product of the idea. The distinction is not in the content but in the way of approach or in the way of speaking. It is a dual affair, esoteric and exoteric. The content is located in the exoteric part. The interest (*Interesse*) of the esoteric part invariably consists in recovering the history of the logical concept in the state. But it is on the exoteric side that the real development takes place. To put it in rational terms, Hegel is saying no more than that the family and civil society are parts of the state. The "state material", that is to say, public business and affairs, is distributed among them through circumstances and caprice. Those who are state citizens are members of a family and of civil society.

Hegel calls the family and civil society the two ideal spheres of the concept of the state. The term "ideal" implies that the division of the state into these two parts is necessary, belongs to the essential being of the state. In other words, family and civil society are actual parts of the state, are actual, mental existences of the will; they are "embodiments" of the state, modes in which it exists, they comprise the state. They are the initiative-takers, the motive force. Yet Hegel puts it precisely the other way round. As he represents it, family and civil society are the passive object of the idea; it is not their own life-process which combines and unifies them into the state, but it is the life-process of the idea that has made them distinct. They are the finite being of the idea; they owe their existence to a spirit that is not their own, they are defined by a third factor, and are not self-defined. That is why they are defined as "finitude", as the finiteness inherent in the actual idea. The end of their existence is not that existence as such; but the idea separates these pre-suppositions from itself, "so that on the basis of their ideality it can be for itself infinite, actual mind"; that is to say, the political state cannot be, apart from the natural basis of the family and the artificial basis of civil society. For the political state they are a *conditio sine qua non*. Thus the condition (*Bedingung*) becomes the conditioned (*Bedingte*), the deter-minator (*Bestimmende*) is posited as what is determined (*Bestimmte*), the productive factor (*Produzierende*) is presented as the product of its product (*als das Produkt seines Produktes*). The actual idea only descends into the "finiteness" of family and civil society in order, through the supersession of that finitude to enjoy and engender its own infinity. "To that end" (that is, in order to attain its goal) "the idea assigns to these spheres the material of this its finite actuality" (this? what actuality? surely these spheres are its "finite actuality", its "material"), "human beings as a mass (the material of the state here is 'human beings, the mass, the multitude' ", it is they who constitute the state, its existence is here formulated as an act of the idea, as a "distribution" of its own material; the fact is this, that the state emerges from the mass, in its existence *qua* the members of family and of civil society; speculation formu-lates this factum as an act of the idea, not as the idea of the mass but as the act of a subjective idea, which is distinct from the fact itself) "so that this assigning to the individual (before, it was only a question of assigning individuals to the spheres of family and civil society) appears to be mediated through circumstances, caprice and so forth".

In this fashion Marx analyses with great precision one sentence of Hegel's that fills an entire section, and he gives us, "in prose", a version of what it contains. Thus he concludes that Hegel manages to absorb empirical actuality as it is; it is also given expression as something rational (*vernünftig*), yet it is not rational by virtue of its own inherent reason (*Vernunft*), but because the empirical fact in its empirical existence has a significance other than itself. The fact forming the basic premiss is not interpreted as such, but rather as a mystic result. What is actual becomes "phenomenon"; but the idea has no content other than this phenomenon. Again, the idea has no goal other than the logical goal: "to be for itself infinite, actual mind". In this section, Marx concludes, is enshrined the whole mystery of the *Philosophy of Right*, nay, of Hegel's entire philosophy.

We have here been able to follow Marx's dissecting knife in its every movement. The hand, and indeed the method of working, is at once recognizable as the one operative in the dissertation. There Marx had succeeded in uncovering, in one apparently trivial detail overlooked by all previous historians and philosophers, the central core of Epicurus' natural philosophy; and in this detail he discovered the key to Greek philosophy as a whole. In much the same way, Marx's scalpel reveals in the anatomy of a single section the mystery of Hegel's *Philosophy of Right*, indeed, of Hegel's philosophy in its entirety.

The choice of this section is the more striking because of the connection Hegel himself made with a section in the chapter on civil society, to which he explicitly refers in a bracketed addition. Marx was not concerned with that reference, because the chapter in question lay outside the frame of his *Critique*. Hegel refers us to a section (185) which I have already had occasion to consider earlier. In it, he outlines the physical and moral corruption to which civil society is prey, torn as it is between the extremes of unrestricted luxury and bitter poverty and wretchedness. He compares this degeneracy with the period of decline in ancient Greece, and affirms that the principle of self-subsistent, inherently infinite personality has an intrinsic connection with the Christian religion and extrinsically was developed in the Roman world: a principle that had brought Plato's philosophy of the state to an impasse. We have seen that this section is really a more detailed working out of a central theme which Hegel had already broached in the *Vorrede*.

Running right through the *Philosophy of Right*, therefore, is a thread linking up with the section (262) in which Marx claims to have uncovered the very core of Hegel's whole philosophy.

It would take us too far afield to continue following Marx's *Critique* in every detail; but the main contours and the structure of his analysis can be illustrated from fragments of the *Critique*. Fundamental to Marx's analytical method is the indissoluble unity of form and content. In the Preface to the *Philosophy of Right* Hegel had himself made much of this principle as the basis of authentic philosophy; but Marx demonstrates that Hegel was true to the principle in appearance only. What Hegel's speculation failed to achieve Marx's *Critique* accomplishes in the unity of its formal and substantive analysis. All the time, the critical handling of the formal structure of Hegel's thought goes hand in hand with a substantive critique of his constitutional law.

First, let us take a closer look at the formal aspect of Marx's analysis. There is, first of all, the peculiar character of Hegel's speculative method, which one can recognize in every part of his system. In the four subsequent sections (263 to 266) Hegel argues that mind is not only, as substantive universality, the external necessity of the private realm but equally, as being conscious of itself as its own end, the inner freedom of the private realm. Marx comments that evidently the transition from the realm of family and of civil society to the political state does not derive from the special nature of the family and so on, from the particular nature of the state, but from the universal relation of necessity and freedom. It is exactly the same transition which is effected in Hegel's logic from the realm of essential being to the realm of the concept. In natural philosophy the same transition is made from an origin in inorganic nature to living nature. It is always the same categories that furnish the soul now for this realm, now for that. It is simply a question of finding abstract characteristics that correspond to the special, concrete ones.

In the next section (267) Hegel argues thus: the necessity in ideality is the inner self-development of the idea. As the substance of the individual subject it is political sentiment; as the substance of the objective world, in distinction therefrom, it is the organism of the state, the strictly political state and its constitution. This Marx analyses as follows: the *subject* here is "the necessity in ideality", the "idea within itself"; the *predicate*—the political sentiment and the political constitution. And Marx adds with a touch of sarcasm: in (plain) German this means that the political sentiment is the subjective, the political constitution the objective substance of the state. Thus the logical development of family and civil society into state is just illusory; for it is not explained how family sentiment, civic sentiment, the institution of the family and social institutions as such relate to political sentiment and the political constitution and how they cohere with them. The main point is that Hegel everywhere makes the idea the subject and makes the real and actual subject, such as "political sentiment", the predicate. The development, however, always occurs on the predicate's side.

We have already, in the context of the *Critique of Heaven*, come across Marx's charge against speculative philosophy that it systematically confuses subject and predicate. The unity of his critique of heaven and earth comes out once again, now that we encounter this same charge within the context of constitutional law. In one of the later sections (270) Hegel declares that the end of the state is the universal interest as such, so that the state is also the substance and means of conserving particular interests; at the same time this substantiality is mind knowing and willing itself, having passed through the forming process of education (*Bildung*). Here again Marx sees the familiar signs of confusion. The sentence does not run "educated mind (*gebildete*) . . . is the substantiality", but on the contrary "the substantiality is educated . . . mind". In this way, mind becomes a predicate of its predicate. The real starting-point, without which the end and the authoritative powers of the state must be so many castles in the air, vacuous, nay, impracticable existences, appears merely as the latest predicate of the substantiality which had already been defined earlier as a universal end and as the various state powers (Crown, Executive, Legislature). If one's starting-point be actual mind, then the "universal end" would be its content, the various constitutional powers, the manner in which it is actualized, its real or material existence, the specification of which would have had to be developed out of the nature of the end being pursued. Since, however, the starting-point is the "idea" or the "substance" *qua* subject, actual being, therefore the actual subject appears only as the final predicate of the abstract predicate.

All this really shifts the discussion with Hegel into the area of logic. After all, the main point is that the concrete content, the actual definition, is manifest as exhibiting form, whilst conversely the purely abstract definition of form is brought in as the concrete content. Thus, the state's characteristics are not treated, essentially, as being what they are in their own right; instead, they are envisaged in their abstract form as logical-cum-metaphysical characteristics. It is not the philosophy of right but logic that is at issue here. The task of philosophy is to ensure not that thinking assumes a form—the form of political realities—but that the existing political realities are volatilized into abstract ideas. Not the logic of the issue, but the issue of logic is the philosophical component. Instead of logic serving to substantiate the state, the state serves to substantiate the logic. The whole philosophy of right, therefore, is merely parenthetical to logic; that is to say, the philosophy has the position in it of a casual observation, an "aside". Naturally, the parenthesis is no more than an *hors d'oeuvre* to the real thing.

With the help of Hegel's construction of state polity, Marx reveals legislature as the "medium", the mediating principle between the two extremes, the principle of monarchy and civil society; but this medium is a composite mixture of them both, an impossible compromise of empirical particularity and empirical universality, of subject and predicate. Hegel interprets the result of his argumentation as a medium, a middle factor. In this methodology the whole transcendence and mystical dualism of his system emerge. The mediating factor is so much "wooden iron", the concealed opposition between universality and individuality. Each element in the cycle is now extreme, on the outside, now the middle factor. The monarch must constitute, in the legislature, the medium between the governmental authority and the "estates" (classes); but the government (the Executive) is itself the mediating factor between the monarch and the estates, and the estates are a similar factor between the monarch and civil society.

It reminds one of the anecdote about the husband and wife who had quarrelled and the doctor who insisted on being the intermediary between them, so that first the wife had to be go-between (*vermitteln*) for the doctor with her husband, and then the husband be go-between for his wife with the doctor. This mediatory system means that the same man who wants to give his opponent a thrashing has to protect him from being thrashed by different antagonists in other directions; with the result that, confronted with this double task, he never gets round to actually doing it.

It is worth noticing that Hegel, who reduces this absurdity of the mediatory principle to its abstract, logical—that is to say, its unadulterated, unwrenchable—expression, at the same time describes it as a speculative mystery of logic, as the rational (*vernünftige*) relationship. Extremes cannot in fact be mutually reconciled, for the simple reason that they *are* extremes. But they require no mediating factor, either, for they are in their essential nature opposites. They have nothing in common, they do not want each other, are not complementary. The one does not cherish a desire for, a need for, the anticipation of the other. But when Hegel treats universality and individuality, the abstract components of his logical argumentation, as *actual* opposites, that is precisely the fundamental dualism of his logic.

Marx rounds off this analysis by remarking that the place for a more detailed discussion is in the critique of Hegel's logic. To the end of his life, in fact, he nursed a plan, never to be realized, for getting down to the task of writing such a critique. The need for it arose out of the critique of Hegel's constitutional law and the realization he had of the all-pervading influence of Hegel's speculative logic.

This did not stop him, however, from pursuing the subject. The conciseness and brevity of his analysis do not make it easy to follow; but it is so pertinent to the heart and centre of Marx's critique of Hegel that it is worth taking the trouble to sketch in the main features of it. He himself imports a counter-argument into the discussion, in the form of the maxim, *Les extrêmes se touchent*, extremes affect each other. North and south poles attract each other; likewise the male and female sexes; and it is only through the union of their extreme differences that human beings come into existence. But over against this

Marx sets the proposition: each extreme *is* its other extreme (*Jedes Extrem ist sein andres Extrem*). Abstract spiritualism (i.e., immaterialism) is abstract materialism; abstract materialism is the abstract spiritualism of matter.

We see here a notional development that typifies Marx's style of thought and the style of his critique of Hegel. Without letting himself be led into the area of purely formal logic, he pierces through in a few sentences to the heart of the issue with which the *Critique of the Philosophy of Right* is really concerned. What for Hegel is the unity of logic and the philosophy of right, Marx treats as the unity of a critique of logic and a critique of constitutional law. We have already followed Marx's critique of Hegel's speculation about the relation between the state on the one hand and the private realm of the family and civil society on the other—a relation envisaged as the assigning of "state matter" by mind to the private realm. Marx turned this speculative way of talking into "prose"; so we know what he is thinking of in the philosophy of right context when he speaks about the polarity between mind and matter.

What Marx's analysis is meant to show is that the extremes which Hegel reconciles *are* extremes and, if they can be reconciled, it is because they are pure abstractions. Indeed, in the realm of abstraction each extreme is the extreme of its opposite. In the realm of abstraction, "mind" is the opposite of "matter". Hegel treats these abstract notions as extremes which can be and must be reconciled with each other. This (merely) apparent reconciliation is brought about between apparent extremes. In fact, the abstract concept, "mind", is only the abstraction of matter. It has no self-subsistent signification, but only as the abstraction of something else, namely, matter. Matter is the object from which mind abstracts. The abstraction of matter is abstract materialism. Thus in the realm of abstraction, abstract mind and abstract matter, or abstract spiritualism and abstract materialism, form each other's counterpart. In Hegel's speculation, abstractions without intrinsic subsistence are made self-subsistent, are then contrasted or opposed to each other as extremes, and finally reconciled. But, in fact, this opposition is illusory; for the concept "mind" does not stand in opposition to real matter, but is an abstraction from it. The polarity is only with the abstract concept "matter"; and this abstract polarity is just a delusion; for abstract "mind" and abstract "matter" are both abstractions from the matter which really exists.

The case is different with polar existences, like man and woman, north pole and south pole. Male and female sexes both belong to a single species, a single being, "human being". North and south are polarized aspects of a single, albeit differentiated, existent. They are not actual, nor real extremes, therefore. Real extremes would be pole and non-pole, human and non-human being. With these real extremes there is a distinction between one being, one existent, and another, a second existent. In the case of the contrast between man and woman, north pole and south pole, on the other hand, the distinction is one of existence within a single reality.

Now Hegel's speculation confuses this distinction of existence within a single mode of being, in two directions, with a quite different distinction. On one hand, it is confused with the contrast between (putatively) self-subsistent abstractions, and, on the other, with the real opposition between two existents which are mutually exclusive. In other words, the polarity between man and woman is confused with that between the abstractions "mind" and "matter", and again with that between pole and non-pole. This confusion gives rise to a two-fold error: (1) A principle is not regarded as a totality in itself, but appears exclusively as an abstraction of something else, as a one-sided, partial thing; (2) Real contrarieties, of which the opposed parties are aware and which lead to conflict, are not acknowledged in their reality but are seen as something injurious, as something to be obviated, if at all possible. An attempt is made to reconcile these real contrarieties.

Marx illustrates this procedure from the relation between Christianity or religion in general, on the one hand, and philosophy on the other. The truth is, there is no real opposition between religion and philosophy; for they are in different planes: philosophy aims to encompass religion, includes and comprehends religion in its illusory actuality. Thus for philosophy, in so far as it sets out to be something actual, religion is resolved into philosophy itself. There is no real dualism here between one existent and another existent; for such a polarity exists only on one side, namely, that of religion; whilst from the other side, from the philosophical viewpoint, the polarity has no genuine reality at all. From this example Marx intends to make it clear that the whole speculative method whereby Hegel first turns abstractions into polarities in order subsequently to reconcile them and supersede the lower in the higher is a charade in which, on the one hand, pseudo-opposites are exhibited as real, and, on the other, real polarities are reduced to mere appearances and then reconciled.

Just as Hegel "dissolves" religion into philosophy (which supersedes it), so does he "dissolve" civil society into the state. In the former case he is cancelling out a contrast that does not actually exist; in the latter case he is "moderating" a real opposition. Marx demonstrates this by analysing Hegel's construction of the legislature, the central, mediating principle of constitutional monarchy. Here again we are dealing with a compound affair. In the legislature are unified: (1) a representation of the principle of monarchy, "the Executive"; (2) a representation of civil society, the "estates" elements; (3) further to that, the one extreme as such, the principle of monarchy, whilst the other extreme, civil society, is not as such subsumed in it. In this procedure the "estates" element is first of all made the opposite extreme to the principle of monarchy: that is, it takes the place of civil society. For it is only in the representative body of the estates that civil society organizes itself so as to assume a political existence. The "estates" element is the transubstantiation of civil society into the political state. Indeed, civil society is the "unreality" of political existence, so that the political existence of civil society entails its own dissolution, whereby civil society is parted from itself.

The legislature is the political state *in toto*. The inner contradiction, therefore, of the legislature brings to light the inner contradiction of the political state as a whole. The political state merges, is resolved, into the legislature. Within the legislature totally discrepant principles collide. In Hegel's construction this contrariety appears as the opposition between the principle of monarchy and that of the "estates" element. In fact, however, it is a question of the antinomy of the political state and civil society, the intrinsic contrariety in which the political state is in conflict with itself. The legislature embodies the revolt against this internally conflicting structure of the political state.

To this analysis Marx appends a conclusion which he again puts in parenthesis, as it were, in order to indicate that its proper place is in the critique of Hegel's logic. For that very reason it is important to reproduce his conclusion here. Hegel's chief mistake, that conclusion says, is that he interprets the contrariety of the appearance (*den Widerspruch der Erscheinung*) as a unity in essence, in the idea (*Einheit im Wesen, in der Idee*). The phenomenal contradiction does indeed have something more profound as its essence (*ein Tieferes zu seinem Wesen*), namely, an essential contradiction (*wesentlichen Widerspruch*), just as for instance in this case the contradiction inherent in the legislature (*Widerspruch . . . in sich selbst*) is only the contradiction in the political state and thus also that which civil society evinces with itself. (*Widerspruch . . . mit sich selbst*).

The vulgar critique falls into an error opposite to Hegel's, that is, into a dogmatic one. It criticizes the constitution, for instance. It points out that the various organs of state authority are opposed to one another, and so on. It finds contradictions everywhere. This is still a dogmatic critique which *combats*, more or less as the people used to do who exploited the "one and three" contradiction in order to wipe the floor with the dogma of the Holy Trinity. Over against that, the true critique shows the inner process, the history of how the Holy Trinity came into being (*innere Genesis*) within the human brain. It describes the "act of birth" (*Geburtsakt*). Thus, a truly philosophical critique of the existing constitution not only shows that contradictions exist, but also explains them, comprehends their genesis, their necessity. It grasps them in their peculiar significance. However, this process of understanding consists not as Hegel supposes in detecting here, there and everywhere determinable instances of the logical notion (*die Bestimmungen des logischen Begriffs*), but in grasping the distinctive logic of the distinctive object (*die eigentümliche Logik des eigentümlichen Gegenstandes zu fassen*).

In this conclusion there beats the very heart of Marx's critique of heaven and earth. The definition of the genuinely philosophical critique as contrasted with the dogmatic one may remind us forcibly of the closing passage of Marx's third letter to Arnold Ruge, published in the *Deutsch-Französische Jahrbücher*. In part I, chapter 8, I explained the socratic character of Marx's critique and the typical engagement with actual politics. In the conclusion as just reported what comes out most of all is the unity of Hegel critique, the critique of religion and the critique of politics.

This brings us to the second aspect of Marx's critique. The first had to do with the formal structure of Hegel's philosophy. Inseparably connected with that is the substantive critique of constitutional law, to which we must now turn.

It would be a serious mistake to regard Marx's *Critique of Hegel's Philosophy of Law* merely as a sample of "Hegel critique"; for the confrontation with Hegel entails the confrontation with the political state. Marx expressly makes this point—and does so in connection with his analysis of the duplicity of Hegel's construction of the legislature, which comes out particularly in the bogus position of the "estates" element as the political representation of civil society. "The function of the estates element," Hegel declares (section 301), "is to ensure that the 'public cause' will come into existence in it not only implicitly (*an sich*) but also explicitly (*für sich*): that is to say, the element of subjective, formal freedom, the public mind as, empirically, a common pool of the ideas and opinions of the many." Marx points out the extraordinary contempt which Hegel displays here for the "spirit politic" where he comes across it in an actual, empirical form—the same Hegel who has such enormous respect for it as "ethical mind". The fact is, the "public consciousness" is here simply equated with the empirical, general pool of the opinions of the many, the totality of views and ideas to be found among the mass. That is the enigma of mysticism. The same fantastic abstraction which identifies the state's consciousness with the completely inadequate form of the bureaucracy unblushingly admits, on the other hand, that the empirical "mind of the state" is simply a pot-pourri of the ideas of the mass. Because he gives the actual content of freedom a mystical basis, therefore the actual subject of freedom assumes a purely formal significance. The division between "in itself" (*an sich*) and "for itself" (*für sich*), between substance and subject, is abstract mysticism.

Marx would be the last to deny that in all this Hegel has

correctly represented the actual nature of modern monarchies, including constitutional ones. On the contrary, the situation in modern states is exactly as in Hegel's *Philosophy of Right*: the true reality of the public cause is only formal, or only the formal is really and actually "public cause". Hegel is not to be blamed for delineating the essential nature of the modern state as it is, but because he presents what is as the essential nature of the state. That the rational is actual is manifest from the contrariness of irrational actuality (*Dass das Vernünftige wirklich ist, beweist sich eben im Widerspruch der unvernünftigen Wirklichkeit*), which is invariably the reverse of what it claims to be, and claims to be the reverse of what it is (*die an allen Ecken das Gegenteil von dem ist, was sie aussagt, und das Gegenteil von dem aussagt, was sie ist*).

Without expressly mentioning it, Marx looks back to the celebrated statement in Hegel's *Vorrede* to the *Philosophy of Right*: *was vernünftig ist, das ist wirklich; und was wirklich ist, das ist vernünftig*: what is rational is actual and what is actual is rational. He holds Hegel to his word, indeed, his analysis confirms the truth of Hegel's proposition: philosophy is its own time, apprehended in thoughts (*ihre Zeit in Gedanken erfasst*). But this confirmation is a confirmation in Hegel's style: it denies what it confirms, or it confirms by denying. It would be wrong to see in this a specimen of Marx's flair for crushing irony, unless one sees that as being rooted in the socratic irony described in the studies preliminary to his dissertation. This philosophical irony is indeed the pulse-beat of Marx's critical method, it has a "maieutic" significance, it assists at the lying-in and is present at the birth of truth. Hegel's principle is correct: the actual is rational, and the rational actual. Hegel saw the essential nature, the rational idea, of the modern state and correctly defined it as the actualizing of the rational will, free will; but he did not see that the actual condition of the modern state flagrantly contradicts its essence, its truth, its rationality. And so he fell into the error of regarding the actual existence of the modern state as the essential nature of the state.

Yet this in itself does not take us to the heart of what Marx is saying. The contradiction in Hegel's philosophy, which sees and at the same time fails to see the essence of the modern state and mistakes the essence for the actuality and the actuality for the essence—that contradiction is not simply Hegel's, but that of the actuality itself. What Hegel asserts (*ausgibt*) about the actual existence of the state is evidenced by (*aussagt*), the actuality itself. Obviously, he has attended carefully to the actuality and is only passing on what he has heard. For the actuality itself is precisely the opposite of what it professes to be. It claims to be rational (*vernünftig*), whereas it is irrational (*unvernünftig*). And this very fact reveals, is sufficient to establish (*beweist sich*), that the rational is actual.

The expression "is established", "is proved" (*beweist sich*) has a profound meaning; and here we do come up against the hard centre of Marx's *Critique*. Hegel's philosophy had no other aim than to furnish proof of the speculative case that what is actual is rational, and what is rational is actual. Marx recognizes the truth of this proposition; but he views the proof from exactly the other side. Hegel set out to furnish his proof through a knowledge of actual reason (*wirkliche Vernunft*) and rational actuality (*vernünftige Wirklichkeit*). Marx on the contrary finds the proof in the contradictoriness of irrational actuality (*unvernünftige Wirklichkeit*) and of actual irrationality (*wirkliche Unvernunft*). That is precisely the distinction between the "matter of logic" (*Sache der Logik*), which Hegel projects on to the actuality, and the "logic of the matter", which Marx develops out of the actuality. In that, Marx follows the guideline of Hegel's own dialectic, which after all has nothing else to do than bring into consciousness the proper work of the reason of the thing in itself (*diese eigene Arbeit der Vernunft der Sache zum Bewusstsein zu bringen*). Hegel did not stick to his own guideline, otherwise he would have made the discovery that Marx now makes in his stead: the discovery that the logic of what is actual is demonstrated in the contradiction of an irrational actuality.

It is the ambiguity of Hegel's *Philosophy of Right* that in it, whenever this radical dialectic is on the point of breaking through, it seems to be dissolved in speculation. In the discussion of Hegel's *Vorrede*, the Preface to the *Philosophy of Right*, I have already referred to the curious context into which the utterance about the rationality of what is actual is incorporated: the context, that is, of the impending world revolution of which Plato did indeed have a presentiment, but which he had no means of resisting other than by taking up a defensive position in an idealized, substantive form of Greek ethical life and the ancient state. We have seen, too, how Hegel returns to this in the chapter on civil society, which represents an analogous world revolution in the modern period; and how, in a combination of Christian and Roman subjectivity, he finds a capacity which Plato in his time did not possess for weathering this revolution (section 185). And, finally, we traced the line through to Hegel's examination of the state, with which Marx begins his *Critique* and in which he finds epitomized the whole mystery of Hegel's *Philosophy of Right* (section 262). In the process the ambiguity of that philosophy is brought to light. More clearly than any thinker before him, Hegel saw just how radical was the character of the revolution, which for him was expressed in the term "civil society". He analysed sharply both the analogy and the fundamental difference with the downfall of ancient civilization and managed to expose the basic flaw in Plato's philosophy of the state. Even so, Hegel himself seems to have been unable to escape from Plato's magic. Where he is describing Plato's failings and also his greatness, it looks very much as though he is describing his own reflected image. Indeed, one even gets the impression that Hegel's picture of Plato has the features to some extent of a self-portrait. Historically, his picture of Plato is greatly overdone. If we read the relevant sentence from the *Vorrede* once again, it would seem more applicable to Hegel himself:

"Still, his genius is proved by the fact that the principle on which the distinctive character of his Idea of the state turns is precisely the pivot on which the impending world revolution turned at that time.

What is rational is actual;
and what is actual is rational".

It is worth noting that the phrase "at that time" (*damals*) was added by Hegel in his own hand to his own copy of the *Philosophy of Right*, as though he were afraid the reader would confuse the former revolution with the modern one and might suppose that Hegel was talking here about himself. That fear was all too well founded; for Hegel's critique of Plato can be taken over word for word as a critique of Hegel. After all,

Hegel too took refuge in an external form, the state, which was an idealized epitome of the nature of the existing ethical life: a defensive position to which he withdrew when faced with the impending revolution. And just as he accused Plato of doing, Hegel also did the deepest possible injury in this way to the underlying impulse of the revolution, namely, to free, infinite personality.

Thus in a sense all that Marx's critique of Hegel has done is to develop Hegel's Plato-critique, which in a secret fashion had already become Hegel's self-critique, into a critique of Hegel. The term used by Marx, "is proved", is the literal equivalent of the one we find in the passage cited above from Hegel's *Vorrede*. Hegel–Plato "has proved himself", or rather his "genius", through the connection of his philosophy with the impending world revolution. Marx confirms Hegel's thesis that the rational is actual, "is proved", finds its proof, precisely in the contradiction of irrational actuality. Marx is, in fact, talking about the contradiction becoming manifest in the impending world revolution, the world, that is, of the nineteenth century, the world of civil society. Hegel himself says of this revolutionary principle of subjective freedom, "This principle is historically subsequent to the Greek world; and the philosophical reflection which gets down to this depth is likewise subsequent to the substantive idea of Greek philosophy" (section 185). It was on this score that Marx moved into his critique of Hegel with his dissertation on Epicurus. Once again we have confirmation of the fundamental importance of the dissertation as the starting-point for Marx's total development. For quite literally, the whole point of it is this "subsequent to", which acquires a form in post-Aristotelean philosophy. What attracts him in this post-Aristotelean philosophy is in fact its subjective character, the philosophical reflection, which is subsequent to Greek metaphysics. For him Epicurus is the revolutionary pioneer of subjective freedom.

Anyone who sets the *Vorrede* to Marx's dissertation alongside the *Vorrede* to Hegel's *Philosophy of Right* must be struck by the close affinity between them. Hegel's *Vorrede* is an express attack on Epicurus. Marx's *Vorrede* is an express attack on Hegel, in a vein almost analogous to Hegel's in the latter's *Vorrede* on Plato. Marx acknowledges Hegel's genius, but

145

insists all the same that Hegel failed to discover the key to the real history of Greek philosophy. That key is to be found in the philosophy of Epicurus—the same Epicurus whom Hegel repudiated.

So the main historical contours begin to become clearly visible. In Hegel, the line of classical philosophy, the line running from Plato through Aristotle, is extended into the modern period. Marx undertakes an independent exploration through the history of Greek philosophy and comes to see that on this line we cannot hope for any answer to the problems of the modern epoch. However, in the history of antiquity he finds three aspects that are plainly on a different footing. One aspect is historical; he opts for the post-Aristotelean period, post-classical philosophy, the end of Greek civilization. The second aspect concerns the philosophical starting-point; he opts for the subjective character, for the subjective freedom of self-consciousness. The third aspect has to do with the interpretation of nature; he opts for the atomistic philosophy.

In the combination of the three aspects lies the originality of Marx's point of departure. The difference between the natural philosophy of Democritus and of Epicurus is the subject-matter of Marx's enquiry. The difference lies in the first aspect: Democritus is pre-, Epicurus is post-Aristotelean. In the second aspect Democritus' theory of atoms is naive metaphysics, Epicurus' theory is subjective reflection, issuing in subjective praxis. The apparently negligible difference between Democritus and his tardy (belated) pupil, Epicurus, is the paramount difference between the blind necessity of nature and self-conscious, subjective freedom. In Epicurus' principle of the declination of the atom, the atom acquires its freedom. The declination is the revolution of the self-liberating individual in the realm of necessity, the realm of nature.

There is a close interrelation between Hegel's philosophy of right and his natural philosophy, an interrelation explicitly confirmed in the *Vorrede* to the *Philosophy of Right*. Hegel's natural philosophy might be described as a Platonic Aristoteleanism: the substance is the living organism of the self-evolving cosmos, the form is akin to Platonic idealism, which finds true reality in the absolute forms of mathematics, which in material reality are adumbrated only as something phenomenal. Hegel's philosophy of right has a similar character. The state is the finished development of the ethical cosmos; but in its absolute perfection it stands enthroned above what is in reality the poor ethical condition of its members. Hegel perceives a direct analogy between the natural universe and the ethical universe, between the cosmos and the state, the *polis*. And so Epicurus' atomistic philosophy is his sworn enemy; for in it this cosmic and ethical organism is pulverized into a chaotic multitude of atoms, and the august necessity of reason, of *Vernunft*, which governs both the natural and the ethical universe, is ground down into blind mechanics, controlled by caprice and accident. Hegel's opposition to Epicurus' theory of atoms is so explicit because his keen gaze has recognized the astoundingly accurate reproduction of it in the poor actual state of ethical life in civil society. The god-forsaken condition of Epicurus' nature, the atheism of his philosophy, the law of accident and caprice—they have all taken form in the modern world revolution, in civil society. Hegel repeatedly describes its essential character in terms borrowed directly from the theory of atoms. At the close of his *Philosophy of History* he rebuts the polity of liberalism, based as it is on the "will of the many", as "the atomistic principle". The *Philosophy of Right* is full of such expressions as "dependence on external accident and caprice", "a mere, atomistic agglo-meration of individuals" (*ein blosser atomistischer Haufen von Individuen*), "an unorganized kind of opining and willing" on the part of "a mass or an aggregate", in contrast to the "organized state", "a mass dispersed into its atoms", an "atomistic point of view". Such expressions are invariably made to refer to a kind of polity or constitutional law which sets out to compose the state as a total entity out of the in-dividual parts, and to the total dissolution that must threaten family and civil society, if the perfect organism of the state as a comprehensive and primary entity were not there.

Marx too observed this analogy between the philosophy of nature and the philosophy of right; and he chose his starting-point at precisely the opposite pole, that is, in the atomistic theory rejected by Hegel. In the studies preparatory to his dis-sertation he describes Epicurus' atomistic world as the *bellum omnium contra omnes*, the Roman war of all against all, celebrated in the famous poem by Epicurus' Latin disciple, Lucretius. Epicurus' natural philosophy heralds and proclaims the arrival of a new culture. Here again Marx takes Hegel as his point of departure; for it is Hegel himself who in his *Philosophy of Right* draws the parellel between the revolution of the Roman period and that of modern civil society; just as the description of the latter as "the battlefield where every man's private interest as an individual competes with that of everyone else" is also to be found in Hegel. As we shall see in a subsequent lecture, the front established by Marx's *Critique* lies precisely along this line.

Hegel sees an ethical world that, like Epicurus' nature, falls apart and disintegrates into atoms as "God-forsaken"; and he indignantly repudiates any such "atheism of the ethical world". True philosophy, surely, must have as its content the speculative knowledge of God, of nature and of mind. Like Goethe's Mephistopheles, the atomistic theory destroys the foundations at once of speculative natural philosophy, the philosophy of right and the philosophy of religion. This Marx does not deny; on the contrary, the *bellum omnium contra omnes*, the battle of all with all, which in Epicurus' theory of the atoms is given form, is the representation of a "de-divinized nature and a de-terrestrialized God" (*eine entgötterte Natur und einen entwelteten Gott*). It was the greatness of Epicurus that he dared to look this de-divinized nature straight in the face and refused to venerate the universe as God, that he had the courage to find the de-terrestrialized God simply and solely in the impalpable freedom of his own self-awareness.

But even this last recourse, this final refuge, has vanished with the culture of the ancient world. Though the modern private person, the individual *bourgeois* of modern civil society, may have his own "private religion", the bottom has dropped out of it. Whereas Epicurus refused to worship the celestial bodies, nowadays the possibility has been removed even from the private person of being a divine egoist. In the actual situation of civil society there are only human egoists. The union of cosmos and *polis*, of the natural and the ethical universe, of natural religion and "state religion", has gone for good, disappeared with the extinction of ancient civilization; and even Hegel is powerless to revive it. But even the last bulwark, the divine unimpeachability of the individual "I", the private religion of the subject, the self-sufficiency of the perfect atom, even this final bulwark disappeared with Epicurus; and no form of modern Epicureanism is capable of resurrecting it. Both the critique of religion and the critique of politics furnish us with the proof that now and for the future this earth is inhabited by men and by men alone.

6

The heaven of the political state

"MAN is the world of man, the state, society (*Sozietät*). This state, this society, produce religion, a perverted world-consciousness, because they are a perverted world."

This passage from the opening part of the "Introduction" to the *Critique of Hegel's Philosophy of Right* is something we encountered in my first series of lectures, that is, in the context of the *Critique of Heaven*, where we put the chief emphasis on the fact that Marx's critique of religion is basically a critique of Hegel. It is no accident that this critique of religion forms part of the *Critique of Hegel's Philosophy of Right*. An extrinsic connection turned out, when we analysed it in more detail, to go back to identical roots.

In this second series we shall stress the other element, namely, the fact that the critique of religion is part and parcel of the critique of the philosophy of *right*, or of *law*, in other words, of the critique of "natural law and political science", as the subtitle to Hegel's work has it. Our analysis has already led us to the preliminary insight that Marx's *Critique of Hegel's Philosophy of Right* is at bottom a critique of the modern state. In Hegel's constitutional law he encounters the actuality of the modern state. So the circle is completed: critique of religion = critique of Hegel = critique of the philosophy of right = critique of the state = critique of religion. It is this cycle that in abbreviated form is reflected in the passage with which this lecture began: "This state, this society, produce religion".

In point of fact, the curious dual character of the phrase, "this state, this society", enshrines the problems raised both by Hegel's *Philosophy of Right* and by Marx's *Critique*. The German term, *Sozietät*, occurs quite a lot in Marx's article—but in the "Introduction" only in the passage cited. Here is a passing indication that the "Introduction" is not to be understood apart from the article itself. In this respect we not only have the advantage as compared with the readers of the "Introduction" in the *Deutsch-Französische Jahrbücher*, but even Franz Mehring in his 1918 biography of Marx had to make do with the "Introduction" alone. Nowadays it is no longer justifiable to discuss the "Introduction" all by itself; for Marx wrote it as nothing more than a preamble to his main article, in some sense comparable to Hegel's *Vorrede*, the Preface to his *Philosophy of Right*.

The term *Sozietät* is evidently used by Marx in distinction from the term *bürgerliche Gesellschaft*. Of the latter term he later declares, in the 1859 *Vorwort* to the *Critique of Political Economy*, that he has borrowed it from Hegel. For the term *Sozietät*, on the other hand, one looks in vain in Hegel's *Philosophy of Right*. Indeed, it is in this difference that the explanation lies for the use Marx makes of this term. Underlying the choice of linguistic form there is a yet deeper one. The term *Gesellschaft* is German; the term *Sozietät* is taken directly from the French *société* and the English "society"; it comes from the Latin *societas*. As a matter of fact, Marx himself points to Hegel's borrowing of the term *bürgerliche Gesellschaft* from French and English thinkers of the eighteenth century. He goes behind Hegel to Hegel's predecessors; but this "retrogression" is a decisive step forward. Marx writes his *Critique of Hegel's Philosophy of Right*, as it were, on the eve of his emigration from the German fatherland, whence he has nothing further to hope for. He writes the "Introduction" from Paris, *en route*, so to speak for London; and he publishes it in a Germano-French journal, expressly aimed at a definite crossing of frontiers.

Behind the French and English source of the term *Sozietät* lies the Latin one. We have already traced the European tradition of the Latin term, *societas civilis*. In so doing, we saw that Rousseau's *société civile* was still aligned with the tradition that draws no distinction between "state" and "society", *civitas* and *societas civilis.* As it turned out, it was Hegel in his *Philosophy of Right* who first established a fundamental contrast between the terms *Staat* and *bürgerliche Gesellschaft*. Marx takes over this terminology and invariably uses both terms in the senses distinguished by Hegel. The term *Sozietät*, on the other hand, goes back to the Latin-cum-European tradition which recognizes no distinction between *civitas* and *societas civilis*. The term *Sozietät* anticipates a future in which the present cleavage between *Staat* and *bürgerliche Gesellschaft* will be obliterated, and in which the sham and falsehood of a divided reality will be abolished by the light of the one and undivided truth. That is the allusion in the passage: "Man, that is the world of man, state, society" (*Der Mensch, das ist die Welt des Menschen, Staat, Sozietät*). The comma between "state" and "society" precisely represents the Latin "*sive*" in the definition, *civitas sive societas civilis*. Marx means that the one, undivided world of man, this *civitas sive societas civilis*, is split into two halves, so that each half distorts the true and real unity, becomes a half truth and therefore a half lie. The world of man has become a perverted world, which can only produce a perverted world consciousness.

It is only right to remind ourselves here of the third term of the Latin definition, the term *res publica*, which the word *sive* in the definition equates with the terms *civitas* and *societas civilis*. With his *Critique of Hegel's Philosophy of Right* in view, Marx points out how impossible it is to find an equivalent for this term in German. He takes over from Hegel the expression *allgemeine Angelegenheit*, a term Hegel uses to denote the objective side of what on the subjective side is known as *öffentliche Bewusstsein* (section 301). A combination of *Angelegenheit* (Latin *res*) and *öffentlich* (Latin *publica*) yields more or less the required parallel to the term *res publica*. This brings us back to the passage quoted in my previous lecture, where Marx is summarizing his *Critique*. "In modern states, as in Hegel's *Philosophy of Right*, the conscious, true actuality of the public cause (*der allgemeine Angelegenheit*) is only formal, or only the formal is the actual public cause (*allgemeine Angelegenheit*)." The *res publica* is reduced from the status of actuality to a formality, its truth has become no more than a shadow, a spectre, in the modern state; and as a conscious actuality it evaporates into an illusion in modern civil society. The unity of the *civitas sive societas civilis sive res publica* disintegrates; and neither the modern state nor Hegel's speculative method turns out to be capable of restoring it.

Admittedly, Hegel's idea of the state is based on that of the organism in which all the parts exist through, and are to be understood in terms of, the living totality. But this idea is a semblance only, it remains purely formal, acquires no actual content. Marx also indicates what is the root of this defect: the idea of the organism is not a *conscious* reality. In the state, conscious reason must prevail (*muss bewusste Vernunft herrschen*); the substantive, purely inward and therefore purely outward necessity, by which the particular functions of the state are linked up with the state as a whole entity, cannot be envisaged as the rational aspect (*die substantielle bloss innere und darum bloss äussere Notwendigkeit . . . kan nicht für das Vernünftige ausgegeben werden*). The term "substantive" (*substantiell*) could be interpreted here as "biological". Hegel's organic idea is a biological model. There is no place in this model, therefore, for the typically human, the conscious reason (*bewusste Vernunft*) of the human individual. There is no bridge from this organic totality to the actual being of society, which consists of self-subsistent, consciously willing and acting individuals. Hegel forgot that the state can only function through individuals, that the affairs and activities of the state are human functions, that specific individuality is of the human variety. He forgot that the essential thing about individual personality is neither beard nor blood nor abstract *physis*, but its social character (*soziale Qualität*) and that the affairs of the state, and so forth, are simply modes of existence and functions (*Daseins- und Wirkungsweisen*) of the social attributes of the person.

What applies to Hegel's philosophy of right applies also to the constitutional state, which his philosophy mirrors. The constitutional state is the state in which the state interest (*Staatsinteresse*) as the actual interest of the people is present only formally, as a particular form beside the actual state; the concern or interest of the state here has acquired, formally speaking, a new actuality as the people's interest; but it is bound to have that formal actuality and that alone. This finds expression in the legislature: as its content it has the general, the universal; but this universal is more a matter of knowing than of will, it is a metaphysical "arm" of the state, a fitting depository for the metaphysical, general, illusory state.

Hegel starts off from the separation of "civil society" (*bürgerliche Gesellschaft*) and political state (*politische Staat*) as two contrasted actualities, two actually separate realms. This separation is indeed a present reality in the modern state. The polarity he tries to resolve through the (mediating) element of the "estates" (*Stände*), which he sees as a synthesis between state and civil society. Yet this speculation of his is a complete fiction. As he admits himself, it was in the Middle Ages that such a synthesis did exist. In those times the "estates" of civil society and the "estates" in a political sense were indeed identical; for during the Middle Ages civil society was the same thing as the political society, the body politic; the organic principle of civil society was the principle of the state. But the Middle Ages are dead and gone. Hegel is harking back to a synthesis which has disappeared for good.

That is why he keeps ending up in self-contradiction. On the one hand, he posits sharply enough the conflict between state and civil society. The actual nature of civil society he defines clearly as the "battleground where each person's individual, private interest encounters that of everyone else" (*Kampfplatz des individuellen Privatinteresses Aller gegen Alle*) (section 289); and Marx is right in regarding this as a translation of Hobbes' *bellum omnium contra omnes*. Hegel's profundity comes out here, in that he is sensible of the cleavage between civil and political society as being one of conflict; but his mistake is to rest content with the mere semblance of a solution.

For there is, in fact, no bridge between the idea of the organic state, on the one hand, and the actuality of "an aggregate dispersed into its atoms", which Hegel presents in outline as the manifest form of civil society (section 303). Between organism and atomistic world no mediation is possible. Civil society, therefore, within Hegel's philosophy and in the context of the modern state, cannot possibly take on a political significance. Hegel describes civil society as the "private class" (*Privatstand*); one fails to see how a private class can promote or have at heart the general interest, which is why Marx calls the political function which Hegel would nonetheless ascribe to this private class a "total transubstantiation" (*völlige Transsubstantiation*). For in this political function civil society is bound to belie itself completely *qua* civil society, *qua* private class, and bring to the fore a side of its nature which not only has nothing in common with the actual, civil character of that nature's existence but is even in direct conflict with it.

In fact, civil society and state are divided; and that is why the state citizen (*Staatsbürger*) and the "civilian" (*Bürger*), in the sense of the member of civil society, is also divided. He therefore has to effect a fundamental division (*Diremption*) within himself. As an actual citizen he finds himself in a dual organization: on the one hand, the bureaucratic organization—an external, formal property of the state "out there" (*jenseitigen*), the ruling authority which does not touch him and his actual, separate and independent being; and, on the other hand, the social organization of civil society. In the latter he stands as a private being (*Privatmann*) outside the state. The former is a state organization, the matter for which he continues to provide. The second is a civil organization, the matter of which is not the state. In the first, the state relates as a formal polarity to him as a private person; in the second, he is related as a material polarity to the state. If then he wishes to assume his role as an actual citizen, to achieve political significance and activity, he must withdraw from his actual civil capacity, abstract from it, retreat out of this whole organization into his individuality; the sole existence that he can find for his role as citizen of the state is his pure individuality; for the state's existence as the government is complete without him, and his existence in civil society is complete without the state. Only at variance with these two communities between which he must choose outright, only as an individual can he be the state citizen. His existence as that citizen is one that lies outside his communal existence: in other words, it is a purely individual existence.

Hegel's idea of the organic state attempts to gloss over this contrariety. He opposes the current liberal view that the citizen as member of the "private class" can participate in the functions of the state only *qua* individual, whether it be through elected representatives or directly. He calls this an "atomistic and abstract point of view". In the state no one of its elements can appear as an inorganic (unorganized) aggregate. The many as single units (what we are pleased to regard as "the people")—are of course connected, but only as an aggregate—a formless mass whose commotion and activity must be elementary, irrational, barbarous and frightening (section 303).

This is indeed, Marx's commentary is saying, an abstract view; but it is the "abstraction" of the political state, as explicated by Hegel himself. This viewpoint is atomistic as well; but the atomism is that of society itself. The interpretation, the point of view, cannot be concrete, as its object is "abstract". The atomism into which civil society in its political action is plunged is a necessary consequence of the fact that the communal mode of being (*das Gemeinwesen*), the communistic mode of being (*das Kommunistische Wesen*) in which the individual exists, is civil society divorced from the state, or the political state as an abstraction from civil society.

When Hegel argues that this atomistic point of view at once disappears in the family, as well as in civil society, because even at these levels the individual is in evidence only as a member of a general group, then it is not in any event true that at the level of the state this atomism is totally superseded. On the contrary, it recurs precisely at this point, simply because the state is an abstraction from the family and civil society.

Hegel opposes the notion that would dissolve the communal relations of family and civil society, where the latter function at the political level, that is, the level of the highest concrete general group, back again into an aggregate of individuals; for this idea thereby holds civil and political life apart from each other and leaves the latter hanging in the air, as it were, because its basis could then only be the abstract individuality of caprice and opinion, not a solid foundation but a basis of chance.

To this Marx replies that it is not this notion which holds civil and political life apart; rather is it the notion, the representation, of a separation which actually exists. It is not the representation itself which leaves political life hanging in the air; but political life is the rarified existence (*Luftleben*), the etherial region (*die ätherische Region*) of civil society.

In Hegel's conception of constitutional monarchy the legislature is composed of the representatives of the various estates.

Marx criticizes thls construction by means of a little historical analysis. It is a sign of historical progress that the political estates or classes have turned into social classes; so that just as Christians are equal in heaven but unequal on earth, so are the individual members of a people equal in the heaven of their political world, unequal in the earthly existence of a society (*Sozietät*). The real change of the political classes into civil ones was completed in absolute monarchy; but even then, side by side with the bureaucracy of an absolute governing authority social distinction between the various classes continued to have a political significance. It was the French Revolution that first achieved the change of political classes into social classes; to put it another way, it turned the class differences of civil society into purely social differences, differences in private life that had no significance in political life. In that way the separation between political life and civil society was made complete.

In this brief historical analysis, what comes out very clearly is the dialectical character of Marx's *Critique*. That *Critique* is a two-edged sword. He acknowledges the division between the political state and civil society as an historical advance, and the importance of the French Revolution as the decisive step on this road. Thereafter there can be no going back. Does this mean that he applauds the separation? No; on the contrary, his *Critique* is aimed at precisely this division, which he exposes as the fundamental distortion of the true reality of the world of man. Must the division, then, be done away with? Yes; but not by putting the clock back. What was done by the French Revolution cannot now be undone. There is no way back, only a way forward. Should the gulf not be bridged, then, the fatal discord not be resolved? Certainly; but not by blurring the contrast, not by some conciliatory measure which would leave the contradiction still there, not by an ideal supersession of opposites that fails to touch the reality of the conflict. Only a ruthless analysis of the real contrariety can lead to a real solution.

In the light of this, it becomes clear why Marx describes the notion of the political state, as an existence divorced from civil society, as the theological notion of the political state. He does not mean by this that the notion is based on a fiction. On the contrary, we have just heard how he rebuts Hegel's speculative

method, which attempts to eliminate the division between
political state and civil society, which Hegel had himself put on
record, by reducing it to something that does not represent or
reflect the real state of affairs. No; the conception is right
enough. The theological idea of the political state is an exact
representation of the modern state as it actually is, divorced
from civil society. The target of Marx's *Critique*, therefore, was
not so much the theological notion as the actuality portrayed in
it, an actuality which in its turn is kept in being by the notion
itself.

When Marx formulates the contrast as one between the
"heaven of the political world" and the "earthly existence of a
society (*Sozietät*)", this expression is not to be understood
metaphorically, but taken literally. The "theological notion"
of the political state is not a religious appendage or sanctioning
of something already actual, which exists independently of it as
a profane actuality; but the theological notion reflects the
actual state of affairs. This itself bears a theological character.
The division between political state and civil society is in itself
a theological division, it derives from the same root whence
comes the division between "heaven" and "earth"; to put it
more precisely, it is itself that division. This is why one might
equally well call the theological notion of the "heaven" of the
political state a reflection, or perhaps a projection, of the
theological notion of "heaven", as *vice versa*. What we have here
is a fundamental analogy, in which image and reality reflect
each other; an identity-relation, where the image amounts to
the reality and the reality is just as much image.

Marx's *Critique* is the analysis which equally reveals in the
theological notion the actual character of political and civil
life and conversely demonstrates from the actuality of political
and civil life the true nature of theology. The effect of his
Critique, therefore, is always double-edged: representation
(notion) *and* reality; theology *and* politics; abstract "heaven"
and abstract "earth"; distorted reality *and* distorting speculation; the impossibility of a conflicting division *and* the impossibility of a kind of bridging which still allows the gulf to exist.

"This anti-critique, this mysticism is the riddle of modern
constitutions (specifically of the class state) as well as the
mystery of Hegel's philosophy, particularly the philosophy of

right and of religion." (*Diese* UNKRITIK, *dieser* MYSTIZISMUS *ist sowohl das Rätsel der modernen Verfassungen* (*Kat'exochèn der ständischen*) *wie auch das Mysterium der Hegelschen Philosophie, vorzugsweise der* RECHTS- UND RELIGIONSPHILOSOPHIE). In this sentence we have a summing up of Marx's whole multi-dimensional critique. *Unkritik*, the absolute opposite of critique (just as inhuman is the complete negation of human), is the root of the modern state and of religion, of the state *and* of Hegel's constitutional law, of Hegel's philosophy of right *and* of his philosophy of religion.

Since Marx's *Critique* is meant to be radical, that is to say, meant to penetrate to this one root of all *Unkritik*, in its terminology it persists in relating the various dimensions to one another. It is not figurative language but the idiom of this radical critique, when he analyses Hegel's construction of constitutional monarchy thus: in the legislature, regarded from the standpoint of the government's share in it, the empirical, impenetrable individuality of the ruler assumes an earthly guise (*sich verirdischt*) in a number of limited, tangible, responsible personalities; and in the share which the classes, the "estates", have in the legislature, civil society acquires its heavenly aspect (*sich verhimmlischt*) in a number of political figures. Just as the ruler has in the governmental authority an intermediary between himself and civil society, has in fact a sort of Christ, so by means of the classes as its priests society is reconciled (*vermittelt sich*) with the ruler.

If the *Unkritik* is the enigma of modern constitutions, then conversely Marx describes democracy as the "solved riddle" of all constitutions (*Die Demokratie ist das aufgelöste Rätsel aller Verfassungen*). Here again the critique of Hegel, of the state and of religion are continually interlocking the one with the other. He starts by opposing Hegel with his own weapons, that is, by showing the organic idea to be incompatible with the idea of constitutional monarchy favoured by Hegel himself. Hegel contends that without its monarch the people is an organism with no centre, no more than a formless mass; and so he rejects the modern idea of the people's sovereignty as the product of a barbarous conception of "the people". Marx exposes this line of argument as a tautology: if one begins by defining "the people" in an organic interrelation with the monarch, then by definition it is a formless mass without the monarch. As opposed to Hegel's derivation of the republic, more specifically of democracy, from the organic idea of monarchy, Marx deliberately opts for what Hegel calls "the barbarous conception of the people".

Democracy is the truth implicit in monarchy, monarchy is not the truth in democracy. Monarchy is of necessity democracy as a self-opposed inconsequence, the monarchical element is not an inconsequence within democracy. Whilst monarchy cannot be comprehended in terms of itself, democracy can. In democracy no element assumes other than its proper importance: each element is actually just an element of the whole *demos*. In monarchy a part determines the character of the whole.

If, at this point, Marx turns Hegel's organic idea against his notion of monarchy, a little later on he goes a step further, demonstrating that Hegel's state is governed by chance, by accident, in other words, by just that element which Hegel's speculation was intended to exclude. Hegel had compared the mystery of the ruler's being predestined through his birth in the course of nature to the status of monarch with the ontological proof of God's existence. There too the absolute concept is converted into being (section 280). Marx's comment on this is that the birth of an individual destined to monarchy no more qualifies to be a metaphysical truth than does the immaculate conception of the Virgin. Whilst Hegel finds the speculative unity, the actual unity, of the state to be rooted in the ostensibly accidental character of the link between the concept of monarchy and the ruler's birth in the course of nature, Marx concludes that caprice, the natural accident of birth, in other words, King Chance, constitutes the real unity of Hegel's state.

In monarchy the whole, the people, is classified under one of its modes of existence, the political constitution; in democracy the constitution as such is in evidence only as a prescriptive enactment, a determination, the self-determination of the people. In monarchy we have the people of the constitution, in democracy the constitution of the people. Democracy is the "resolved riddle" of all constitutions. The constitution here is not only in itself, essentially, but in its existence, actuality, reduced to its true ground, the actual human being, the actual people. The constitution appears for what it is, the free product of man.

Hegel takes the state as his starting-point and turns man into the state subjectivized; democracy starts with man and makes the state objectivized man. Just as religion does not make man, but man makes religion, so the constitution does not make the people, but the people the constitution. In a sense, democracy relates to all the other forms of state, just as Christianity relates to all other religions. Christianity is the religion *par excellence* (*Kat 'exochèn*), the essence of religion, divinized man as a particular religion. So democracy is the essence of all polity, all forms of government, socialized man as a specific polity. Democracy is related to all other forms of state as to its Old Testament. Man does not exist for the sake of the law, but the law exists for man's sake. The point and concern of democracy is man's existence as man, whereas in the other forms of state man is "legalized being", is existence under the law. That is what fundamentally distinguishes democracy.

Hegel says, fairly enough, that the political state is the constitution; in other words, the material state is not political. Of the different elements of national life the most difficult to develop was the state as a political entity, the constitution. It did develop as universal reason (*Vernunft*) over against the other realms, as something situated way beyond the rest (*als ein Jenseitiges derselben*). Historically, the task was to retrieve this universal reason from way and beyond (*Revindikation*); but the several spheres have not been aware in this connection that their individual essence stands or falls with the essentially remote nature (*jenseitige Wesen*) of the constitution, and that the detached existence (*jenseitiges Dasein*) of the constitution is nothing other than the corroboration of their own estrangement (*Entfremdung*). The political constitution was up to this point the religious sphere, the religion of the national life, the heaven of its universality as over against the earthly existence of its actuality. The political sphere was the sole public sphere in the state, the only sphere in which the content as well as the form was the content of the general group (*Gattungsinhalt*), the truly universal; but at the same time this solitary sphere persisted over against the rest, so that its content also became a formal and particular content. Political life in the modern sense is the scholasticism of the life of the people. Monarchy is the perfect expression of this alienation (*Entfremdung*). The republic is the negation of this within its own sphere. Obviously, the political constitution as such first begins to develop where the several private realms have achieved an independent existence. Where trade and land-ownership are not free, have not yet become self-reliant, there too the political constitution is not as yet free, not yet self-subsistent. The Middle Ages were the "democracy of unfreedom".

The abstraction of the state as such is a product solely of modern times because the abstraction of private life is a product solely of modern times. The abstraction of the political state is a modern product. In the Middle Ages the life of the people, the nation, and the life of the state are identical. Man is the actual principle of the state, but unfree man, man under constraint. He is therefore the democracy of unfreedom, the consequent alienation (*Entfremdung*). The abstract, reflected polarity is a product only of the modern period. The Middle Ages are an actual, *de facto* dualism, the modern period is abstract dualism.

Marx pursues a similar train of thought when it comes to the other half of the divided, self-alienated unity of man's world, civil society. The separation between political state and civil society, accomplished by the French Revolution, also served to change the character of the social classes, the "estates". Civil society became the private class. In his political capacity the member of civil society detaches himself from his private class; only in his political capacity does the member of civil society acquire significance as a human being, only here is his function as a member of the state, as a social being, revealed as his human destiny. Modern civil society is the logical principle of individualism, existence at the individual level being the ultimate goal.

In the Middle Ages, class was based on the division of society (*Sozietät*); and so the human being becomes divorced from his general nature, is made an animal immediately identical with its specification in nature. The Middle Ages form the animal history (*Tiergeschichte*) of mankind, its zoology.

The modern epoch, civilization, commits the opposite mistake. It separates off the objective being of man, as a merely external, material aspect. It fails to take the content of man as his true reality.

The mistake of the modern epoch, of civilization, is the basic error of Hegel's philosophy. In his *Critique* of it Marx criticizes the modern age, civilization. At the end of his article he returns to it yet again. It is a fault common to Hegel and to *de facto* modern conditions that they presuppose the division between "real life" and public life and turn the public capacity into an abstract capacity of the actual member of the state. As over against the abstraction of the "state idea", the qualities of the actual, empirical state-formalism appear as content, and in consequence the real content appears as formless, unorganized matter (in this case the actual human being, actual society (*Sozietät*), and so forth).

This basic error also makes it impossible for Hegel to resolve the dilemma which he sees residing in the contradiction between Rousseau's *volonté de tous* and *volonté générale*. If one's starting-point is the divorce between civil society and the state as a political entity, then obviously the atomistic mass of isolated individuals who constitute civil society can never promote the general cause, the public cause (section 308). But the dilemma is one produced by Hegel himself: it is an abstract political problem within the abstract political state. In an actually rational (*vernünftige*) state the "individuals" who take part in the public cause are at the same time "everybody", that is, they take part as members of the society and within the whole of that society (*Sozietät*). Not everyone individually, but individuals *qua* "everyone". The very notion of a member of the state implies that they are limbs, are members, are a part of it, that the state takes them as its "share". Thus if they are a part, a portion, of the state, then naturally their social existence is already their *de facto* sharing in the state. They are not just a portion of the state, but the state is their portion. Consciously to be a part of something, that is deliberately to take a share of it, to take a share, to participate in it. Without this consciousness the member of the state must be an animal. The expression "political matters of general concern" makes it look as though "matters of general concern" and "the state" are different things. But the state is the "public cause", the general concern (*allgemeine Angelegenheit*), and thus in reality "matters of general concern".

The striving of civil society to turn itself into political society, or to make the political society the society that actually exists, comes to expression in the struggle for the most universal participation possible in the legislature. If civil society is actually political society, then the importance of the legislature as a representative power vanishes. The legislature is a representation here in the sense in which any function is representative, just as the shoemaker, for instance, in so far as he fulfils a social need, is my representative agent, just as each particular social activity as an activity of the species simply represents the species, that is to say, a characteristic of my own being, just as each and every person is the representative of the rest. He is a representative here not through something else that he proposes or envisages, but through what he *is* and *does·*

So the *Critique of Hegel's Philosophy of Right* allows us a glimpse into the true and actual world of man, of the human being who at the same time is fully a member of the state, *citoyen*, and a member of civil society, *bourgeois*; the whole man in a complete *res publica* which is both *societas civilis* and *civitas*.

This scheme comes to maturation in Marx's thinking when in 1844 he writes the two articles for the *Deutsch-Französische Jahrbücher*, the critique of Bruno Bauer's discussion of the Jewish question and the "Introduction" to the *Critique of Hegel's Philosophy of Right*. The two articles are closely interrelated, modulations and elaborations of the main theme.

The article on the Jewish question (*Zur Judenfrage*) is, over Bruno Bauer's head, really a critique of Hegel and to that extent a continuation of the critique written in the two previous years. The main charge against Bauer is that he simply takes over from Hegel the cleavage between the political state and civil society and lets the division persist as a profane polarity, whilst attacking only its religious expression.

In a sense, Marx's article on the Jewish question fills in a gap which he had deliberately left open in his *Critique of Hegel's Philosophy of Right*. In his chapter on constitutional law, Hegel devotes a lengthy section (section 270) to the relation of the state to religion. Marx leaves out this section, promising to return to the problem later on. The fact that provisionally he sets this question aside is in itself typical of his approach, in which the issue plays only a subordinate role.

Entirely in keeping with his philosophy of religion Hegel treats religion as a relation to the absolute in the form of feeling, representational thinking and faith, over against which the state is posited as the divine will, which actualizes itself as the shape and organization of Mind, unfolding itself to the world. On this basis, the state is related to the diversity of churches as is the principle of universality to particular elements. Marx endorses this thesis, but sets it within the broader context of the relation between state and civil society; of this latter, religion is merely a special expression. In a divided reality man leads a dual existence, a heavenly life and an earthly one, life in the politico-communal mode of being, in which he is aware of himself as a being-in-community (*Gemeinwesen*), and life in civil society, in which he is active as a private person (*Privatmensch*), regards other human beings as a means, reduces himself to a means and becomes the plaything of alien forces. The political state has the same spiritualistic relation to civil society as heaven has to earth. The Jewish problem is only a component of the problem of religious man, which in turn is no more than an aspect of the question of civil society. It is only on a sophistic basis that the bourgeois, like the Jew, persists in the life of the state, just as it is only on such a basis that the *citoyen* can continue to be Jew or bourgeois; but this sophistic is not personal. It is a sophistic entailed by the life of the state, public life itself. The distinction between religious man and state citizen is the distinction between the living individual and the citizen. The situation of conflict in which religious man finds himself with political man is the same as that in which the *bourgeois* finds himself with the *citoyen*, and the member of civil society with his political lion's skin.

Man emancipates himself politically from religion by banishing it from public law to private law. The "disintegrating" of the human being into Jew and public citizen, religious man and citizen, does not belie the value of citizenship, it is not a way of evading political emancipation; it is the political means of emancipating oneself from religion. Indeed, in times when the political state *qua* political state is being violently born out of civil society, times in which the self-liberation of man is trying to fulfil itself in the form of political self-liberation, the state can and should do its utmost to supersede, to abolish religion; but it does this only in the same way that it does its utmost to put an end to private ownership, and so on, as far as to take away life, even as far as the guillotine. At the exceptional moments of an intensified self-esteem political life endeavours to suppress its premise, civil society, and *its* elements, and to constitute itself as the real, incontradictory (*widerspruchslose*) life of human kind. But it is in a position to do this only at the cost of a violent contradiction (*widerspruch*) with the pre-conditions of its own life, only by proclaiming the permanence of revolution; and the political drama ends just as inevitably, therefore, with the restoration of religion, of private ownership, of all the elements of civil society, just as war ends in peace.

Indeed, it is not the so-called Christian state, which professes Christianity as its basis, as the state religion, and on that ground excludes other religions, that is the complete Christian state, but rather the atheistic state, the democratic state, the state which makes a place for religion among the other elements of civil society. The state which still plays the theologian, which still officially professes Christianity, which does not yet venture to proclaim itself a state, that state has not as yet succeeded in expressing in a profane, human form, in its reality as a state, the human basis of which Christianity is an immoderate expression. The so-called Christian state is simply the non-state, because what can find expression in man's actual creations is not the Christian religion, but only the human background to that religion.

The so-called Christian state is the Christian negation of the state, and not the political realization of Christianity at all. The state which continues to profess Christianity *qua* religion does not profess it *qua* state; for it is relating itself to religion on a religious basis, that is to say, it is not a real expression of the human basis of religion, because it still appeals to the unreality, to the imaginary form of this human substance. The so-called Christian state is the defective state; and the effect of the Christian religion is to complete it and lend sanctity to its imperfection. Religion therefore becomes necessary to it as a means; and it is the state hypocritical, caught in dissimulation. It makes a big difference whether the completed state includes religion among its presuppositions because of the deficiency inherent in the general nature of the state, or whether in view of the defect inherent in its particular existence the incomplete state, *qua* defective state, declares religion to be its very foundation. In the latter case, religion becomes an imperfect, defective kind of politics. In the former case, what manifests itself in religion is the actual imperfection of a complete kind of politics. The so-called Christian state needs religion in order to be complete as a state. The democratic state, the real state, has no need of religion in order to be perfected politically. Rather it is able to abstract from religion, because the human basis of religion finds a profane expression in it. The so-called Christian state, on the other hand, relates politically to religion, and religiously to politics. In reducing the forms of the state to a mere show, it equally reduces religion to the same condition. In the so-called Christian state, in particular the Germano-Christian state, alienation prevails, surely enough, but not the human being. The one person who does count, the king, is a being specifically distinguished from other men, but all the same himself a religious being, allied directly with heaven, with God. The genius of religion is not yet really secularized here. It cannot be; for what is it other than the unworldly form of a phase of development of the human mind? The genius of religion can be secularized only to the extent that the phase of development aforementioned, of which it is the religious expression, emerges and is constituted in its profane form. That takes place in the democratic state. Not Christianity but the human foundation underlying Christianity is the basis of this state. Religion persists as the ideal, unworldly consciousness of its adherents because it is the ideal form of the phase of man's development represented in this democratic state.

The members of the political state are religious, thanks to the dualism between individual and collective (public) life (*Gattungsleben*), between the life of civil society and political life; religious, because the individual person relates to public life, to the life of the state which goes on way beyond (*jenseitigen*) his real individuality, as to his true life; religious, in so far as religion is here the genius of civil society and an expression of the fact that man is divided and estranged from man (*Entfernung des Menschen vom Menschen*). Political democracy is a Christian thing, because in it man—not just *a* man but every man—counts as sovereign, as a creature supreme; but man in his contingent existence, man taken all in all, without qualification, man as he is corrupted by the whole organization of our society, has lost and abandoned himself, is exteriorized, is delivered up to domination by inhuman circumstances and elements, in short, man who is not yet a really *human* species of being (*Gattungswesen*). The fantasy-image, the dream, the postulate of Christianity, the sovereignty of man, albeit as a peculiar creature divorced from the real human being, is in democracy a palpable reality, a presence, a secular axiom. The religious and theological consciousness in itself will be deemed in the complete democracy all the more religious, all the more theological, as it is evidently without political significance, without temporal aims, a matter of unworldly sentiment, an expression of a cramped, narrow-minded intelligence (*Verstandes-Borniertheit*), the product of caprice and fantasy, and as it really is a "life beyond" (*Jenseitiges*). Political emancipation from religion leaves it in existence, but not of course with any privileges. The conflict in which the adherent of a particular religion finds himself involved, the conflict with his role as citizen of the state, is only part of the general, profane conflict between the political state and civil society. The completion of the Christian state is the state which professes to be a state and abstracts from the religion of its members. When the state emancipates itself from religion, that does not mean that the individual human being is actually emancipated from it.

It is only in the Christian world that civil society attains its completion. Only under the dominating influence of Christianity, which turns all national, natural, ethical and theoretical relations into relations that pertain only extrinsically to man (*dem Menschen äusserlich macht*), could civil society sever itself completely from public life, rend all the ties typical of human kind (*Gattungsbande*), put egoism and private gain in the place of such ties, and dissolve the human world into a world of atomistic, mutually hostile individuals.

One has to have read Marx's article on the Jewish question in order to be able to understand the other one, the "Introduction" to the *Critique of Hegel's Philosophy of Right*, and to penetrate to the paradox at its heart. For in the analysis of the Jewish question and the indirect critique of Hegel's conception of the political state therein contained Marx illuminates the deepest meaning of his *Critique of Hegel's Philosophy of Right*: namely, that his critique is essentially a critique of religion, and on two levels at that. In the first place, his critique focuses not on the Christian state but on the atheistic, democratic one; not on the defective, incomplete state which still needs a religious basis, but on the completed political state, which is a religion unto itself. The completion of religion is atheistic democracy, the political state is the mature fruit of theology. In the second place, and at a deeper level, he discloses the structure of civil society in its atomistic existence, separated from the political state, as the historical consequence of Christianity, as an expression of Christianity's human basis, as the political realization of the Christian principle that man is the sovereign and supreme being, as the product of man's self-alienation (*Selbstentfremdung*) and his alienation from nature, which has reached its theoretical completion through Christianity.

Here, then, in outline is the paradoxical structure of Marx's critique. The critique of heaven and earth is summed up in the passage from the "Introduction" to the *Critique of Hegel's Philosophy of Right*, which is the principal theme of my two series of lectures: "Thus the critique of heaven is transmuted into the critique of earth, the critique of religion into the critique of law, the critique of theology into the critique of politics." However, when we have read his article on the Jewish problem, then the question arises whether we should not stand this sentence on its head. For in this article the critique of politics is transmuted into the critique of theology, the critique of law into the critique of religion, the critique of earth into the critique of heaven.

"It is in the first instance the task of philosophy, which is intended to serve history, once the sacred guise of man's self-alienation has been exposed, to expose the self-alienation in its unholy guises." Marx makes it appear as though the former (the unmasking of the sacred aspect) were the critique of heaven, religion, theology, whilst the latter (the unmasking of the unholy aspect)—is the critique of earth, law, politics. That is not, however, his deepest aim and purpose. For his critique of the political state consists precisely in the exposure of the religious essence lurking behind the seemingly irreligious form of the democratic state. On closer inspection, the paradox turns out to be already implicit in the term "unmask" (*entlarven*). Man's self-alienation, it seems, shelters behind a Janus-like mask: a holy mask and an unholy one. The "unmasking" implies that behind the mask the true face appears that differs radically from, is indeed the exact opposite of, what the mask displays. It would seem that behind the fool's mask there lurks a saint, and behind the saintly mask a fool. Unmasking of the saintly form reveals the unholy character of human self-alienation, whereas, when the unholy mask is torn away, the sacred character of the self-alienation emerges.

"It is the task of history, once the world beyond (*das Jenseits*) the truth has disappeared, to establish the truth of this world (*das Diesseits*)." What this seems to say is that after the critique of heaven, religion, theology, has been completed, the critique of earth, law, politics, can begin its constructive work. But that cannot possibly be Marx's real meaning. For the *Critique of Hegel's Philosophy of Right* is full of such expressions as "the heaven of the political world", "the heaven of the political state", the "heavenly exaltation of civil society into the political state", the political constitution as the "religion of the national life, the heaven of its universality over against the earthly existence of its actuality", the state as "the religion of private ownership", the "theological notion of the political state", the political state as a "world beyond" (*Jenseitiges*), and so forth. Such expressions indicate in a nutshell the general tenor of Marx's critique of law, of politics, which consists in bringing out from behind the profane mask of the modern state the religious countenance.

Here, evidently, we come up against an ambiguity in Marx's critique. At the root of this ambiguity lies the essentially paradoxical character of his critique of heaven and earth; but on the surface it manifests itself in an ambiguous use of language. We can see this particularly well in a passage from the article on the Jewish question, comparing the situations in Germany, France and the United States.

"In Germany, where no political state, no state *qua* state, exists, the Jewish problem is a purely theological one. The Jew finds himself in a religious contretemps with the state which professes Christianity as its basis. Such a state is a professed theologian. The critique here is a critique of theology, a double-edged critique, a critique of Christian and of Jewish theology. Thus we are still moving all the time in the realm of theology, however critical we may be in doing so."

"In France, in the constitutional state, the Jewish problem is that of constitutionalism, the problem of political emancipation only half achieved. Because the semblance of a state religion, albeit in an empty and intrinsically contradictory formula, in the formula of a 'majority religion', is maintained in this case, the relation of Jewish people to the state presents the appearance of a religious-cum-theological contrast."

"Only in the free states of North America—or at any rate in a part of them—does the Jewish question lose its theological implication and become a purely secular problem. Only there, where the political state has reached a stage of full development, can the relation of the Jew and of the religious person generally to the political state—in short, the relation of religion to the state—become clearly manifest in its pure and distinct character. The critique of this relationship ceases to be a theological critique, the moment the state ceases to relate itself to religion theologically, the moment it relates *qua* state, that is to say, on a political basis to religion. The critique then becomes a critique of the political state."

In its tone, this passage is an exegesis of the proposition that the critique of theology is transmuted into the critique of politics. Marx illustrates the process from the path that runs from Germany, the incomplete, Christian state, *via* France, the half-complete democracy, to the United States, the complete state, emancipated from religion. So here is the terminus of the critique of religion, and the starting-point of the critique of politics. Marx then takes a closer look at the situation in the United States. He notices that religion none the less leads a flourishing existence in that country and concludes that the existence of religion is evidently not in conflict with the completion of the state. But since the existence of religion is the existence of a defect, a flaw, the cause of it can only be sought in the essential character of the state.

"Religion we can no longer regard as the cause, but only as the phenomenal outcome of a profane limitation ... We would argue that free citizens put an end to their religious restriction as soon as they do away with their profane restriction. We are not turning profane issues into theological ones, but *vice versa*. After history has been merged in superstition long enough, we merge superstition in history . . . The conflict of the state with a particular religion, such as Judaism, we transmute into human terms as the conflict of the state with certain profane elements, its conflict with religion as such, its conflict with its own presuppositions as such."

Here Marx's terminology begins to take on a recognizably ambiguous character. The transition from "a particular religion" to the "presuppositions of the state as such" is intended as the transition from religion to politics, as the transmutation of theological into profane issues. But the transition runs *via* "religion as such" (*die Religion überhaupt*, religion in general), a curious middle term between religion and politics, between theology and state. That becomes clear when Marx further develops his argument about the situation of the complete state, the state totally emancipated from religion, as we find it in North America. The relation of this state to religion is nothing other than the relation of the people who form the state to religion.

"From this it follows that through the medium of the state, by political means, man liberates himself from a restriction, since being in conflict with himself, he elevates himself in an abstract, limited and partial way above this restriction. It further follows that by liberating himself politically, man liberates himself by a detour, a roundabout route, a medium, albeit a necessary one. Finally, it follows that man, even when through the state as intermediary (*Vermittlung*) he proclaims himself an atheist, that is, when he proclaims an atheist state, is still in the grip of religion, precisely because it is only in an indirect way, only through a medium, that he recognizes himself. Religion is simply the recognition of man in a roundabout way. Through a mediator (*Mittler*). The state is the mediator between man and man's freedom. Just as Christ is the mediator on whom man loads his whole divinity, his whole religious self-consciousness and constraint, so the state is the mediator in which he invests all his non-divinity, all his detachment and open-mindedness as man."

So this is "religion as such": the recognition of man in a roundabout way, through a mediator. The detour can take either of two routes: it can run by way of "religion" in the accepted sense *and* it can run by way of irreligion, atheism. To put it differently, by way of the "beyond" (*Jenseits*) *and* of the "here and now" (*Diesseits*), by way of "religion" *and* of "politics". The vital point is that the feature common to *both* detours is that they require mediation, a medium, that they need a mediator; and so both detours are by definition religion.

Equipped with this exegesis, we can return to the "Introduction" to the *Critique of Hegel's Philosophy of Right*. We shall find that it bears the full brunt of the ambiguity. It opens with the statement: "For Germany the critique of religion is in the main complete, and the critique of religion is the premise of all critique." The argument leads up to the conclusion: "The struggle against religion, therefore, is indirectly the struggle against that world of which religion is the spiritual aroma." Here, then, we find the mediating factor on the opposite side from where it is in the above-quoted definition of religion. If the critique of religion is the premise of all critique, then the critique of religion is immediate or direct, and all other critique mediate or indirect. Hence the conclusion that the struggle against religion is indirectly, mediately (*mittelbar*), the struggle against the world of which it is the spiritual aroma. In the above-quoted definition, however, the relationship is exactly reversed: there religion is the medium, the mediator, whereby man mediately recognizes himself or, to put it more precisely, religion is this mediate self-recognition on man's part. In terms of that definition, the conclusion would have to be put just the opposite way round: the critique of earth is the premise of the critique of heaven, the struggle against the world of which religion is the spiritual aroma is mediately, indirectly, the struggle against religion.

If we look more closely, we should be able to follow this turn of thought quite accurately in the course taken by Marx's line of argument. The initial assertion that religion is the premise of all critique is illustrated thus: who found in the fantastic reality of heaven only the reflection (*Widerschein*) of himself, will no longer be disposed to find only the semblance (*Schein*) of himself where he seeks and must seek his true reality. This illustrative comment is of a psychological kind: it explains the idea of a "premise" in the sense of psychic motivation. A propos of this, the explanation continues a little later on to the effect that the critique of religion disillusions, undeceives (*enttäuscht*) man.

The next sentence, however, exactly reverses the relation. "The basis of an irreligious critique is: man makes religion, religion does not make man", which statement leads to the conclusion, "Man is the world of man, state, society. This state, this society, produce religion, a perverted world-consciousness, because they are a perverted world." Here we have the term "basis", which term is apparently parallel or counterpart to "premise".

Marx's argument would appear to be saying this. The critique of heaven is the presupposition or *premise* of the critique of earth; the critique of earth is the *basis* of the critique of heaven. The category "premise" lies in the plane of the perverted consciousness, the category "basis" in the plane of perverted being, perverted man, perverted world. The stress here must be on the fact that both are perverted; that is to say, the perverted consciousness is the premise of a perverted mode of being, and perverted being is the basis of the perverted consciousness. The perverted consciousness is the "reflection" (*Widerschein*) of a perverted mode of being, whilst the perverted being is the "semblance" (*Schein*) of a perverted consciousness. "Religion is the self-consciousness and self-feeling of man (*das Selbstbewusstsein und das Selbstgefühl*) who has either not yet found himself or has already lost himself again." It is "the fantastic realization of the human essence because the human essence has no true reality." "Religion is only the illusory sun which revolves round man as long as he does not revolve round himself." The critique of religion disillusions (*enttäuscht*) man to such effect that "he will revolve round himself and therefore round his true sun."

Here the vicious circle is complete. We recall a comparison Marx makes elsewhere between the speculative method and the delusion of the man who struggled all his life against the awareness of gravitational force so that human beings might keep afloat in the water. In that context we may also remind ourselves of the passage in the preliminary studies for the dissertation, where the end of classical antiquity is envisaged as an annihilation of the "gravitational force of religious and political existence". And finally we may recall a passage from one of Marx's articles, where the argument is put forward that, shortly before and after Copernicus' great discovery of the true solar system, the gravitational law of the state was also discovered, in that the gravity of the state was found to be in the state itself. Against the background of this metaphor the problems stand out quite clearly. The critique of heaven awakens man out of his stupor, into which the opium of religion has plunged him; but when he comes to his senses, he observes that he has no true reality. He moves round his true sun, around himself, but he is himself a sham creature. He moves round an illusory self. Thus man must recover his true self, the world of man its true reality, if the restoration of true consciousness is to produce any effect. Otherwise the operation resembles the realization of the force of gravity in the brain of a cosmonaut who finds himself in the phase of weightlessness; he can do nothing about his awareness. But his becoming aware is, of course, necessary in order to make him perform the right actions to bring his spaceship down to earth again. His realizing, becoming aware, is the "premise" of his return; but the earth's actual gravitational pull is its "basis".

This dilemma determines the structure of the "Introduction" to Hegel's *Philosophy of Right*. Marx presents this *Critique* as a contribution to the transmuting of the critique of heaven into a critique of earth. But, he at once goes on to say, this contribution "does not in the first instance bear on the original, but on a copy, namely, on the German philosophy of state and of right, and for no other reason than that it has reference to Germany". Hegel's philosophy is therefore a copy of the actual political state of affairs. And in this it appears to occupy the same position as religion, which after all was described earlier as "the general theory of this world". Indeed, even in the first series of lectures we reached the conclusion that Marx's critique of religion is fundamentally a critique of Hegel, and conversely, his critique of Hegel fundamentally a critique of religion. But that is not what is said. On the contrary, the whole point here is the transition from the critique of religion to the critique of law; and that is why the subject of his critique is not Hegel's philosophy of religion, but his philosophy of right (or law). On the other hand, the transition is not really made; for it is not law but the philosophy of law that is subjected to criticism; it bears not on the original, on earth, on politics, but on a copy of all this.

Why does Marx choose this circuitous route? Only because his critique has reference to Germany. It now becomes evident that his critique of Hegel is really a critique of Germany. "For Germany the critique of religion is in the main complete." What does this opening proclamation signify? It signifies that for Germany the critique of religion is finished, so that the critique of politics can now begin. The critique of politics is the critique of Germany, the German state. But, as we have heard Marx contend, no political state, no state *qua* state, exists in Germany. The German state is professedly a theologian, the critique in this case is a critique of theology. The German state still turns around an illusory sun, not yet having made the discovery that it is itself the centre of its force of gravity. Must the critique of the German state begin, then, with the critique of religion? Yes, because the critique of religion is the premise of the critique of politics. No, because for Germany the critique of religion *is* fundamentally (*im wesentlichen*) already ended. But at the very moment one wants to take the next step, that is, to affirm the truth of this earth, one discovers that the foundation is missing; for Germany is not a political state, has no true reality. Establishment of the truth amounts to no more than the fantastic realization of the German essence.

This fantastic "essence", between heaven and earth, between religion and law, between theology and politics, between *Jenseits* and *Diesseits*, between copy and original—this fantastic essence is the subject of Marx's critique.

7

Jenseits des Rheins—*Beyond the Rhine*

THE title of Nicolaus Copernicus' famous astronomical work of 1543, *De revolutionibus orbium caelestium*, is rendered in the German translation somewhat differently from the French. In German the work is called *Über die Kreisbewegungen der Weltkörper*, whereas the French title runs *Des révolutions des orbes célestes*. The German *Kreisbewegung* renders exactly the meaning of the Latin *revolutio*, which in the tradition of astronomy had become the standing expression for the cyclical movement of the heavenly bodies. On the other hand, anyone reading the French word *révolution* will think first of its social and political meaning, which the German *Kreisbewegung* does not suggest. Curiously enough, each translation preserves a particular aspect of the Latin term *revolutio* and its development. Actually, it goes back to the Greek notion, found already in Polybius and Aristotle, according to which change in the forms of political government happens in conformity to the law of cyclical movement, *anakuklosis*; and it is this basic idea of a cyclical movement, transferred as a metaphor from astronomy to politics, that has been passed on in the European tradition of the term *revolutio*. Even in the seventeeth century, the Glorious Revolution of 1688 was hailed by the English Whigs as a true "restoration", that is to say, as a completion of the return of the legitimate *form* of government, and of the lawful government, which Cromwell's Great Rebellion had overthrown. Not until the French Revolution of 1789 did there emerge the new meaning of *révolution* as a radical break with

M

earlier history and the inauguration of an entirely new epoch in the history of mankind. The new content of the term was itself a creation of the revolution, brought to birth under the extreme pressure of the irresistible force of events. *Revolutio* changed from being *Kreisbewegung* to become *révolution*.

"German history enjoys the privilege of a movement which no people on the horizon of history went through before it or will go through after it. We have shared the restorations of the modern nations, without having undergone their revolutions. We were restored, first because other nations dared to carry out a revolution and second because other nations suffered a counter-revolution; the first time because our rulers were afraid, and the second because our rulers were not afraid. Led by our shepherds, we never found ourselves in the company of freedom except once—on the day of its burial."

In this pithy summing up of the dilemma inherent in Germany's situation the "Introduction" to the *Critique of Hegel's Philosophy of Right* mirrors accurately the development of the European *revolutio*-concept. Although Marx does not bring the historical complications of the terminology into his analysis, it is certainly encumbered with them. As we have seen from English history, "restoration" was originally another word for "revolution". Equating "restoration" with "counter-revolution" only became possible as a result of the French Revolution. According to the traditional conception, Napoleon's emperorship and the course of events consequent upon it were a normal "restoration" in the eternal cycle or *revolutio* of forms of government. The dilemma of the German situation, therefore, according to Marx's analysis, was that, on the one hand, the ancient and medieval tradition was still alive in it, whilst, on the other hand, Germany felt the reaction, the repercussions of the "counter-revolutions" which followed on the real revolution that other modern nations had undergone. The *Kreisbewegung* participated in the reversion without really having had any share in the advance, the forward movement, that is to say, without having been a *révolution*.

The crucial question of how the German "vicious circle" might be broken through, in other words, the metamorphosis of *Kreisbewegung* into *révolution*, dominates Marx's life in the years 1842 to 1844. The question is concretized and given a historical location in the relation of Germany, on the one hand, to France and Britain, on the other. In this relation, there occurs the transition from the critique of theology *via* the critique of politics to the critique of political economy. Marx emigrates from Germany *via* France to England; his physical emigration is an embodiment of the emigration of his thinking, as conversely the development of his thinking follows closely in the wake of his European wanderings.

In this historical-cum-strategical thinking the Rhine plays a critical role. It was not for nothing that in the preliminary studies for the dissertation he had recalled that politician of the ancient world, Themistocles, who, when Athens was being threatened with destruction, chose a new element, the sea. Marx's decision to emigrate to Paris, "the new capital of the new world", has the same dramatic quality about it as Julius Caesar's *alea jacta est* (the die is cast) at his crossing of the River Rubicon. Or to draw another parallel, the exodus from Egypt was followed by the crossing of the Jordan and the entry into the promised land.

Himself a Rhinelander by birth, Marx found it hard to breathe the academic and political air of Berlin. When his editorship of the *Rheinische Zeitung* fell foul of the Berlin censor, and the voice of progress in the Rhineland was consequently silenced, there was no place left for Marx in Germany. His final act is to write the *Critique of Hegel's Philosophy of Right*, completed in Kreuznach, where he had just married and was looking forward to leaving for Paris. Having arrived there, he composed the "Introduction", which is very much dominated by the emigration from Germany to France. He has crossed the Rhine and now looks back on the past, to which he has definitely said farewell. It is a look back from the further side. The "Introduction" was published in the *Deutsch-Französische Jahrbücher*, a German-language periodical, edited and brought out in Paris. The title of the journal epitomizes the programme; it is a watchword of pioneers *en route* for the new country. Had not Feuerbach declared already that the true philosopher must be of Gallo-German blood? The heart must be French, the head German; the head must reform, the heart inspire to revolution.

The theme is a guiding principle of Marx's thinking and

living. We have already drawn a parallel between Marx's critique and that which underlies the philosophy of Immanuel Kant. Marx's description of Kant's philosophy as the German theory of the French Revolution enshrines the correspondence and the distance between the two forms of critique. Whilst Kant's critique remained theory, Marx actually crossed the Rhine; the German theory of the French Revolution was transcended by a practical critique. The fierceness of his attack on Proudhon derives from the fact that in the theories of that Frenchman he met and recognized once more the original sin of German speculation. If Proudhon did not follow through to the extreme consequences of his own theory, he had only to thank his ill luck for being born a Frenchman and not a German. Proudhon's principle of equality is nothing other than the French counterpart to the German principle of self-consciousness. Equality is simply the German *Ich = Ich* in a French, that is to say, a political version. The ending of alienation always happens in the context of that form of alienation which is the prevailing factor: in Germany self-consciousness; in France equality as a political principle; in England the actual, material, practical need that is its own yardstick, and knows no other.

Marx is continually occupied during these years with this comparison between Germany, France and England. In a letter to Ludwig Feuerbach, sent from Paris, he gives a description of the French as opposed to the German character, taking his cue from a saying of Fourier's, "*L'homme est tout entier dans ses passions*", *i.e.*, man's passionate feelings comprise his whole being. The Frenchman contrasts his *passion* with the *actus purus* of German thought. In the *Deutsche Ideologie* the Germans are charged with never having had as yet a mundane, earthly basis for history, and consequently with never having had a historian. Although the French and the British are still caught up in political ideology, they at any rate have the merit of having made the first attempt to give the writing of history a material basis.

The comparison has a reverse side that brings out the positive significance of the German bent for theory. Hardly six months after the publication, in February 1844, of the first and only number of the *Deutsch-Französische Jahrbücher*, Marx rounds upon the co-editor and co-founder of that journal, Arnold Ruge. In the German weekly, *Vorwärts!*, published in Paris, Ruge had written an anonymous article, *Der König von Preussen und die Sozial reform*, signed *Von einen Preussen*. In his attack, published in the same weekly, Marx analyses the recent uprising of the Silesian weavers, and concludes that none of the insurrections by French or British workers had had such a theoretical and deliberate character as this German uprising of June 1844. The German proletariat is the theoretician of the European proletariat, just as the British proletariat is its *National-ökonom* and the French proletariat its politician. Germany has as much a classic aptitude for social revolution as it is powerless and unfit to achieve a political one. For just as the impotence of the German bourgeoisie is Germany's political impotence, so the bent of the German proletariat, even apart from German theory, is the social bent of Germany. The disproportion between the philosophical and political development of Germany is not something abnormal. It is a necessary disproportion. Only in socialism can a philosophical people find its adequate praxis; or, in other words, only in the proletariat can it find the active element of its liberation. For an exposition of the main elements relevant to an understanding of this, Marx refers us to his recent "Introduction" to the *Critique of Hegel's Philosophy of Right*.

The key to the "Introduction" does indeed lie in the dialectical critique of Germany as the historical embodiment of the theory. Not only Kant but Hegel, really, is the German theoretician of the French Revolution. The theory, however, is not theory pure and simple; it is the reality presented by Germany. That is why Marx is unable to criticize the reality of the German state and of German law directly, but is forced to take the indirect way, the critique of the German philosophy of state and law. If one wanted to proceed from the German *status quo* itself, even in the only appropriate way, i.e., negatively, the result would still be an anachronism. Even the negation of our political present is already covered with dust in the historical lumber-room of modern nations. If I negate the powdered pigtail, I still have an unpowdered pigtail. If I negate the German state of affairs in 1843, then according to the French computation of time, I am hardly in the year 1789, and still less in the focus of the present.

As the ancient peoples went through their pre-history (*Vorgeschichte*) in imagination, in mythology, so we Germans have gone through our post-history (*Nachgeschichte*) in thought, in philosophy. We are philosophical contemporaries of the present without being its historical contemporaries. German philosophy is the ideal prolongation (*die ideale Verlängerung*) of German history. If therefore, instead of the *oeuvres incomplètes* (the unfinished works) of our real history, we criticize the *oeuvres posthumes* of our ideal history, philosophy, then our critique is in the midst of the questions of which the present says, that is the question. What in progressive nations is a practical break with conditions presented by the modern state is in Germany, where such conditions simply do not as yet exist, a critical break in the first instance with the philosophical reflection (*Spiegelung*) of those conditions.

German philosophy of right and state is the only German history which is *al pari* (on a level) with the official modern present. The German nation must therefore join this its dream-history to its present conditions, and subject to a critique not only those conditions but also their abstract continuation. Its future cannot be limited either to the immediate negation of its real conditions of state and right or to the immediate implementation of its ideal conditions of state and right; for it has the immediate negation of its real conditions in its ideal conditions, and it has almost outlived the immediate implementation of its ideal conditions in the contemplation of neighbouring nations. We cannot abolish philosophy without making it a reality, any more than we are able to realize, to implement, philosophy without abolishing it.

Now the critique of the German philosophy of state and right, which acquired its most consistent, richest and latest form through Hegel, is both a critical analysis of the modern state and of the reality connected with it, and the resolute negation of the whole manner of the German consciousness in politics and right as practised up to now, the most distinguished, most universal expression of which, raised to the level of a science, is the speculative philosophy of right itself. If the speculative philosophy of right, that abstract, extravagant (*überschweng-*

liche) thinking on the modern state, the reality of which remains a thing of the beyond (*ein Jenseits*), if only beyond the Rhine (*jenseits des Rheins*), was possible only in Germany, inversely the German thought-image of the modern state which abstracts from real man was possible only because and in so far as the modern state itself abstracts from real man or satisfies the whole of man only in imagination. In politics the Germans thought what other nations did. Germany was their theoretical conscience. The abstraction and presumption (*Überhebung*) of its thought was always in step with the one-sidedness and stunted character (*Untersetztheit*) of its reality. If therefore the *status quo* of German statehood (*Staatswesen*) expresses the completion of the *ancien régime*, the completion of the thorn in the flesh of the modern state, then the *status quo* of German political science (*Staatswissen*) expresses the incompletion of the modern state, the defective condition of the flesh itself.

"In politics the Germans *thought* what other nations *did*." In this aphorism is summed up the whole ambiguous relationship of Germany to the French Revolution. Because the Germans did not implement their theory themselves, it has therefore remained a *Jenseits*, a "world beyond". Marx adds, "even though this 'beyond' lies only beyond the Rhine". In this play on words the full ambiguity of the term *Jenseits* is plain to see. Marx has emigrated from Germany, he is criticizing his fatherland from beyond the Rhine (*jenseits des Rheins*), that is to say, he is living in the reality of the modern state, which German philosophy has merely *thought*, a reality, in other words, that for German philosophy remains a "beyond". But the reality of the modern state is not just a "beyond" for German philosophy; it is a beyond also for real man, whom it satisfies only in imagination. In this respect, too, it is the case that other nations did in politics what the Germans had thought. Thus the modern state itself rests on a thought, it is a "thought reality", a state "of the beyond", which does not affect the real man.

Marx elaborates further on this pronouncement in both directions. If the other nations have done in politics what the Germans have thought, then German thinking would appear to have practical consequences, albeit "beyond" the Rhine. Thus the critique of the speculative philosophy of right is not an end in itself, but as the antithesis of German political consciousness the critique issues in problems (*Aufgaben*) which there is only one means of solving—practice.

However, what other nations have done as a result of German thinking is defective in the extreme; nor could it be otherwise, for their practice is based on a (German) idea, it abstracts from real man. Conversely, therefore, the question is: can Germany attain a practice *à la hauteur des principes* (at the level of principles), *i.e.*, a revolution which will raise it not only to the official level of the modern nations but to the height of humanity, which will be the near future of those nations?

Thus Marx searches for the archimedian point whence the actual condition of Germany can be set in motion, a movement that will transform the "dream phase" of German politics into a human reality. In the political present this archimedian point is not to be found, not even in its negation; for the struggle against German politics today is a struggle against the past of the modern nations. So far as German history is concerned, those Germans who make it their occupation have completely frustrated any hope of a rebirth of Germany. The so-called "historical school" of jurisprudence (*die historische Rechtsschule*) declares every protest of the serf against the knout to be rebellion, once the knout is a time-honoured, historical one; just as the God of Israel only allowed His servant Moses to see Him from behind, after He had passed by (Exodus 33:23), so does history allow the "historical school" to see it only *a posteriori*. And then it is better perhaps to say nothing about those enthusiasts, Germanomaniacs, who seek the history of our freedom beyond (*jenseits*) our history, in the ancient Teutonic forests.

However, for Marx this does not conclude the search after German history. After all, there had been a time when the Germans did not leave "praxis", the practical side, to other peoples, and when theoretical emancipation had a specific, practical significance for Germany. Germany's revolutionary past is in fact theoretical, it is the Reformation. Evidently, there really is in German thinking a practical, revolutionary potency.

Is it anything more than a potency? Marx's analysis of the Reformation reaches a negative conclusion. Luther overcame the bondage that arises from devotion, but only by replacing it with a bondage arising from conviction. He shattered faith in authority because he restored the authority of faith. He turned the papist priests into laymen because he turned laymen into priests. He freed people from an outward religiosity because he made religiosity the inner man. He freed the body from chains because he enchained the heart.

All the same, though protestantism was not the true solution, it did at least pose the problem correctly. It was no longer a case of the layman's struggle against the priest outside himself, but of his struggle against his own priest inside himself, his priestly nature (*pfäffischen Natur*).

The theoretical revolution which Germany underwent in the form of the Reformation was really a step forward, therefore, albeit a dialectical step, a sharpening and accentuation of all the problems. The Reformation shifted the field of battle to the inner man. The task now is to solve the problem posed by the Reformation. This subsequent step again starts with a theoretical revolution, simply because Germany is the stage of that revolution. As the revolution then began in the brain of the monk, so now it begins in the brain of the philosopher. This philosophical revolution has already begun, nay, in principle is already completed by the critique of religion, which ends with the doctrine that man is the highest being for man. And where the theoretical revolution ends, there the practical revolution begins; for the doctrine that man is the highest being for man is on a par with the categorical imperative to overthrow all conditions in which man is a debased, enslaved, abandoned, despicable being.

The Reformation did not achieve this revolution in man's condition. Admittedly, the Protestant transformation of the German laymen into priests did emancipate the lay popes (*Laienpäpste*), the princes together with their clerisy (*Klerisei*), the privileged and the philistines. The philosophical revolution will complete this semi-emancipation, the philosophical transformation of priestly Germans into men will emancipate the people. Yet secularization will not stop at the confiscation of church estates, set in motion mainly by hypocritical Prussia, any more than emancipation stops at princes. At the time of the Reformation, the Peasant War, the most radical fact of German history, came to grief because of theology. Today, when theology itself has come to grief, the most unfree fact of German history, our *status quo*, will be shattered against philosophy. On the eve of the Reformation, official Germany was the absolute slave of Rome. On the eve of its revolution, it is the absolute slave of less than Rome, of Prussia and Austria, of country squires and philistines.

With this radical conclusion the "Introduction" to the *Critique of Hegel's Philosophy of Right* lands up at the opposite pole to Hegel's *Vorrede*, the Preface to his *Philosophy of Right*. Hegel also draws the line from the Reformation through to his own time. What Luther initiated as faith in feeling and in the witness of the spirit is what the fully mature spirit has actually come to apprehend. Luther's emblem of the cross in the centre of a heart encircled by roses, Hegel interprets as the reconciliation with the actual, effected by speculative philosophy. Reason (*Vernunft*) is apprehended as the rose in the cross of the present. Whilst a half philosophy leads away from God, true philosophy leads to God; and so it is with the Prussian state, the true rationality of which Hegel perceived and demonstrated.

Marx comes to a radically opposite conclusion. The reconciliation with the actual, which Luther brought about in the heart of man, in faith, was not a real reconciliation, but it did radicalize the cross of actuality. In place of the religious yoke of Rome there came the profane yoke of the Prussian state; and the Reformation, far from liberating the German people, allied itself with the élitist emancipation of the German princes and violently crushed the peasants' revolt, the emancipation of the people. Whereas the outcome of Hegel's "true philosophy" is the Christian-German state, Marx's philosophy, which finishes off the monk Luther's half-completed work, ends in revolution.

And thus he completes Hegel's task as well. Hegel's philosophy is after all the only German history that stands on a level with the official modern present, the level of the French Revolution. If Hegel contends that philosophy is simply its own time apprehended in thoughts (*ihre Zeit in Gedanken erfasst*), then this must apply to the modern period which in Germany has not yet dawned. Genuine philosophy can do no other, therefore, than declare war on the present German situation; for it stands below the level of history, beneath all criticism; at the same time the circumstances of Germany are still the object of criticism, just as the criminal, who is below the level of humanity, is still an object for the executioner. Furthermore, the struggle against the current state of affairs in Germany is even of concern to the modern nations; for the German *status quo* is the straightforward completion of the *ancien régime*, and the *ancien régime* is the hidden flaw in the modern state.

This brings Marx to the crucial question: how, where and by whom are the present conditions in Germany to be overthrown? If speculative philosophy thought what the French Revolution did, how then is what is now being thought by genuine philosophy, that is, by the critique of speculative philosophy, to be done in Germany itself? Of course, the critique issues in problems to which only praxis, action, can provide a solution. But who is the subject of this praxis?

Systematically he sets about his enquiry. If Germany is an anachronism, then it can only attain the level of the modern nations by even now undergoing a "French Revolution". In a sense that is indeed the task; which is why the "Introduction" finishes with a prediction of the day of German resurrection, which will be proclaimed by "the crowing of the cock of Gaul". The rebirth of Germany will have to come, therefore, from a "French Revolution" in Germany. But the day of German resurrection will only come "when all inner requisites are fulfilled". So the question is whether those "inner requisites" are present in Germany. Marx's enquiry leads to an unequivocally negative conclusion. In Germany there just is no common ground, no point of contact for a "French Revolution". The French Revolution was brought about by the bourgeoisie, the third estate, which, with the opening of the celebrated instrument of Sieyès, flung in the face of its opponents the proud words, "I am nothing but I must be everything." Certainly, the emancipation of the French bourgeoisie is only a partial emancipation of the French people, but this partial emancipation is a step on the way to universal emancipation. In Germany even this partial emancipation is inconceivable, because the German middle class entirely lacks the necessary courage and ruthlessness. Its moral self-respect is based solely on an awareness of being the general representative of the narrowness and mediocrity of all the other classes. In France every class of the nation is a political idealist and becomes aware of itself, not in the first instance as a particular class, but as a representative of social requirements generally. In Germany, on the other hand, where practical life is as spiritless as spiritual life is unpractical, no class in civil society has any need or capacity for universal emancipation until it is forced by its immediate situation, by material necessity, by its very fetters in that direction.

Thus in Germany the conditions for a "French Revolution" are absent. But even approached from the other side, the problem would seem to present an insoluble dilemma. The fact is, even if Germany were to have caught up with the French Revolution, still nothing would be achieved by that. For "it has almost outlived the immediate implementation of its ideal conditions in the sight of the neighbouring peoples." Even in France the French Revolution is again almost a time past. It achieved a political emancipation, but not an emancipation of civil society. It was in no position to end the discord between the political state and civil society, which itself arises out of the inner conflict of civil society; on the contrary, it was responsible for creating that discord. Hegel saw it clearly enough; but he offered the mere semblance of a solution. In it he imitated in theory the practice of the modern state; for the *status quo* of German speculative political philosophy is an expression of the imperfection of the modern state. An implementation of philosophy was therefore to mean no benefit for Germany; it would only fall, half a century later, into the same trap as did France by means of the French Revolution. Thus Germany is not only powerless to take this revolutionary leap, but the leap itself is as yet without meaning and purpose. The crucial question remains, therefore, whether Germany can do a somersault that at one go will take it over the level of the modern nations on to the heights of real humanity. The very question seems senseless; for if Germany is in no state to pull itself out of the morass of the *ancien régime*, how could it ever at a single stretch outstrip the modern nations?

No, Marx replies, it is not the somersault, not the double leap, that is impracticable, but the *single* one. If a short vaulting-pole is going to land one in the ditch, then one must make the jump with a long pole; but in any event one has to do it in one go. It is not the radical revolution, not the general human emancipation which is a utopian dream for Germany, but rather the partial, the *merely* political revolution, the revolution which leaves the pillars of the house standing.

At this point the problem returns in the dilemma that in Germany the basis for a revolution is absent. The theory is all there: in principle the critique of religion is completed for Germany; but for the necessary and logical transition to practice no point of contact would seem to exist. In fact, the theory will be implemented in a nation only to the extent that it is a realization of its needs. It is not enough that thought should incite to fulfilment; reality itself must incite to thought. Revolutions require a passive element, a material basis.

In its most extreme form the dilemma might be expressed as follows: are the theoretical needs going to be directly practical needs? The theoretical needs are the demands of German thought; but those demands are a long way ahead of the responses coming from the actual situation in Germany. Between the two there is an enormous dichotomy; yet in itself that is not enough to trigger off an explosion. The inner conflict has to be of similar intensity to the conflict inherent in civil society and the contradiction between civil society and the state; for only that kind of contradiction, which will cause the modern nations to explode, will be able to engender the rebirth of Germany.

The hard core of Marx's contention resides in the relationship between mind and matter, between thought and actuality. He is explicit in describing matter as a passive element; but "passive" is not the same thing as dead, inorganic. Even passivity may be a highly active element, different though the activity may be from that of mind. This specific activity of matter is expressed in the term "need" (*Bedürfnis*). Consciousness in itself, abstracted from being, cannot produce anything real. Only as conscious being, that is to say, only when passive matter has become conscious, active matter, can consciousness give rise to something actual, something real. That "potency" is enshrined in the "need"; for it is the urge to something else, to something more, by which the need can be satisfied. In this respect, hunger is an active element, if only in a negative sense. It is a material void that demands to be filled.

In a work written a year later, *Die Heilige Familie* (The Holy Family), Marx works out this idea in greater detail, in a historical analysis of materialism. I have already referred to that passage in my first lecture. In it he takes up again the question posed by the scholastic Duns Scotus, "whether matter can think" and the notion of the mystical thinker, Jakob Böhme, that the most important of the inherent qualities of matter is motion, not only mechanical and mathematical motion but still more impulse (*Trieb*), vital life-spirit (*Lebensgeist*), tension (*Spannkraft*) or the throes (*Qual*) of matter.

Although Marx makes no use of terms like "birth" or "rebirth" here, they come nearest to what he is getting at. In the process of birth, mother and child are in an extremely dire situation, they are surrendered to absolute passivity; yet it is precisely this process that represents the greatest activity, precisely this extreme "need" that is in a real sense productive and creative. In the birth-process "matter" is manifested as a fertile womb. Literally, what he says is this, "Only a revolution of radical needs can be a radical revolution; and it seems that precisely the preconditions and breeding-places for such needs are absent." What in the spiritual and mental plane he calls a "precondition" is in the material plane a "breeding-place" (*Geburtsstätte*).

The preconditions and breeding-places of a radical revolution for Germany turn out on closer examination to be present indeed in the passive element, and to be so in two ways. In the first place, the very anachronism of Germany's situation provides a basis for the somersault that is to carry it at one go over the top of the modern nations on to the level of humanity. If Germany has gone along with the development of the modern nations only in theory, by means of abstract activity, it has, on the other hand, shared the sufferings entailed by that development without enjoying the advantages, without having participated in the partial satisfaction which the development provides. Corresponding to the abstract activity on the one hand is the abstract suffering on the other. That is why Germany will one day find itself on the level of European decadence, before ever having been on the level of European emancipation. It will be like a fetish-worshipper, pining away with the maladies of Christianity. As you could find the gods of all nations in the Roman Pantheon, so you will find in the Germans' Holy Roman Empire all the sins of all forms of state. Germany, as the flaw in modern politics which have constituted themselves a world of their own, will not be able to throw off the specific German limitations without overthrowing the general limitation of the modern political scene.

As a conclusion to Marx's argument, this train of thought would appear to point to a messianic role for Germany, which at the very moment it threatens to fall total victim to the diseases of the political present rises, as a desperate last measure, to unprecedented heights, to become the saviour of the modern world. This would indeed have to be the conclusion, if Germany's total development extended no further than to the boundaries of political development. Up to this point the argument has, after all, taken place within a political context. But almost unnoticed, a new element appears on the horizon. Entirely within the general line of argument Marx brings in this new element, first of all in a negative way, as an example of the German inability to conduct its affairs at the level of the modern nations.

The new element is industry and its associated science of modern economics. The relation of industry, of the world of wealth generally, to the political world is one of the major problems of modern times. With this definition Marx almost inadvertently introduces a new problem and adds a new dimension to his critique. The main theme of the "Introduction", after all, is Germany's relation to the French Revolution, in other words, Germany's powerlessness to achieve a political revolution that could bring it on to the level of the modern nations. To that is now added a new dilemma: the relation of the French Revolution to the Industrial Revolution or, in Marx's words, the relation of the world of politics to the world of industrial wealth. That takes us from politics into the sphere of economics.

No wonder that, in this field too, Germany turns out to be hopelessly inadequate. In what form, after all, is this leading problem of modern times beginning to engage the Germans? In the form of protectionism, of the so-called "national economy". Germanomania (*Deutschtümelei*), the bogey of the German nation, has passed from men to matter; and quite suddenly our cotton barons and iron heroes, the leaders of an up-and-coming modern capitalism, have turned into patriots. Thus people in Germany are beginning to acknowledge the sovereignty of monopoly on the inside through investing it with sovereignty on the outside. In other words, people in Germany are beginning precisely at the point where in France and Britain they are about to make an end. Whereas the problem in France and Britain is: Political economy or the rule of society (*Sozietät*) over wealth, in Germany it is: "national economy" or the mastery of private property over nationality. In France and Britain, then, it is a case of abolishing a monopoly that has been taken to its extreme consequences; in Germany it is a case of carrying through monopoly to its ultimate consequences. This will suffice as an example of the German form of modern problems, an example of how our history, like a raw recruit, still has to do extra drill in order to keep up with events already hackneyed and old.

Even on this new terrain, therefore, any point of contact for a German emancipation would seem to be lacking. Indeed, on the part of industrial wealth it is not to be expected; the activity in Germany is as hopelessly inadequate as is German economic theory. But Marx's argument comes out once more on the other side, with the passive element. Here the hopelessness of Germany's political situation would seem to converge with the hopelessness of its economic situation. Whilst industrial wealth affords no prospect of emancipation, the light of resurrection glimmers in the darkness of industrial poverty.

In Marx's first economic essay, his article on the legislation against wood-stealing, this theme is already adumbrated. There he takes up the cause of the poor, a class who occupy the same position in civil society as dead wood does in nature; so far, the very existence of an impoverished class is purely a custom of civil society, one that has not as yet found an adequate place within the orbit of the deliberate structuring of the state. Although as early as this article of 1842 he is championing the poor as a class against a rising capitalism, his argument concentrates entirely on their traditional rights of custom. Now, several years later, he takes a further crucial step—in fact, by introducing a new term, the proletariat. As opposed to poverty of the traditional kind, the proletariat is a fundamentally new phenomenon, the product of a new historical epoch. The proletariat begins to appear in Germany as a result of the rising industrial movement; for it is not the naturally arising (*naturwüchsig entstanden*) poor but the artifically impoverished (*künstlich produzierte*), not the human masses mechanically oppressed by the gravity of society but the masses resulting from the drastic dissolution of society, mainly of the middle estate, that form the proletariat, although the naturally arising poor and the Christian-Germanic serfs are of course slowly but surely joining its ranks.

The proletariat is introduced into Marx's argument in one way for Germany, in another for France. In the first instance the French proletariat plays a political role, for it is the fourth estate, whose task is to complete the revolution only half accomplished by the third estate. The role of emancipator therefore passes from one class of the French nation to another, in rotation, until it ends up with the class which implements social freedom no longer with the provision of certain conditions lying outside man and yet created by human society, but rather organizes all conditions of human existence on the basis of social freedom. In France, even the proletariat is a political idealist, like the bourgeoisie; and so emancipation comes about there through mental and spiritual activity. Conversely, in Germany emancipation is the product of material passivity; it is not the way of conscious revolution, but merely the negative result of a completed process of dissolution.

The total decadence of German history converges with the process of dissolution set going by the industrial movement. It is by this negative means that the cleavage between the state and civil society, which Hegel had tried in vain to find a positive way of bridging, is actually superseded; for the dissolution of the state, the *ancien régime*, and the dissolution of civil society, modern society, at the same time signify the end of the conflict between the two. The proletariat is identical with the dissolution of a civil society isolated from the state; the proletariat no longer stands, like the bourgeoisie, in a one-sided antithesis to the consequences, but in all-round antithesis to the premises of German statehood. The proletariat is a sphere of society which cannot emancipate itself without emancipating itself from all other spheres of society, which, in a word, is the complete loss of man, and so can win itself only through the complete winning back of man.

So the Industrial Revolution achieves for Germany what the French Revolution could not: the emancipation of the German, which is the emancipation of man. But this point is reached by a negative route. By heralding the dissolution of the present world order, the proletariat merely proclaims the secret of its own existence; for it is the factual dissolution of that world order. By demanding the negation of private property, the proletariat merely raises to the rank of a principle of society what society has raised to the rank of *its* principle, what was already incorporated willy-nilly in the proletariat, as the negative result of society.

With this the circle of the argumentation is completed. The case started with the proposition that for Germany the critique of religion is essentially finished. Indeed, as appeared in a later part of the argument, the critique of religion turns out to be the premise of all critique; for the critique of politics (the French Revolution) and the critique of economics (the Industrial Revolution) are merely the unmasking of the unholy guise of self-alienation, which in religion conceals itself behind a saintly mask. What was still lacking was the material complement, which corresponds to the theoretical subject of the critique, radical philosophy. Without this complement, theory could not pass over into the necessary practice.

Now, at the conclusion of the argument, the upper and lower halves of the complete circle have come together: mind and matter, consciousness and being, action and passivity, freedom and necessity. As philosophy finds its material weapon in the proletariat, so the proletariat finds its spiritual weapon in philosophy; and once the lightning of thought has squarely struck this ingenuous soil of the people, the emancipation of the German into the man, the human being, will be accomplished. The only *practically* possible liberation of Germany is liberation from the point of view of that theory which proclaims man to be the highest mode of being for man. The head of this emancipation is philosophy, its heart is the proletariat. Philosophy cannot be made a reality without the abolition of the proletariat, the proletariat cannot be superseded without philosophy being made a reality. When all inner requisites are

fulfilled the German day of resurrection will be proclaimed by
the crowing of the cock of Gaul.

So ends the "Introduction" to the *Critique of Hegel's Philosophy
of Right*. A radical critique, which stands in radical contrast to
Hegel's philosophy and yet, in its form as a critique, presupposes that very philosophy. Hegel's *Vorrede* (Preface) to his
Philosophy of Right hails the Christian-Germanic state as the
rose in the cross of the present, as terminating through reason
the discrepancy between the state and modern society. Marx
propounds the total decadence of the Christian-Germanic and
the completing of the discord, the discrepancy. Hegel sees philosophy as an apprehending of its own time, in thoughts; as a
pointer to the future it always comes too late, for only completely formed actuality lends itself to being apprehended in
thought, and the owl of Minerva spreads her wings only as
twilight is descending. Marx's philosophy agrees that German
philosophy does indeed always come too late; but whereas
Hegel's *Vorrede* ends with the nocturnal flight of Minerva's owl,
Marx's "Introduction" ends with the crowing of the cock of
Gaul, which calls for the light of morning to appear. At the
close of his *Philosophy of History* Hegel salutes the glorious sunrise of the French Revolution, the first attempt in human
history to base the state wholly and exclusively on thought.
Marx sees the French Revolution as indeed the sunrise of
thought, but for that very reason as the illusory sun which
revolves around man as long as he does not revolve round himself. The cock of Gaul does not crow to greet the dawn light of
the French Revolution, for that sun has almost set again, and
in the evening twilight it is the owl of Minerva who feels at
home. No; the cock of Gaul salutes the day of German resurrection, that is the emancipation of man, of real man and real
human society, universal man, who has ceased to recognize
national frontiers.

The distance which separates Marx from Hegel is that
between the radical critique of the Industrial Revolution, on
the one hand, and the German theory of the French Revolution, on the other. If we were to leave it at that, however, we
would be doing an injustice to Hegel's philosophy and at the
same time misrepresenting Marx's relation to Hegel. For even
Marx's critique of the Industrial Revolution links up with

Hegel's philosophy of right, in particular with Hegel's analysis of civil society. It is much to the point that in the third part of Hegel's *Philosophy of Right* civil society is the subject of the second chapter, as the middle factor between the family on the one hand and the state on the other. In the totality of objective ethical life, civil society is the antithesis, following on the thesis of the family and followed by the synthesis of the state. Civil society is the radically negative element. In this Marx agrees with Hegel. That is why it is in Hegel's analysis of civil society that we find the principles of Marx's *Critique of the Industrial Revolution*.

Hegel depicts civil society as the "system of needs" (*System der Bedürfnisse*); but this system is the system of the "ethical order, split into its extremes and lost" (*in ihre Extreme verlorenen Sittlichkeit*). The system is the product of the dissolution of the system of the natural ethical order which assumes a form in the family and was embodied in the ancient state. What emerges from this process of dissolution is an assemblage of atoms, which is the battlefield where everyone's individual private interest encounters everyone else's, the model of Hobbes' *bellum omnium contra omnes*. Of course, individual egoism, which is the basis of civil society, is a totality of needs that can only be satisfied in the all-round interdependence of all individuals; and to that extent civil society does indeed form a system whereby the material well-being and rights of the individual are protected. But Hegel at once defines this system as "the external state", as the "state based on need" and the "state as envisaged by the understanding" (section 183). That is to say, the system is not, like an organism, governed by an inner principle of organization, it has no mind or heart whence all the parts are derived; the cohesion is merely an external one, it rests on the well-understood private interest of individuals, in short, it is a system of needs. Individual needs are, on the one hand, dependent on individual caprice, are insatiable and unlimited, so that the individual in the pursuit of gratifications ruins both himself and the substance of his personality. On the other hand, the satisfaction of needs, of necessary as well as accidental needs, is subject to the quirks of external accident and caprice and is held in check by the power of universality. In these contrasts and their complexities civil society provides a spectacle of repellent luxury alongside want and of the physical and ethical degeneration common to them both (section 185).

Having stated at the outset these pernicious consequences of the rise of civil society, Hegel begins systematically to unravel the structure of this system of needs. Various writings of the young Hegel already point to a deep concern on his part with the study of political economy. In the *Philosophy of Right* he starts his analysis of "the system of needs" by unfolding the significance of this relatively young science, mentioning as he does so the names of the British economists, Adam Smith and David Ricardo, and that of the Frenchman, Jean Baptiste Say. Ricardo's *On the Principles of Political Economy and Taxation* had in fact been published only three years before, in 1817—an indication of just how intensely Hegel was following the development of economic science in Britain (section 189).

Hegel defines in some detail the relevant function of political economy (*Staatsökonomie*). The system of needs comprises a network of means to their satisfaction, means which, on the one hand, are external things, the property and product of the needs of others, while, on the other hand, they are produced by one's own work and effort. The universality of reciprocal relations which constitute this system is at the level of the understanding (*Verstand*). Hegel expressly limits the significance of political economy to the level of the understanding, just as he describes the system of needs as the state or sphere of the understanding. The understanding is the "show of rationality in this sphere of finitude" (*das Scheinen der Vernünftigkeit in diese Sphäre der Endlichkeit*), where the term "show" renders the Greek *phainomenon*, itself suggestive of the idea of "appearance" (phenomenon) *and* the idea of a "semblance". Reason (*Vernunft*) "seems to be manifest" and "is manifest" in the understanding (*Verstand*), just as conversely the understanding is the "manifestation" and the "show" of reason (*Vernunft*).

It is in this plane of the understanding that political economy operates. Its task is to explain the interrelations and movements of the system of needs in their qualitative and quantitative character and all their complexities. From the infinite multiplicity of particular data this science extracts certain simple, basic principles; in other words, it reveals the understanding operative in this multiplicity and directing it. This is enough to show the importance and the limitations of political economy. In the act of recognizing the show of rationality (reason) in the sphere of needs is vested a reconciliation with reality; but conversely, this is the field in which the understanding with its subjective aims and moral sentiments gives vent to its discontent and moral frustration.

Having thus assigned to political economy its limited function, in a manner which Marx's *Critique of Political Economy* is later on to take as its starting-point, Hegel begins to work out systematically, on an anthropological basis, the distinctive character of the system of needs. That character is intrinsic to the distinction between man and animal. An animal's needs and its ways and means of satisfying them are both alike restricted in scope (section 190). Though man is subject to this restriction too, yet at the same time he evinces his transcendence of it and his universality, first by the multiplication of needs and means of satisfying them, and second by the differentiation and division of concrete needs into single parts and aspects which in turn become different needs, particularized and so more abstract.

In Hegel's account of things, this distinction between man and animal has yet another special point to it, in that the force of the term "man" first becomes fully apparent here. Following the division made in the *Philosophy of Right*, he explains that in (abstract) right, in law, we are concerned with the person, in the sphere of morality with the subject. In the sphere of ethical life (*Sittlichkeit*) (the theme of the third part) we have before us, in the family, the family-member, in civil society as a whole, the citizen (burgher, *bourgeois*); here, from the standpoint of needs, we have the composite idea we call man. Thus this is the first time, and properly speaking the only time, to speak of man in this sense.

In an earlier context I lingered over this remarkable statement; and now I come back to the passage, because it contains a key to the understanding of Marx's *Critique of Political Economy*.

Hegel does not complete the summary; but it is obvious enough that it in fact leads on to the sphere of the state, where we are concerned with the burgher or citizen (*qua citoyen*).

Hegel's thinking leads him to insert between the citizen as *bourgeois* and the citizen as *citoyen* a further term, the term "man". We are in the area of civil society here, but only in one component part of it; for besides the "system of needs" aspect there are also those of the administration of justice (*die Rechtsplege*) and of "the police and the corporation" (*die Polizei und Korporation*). All the more significant, then, that in this special sphere of "the system of needs", and really in this case alone, we are to speak of "*man*", that is, of the composite idea we call "*man*".

Thus Hegel reserves the term "man" especially for "*homo economicus*", in so far as what is here in question is the "kind of need and satisfaction". This *homo economicus* is also *homo faber*. He is distinguished from the animal by his typically human form of labour, which consists in the division of labour and, going along with that, the multiplication of needs and the means of satisfying them. On closer reflection we see that there is a polemical point to Hemel's terminology, aimed in particular at Rousseau. Without mentioning his name, Hegel attacks the idea that man in a so-called state of nature, in which he knew only supposedly simple, natural needs and means of satisfaction, once lived in freedom, that is to say, quite apart from the element of liberation intrinsic to work. As against that he argues that the natural need as such and the direct satisfaction of such need is no more than the condition of "the mental plunged in the natural", in short, the condition of savagery and unfreedom. Freedom is to be found only in the reflection of mind into itself, that is, in the way the mental is distinguished from the natural and the way in which mind reflects on this distinction (section 194).

Man only comes to be man when he distinguishes himself from what is purely natural. When man frees himself from the strict natural necessity of need, he enters into relation to a necessity of his own making; he is no longer exclusively dependent on external contingency but instead acquires a relation to an inner contingency, to arbitrary choice, his own conscious choice.

Man rises above the animal through his ability to achieve, in principle *ad infinitum*, a multiplication and particularizing of his needs and of the means of satisfaction (section 191). Regarded from the standpoint of the individual, this leads to a progressive specification and abstraction of his needs; but in fact this particularizing and abstraction are just what leads to typically human society. For needs and means, as things existent *realiter*, become something that has being for others, by whose needs and work satisfaction for all concerned is defined. When needs and means become abstract in quality, abstraction is also a property of the relation between individuals. It is through this reciprocal relation that abstract needs and means become concrete, that is to say, social needs and ways and means of satisfaction (section 192).

Thus the "composite idea we call man" is *homo socius*, man in society, man as society. One might express Hegel's train of thought by saying that "civil society" has two aspects: the "civil" aspect of the citizen *qua bourgeois* and the aspect of "society", that is, of man as the concrete totality of economic transactions, *homo economicus*.

Just as *homo economicus* can only exist as *homo socius*, so does the same thing apply to *homo faber*. The unlimited multiplication of needs leads to an infinite increase of dependence and want; for man is dealing with a material that offers infinite resistance (section 195). The answer to this want is work, which couples with the multiplication of needs a corresponding multiplication of the means of satisfaction. Through work the material directly supplied by nature is specifically adapted to these numerous ends by all sorts of different processes. In this way, the means of satisfaction acquire their value and utility, so that in what he consumes man is mainly concerned with the products of men. If this is the case with the multiplication of needs, it applies equally to the division of labour. Increasing abstraction is the very thing that intensifies the dependence of men on one another and their reciprocal relation. As *homo faber*, too, man is more and more man-in-society. At the same time, the abstraction of the production process makes work more and more mechanical, until finally man is able to step aside altogether and install the machine in his place (section 198).

With no less precision than the aspect comprising the "system of needs", Hegel sketches the inner dynamic of the other aspect, the "civil" aspect of "civil society". Originally, the family is the substantive whole; but civil society tears the individual from these ties, estranges the members of the family from one another and recognizes them as self-subsistent persons. Further, for the paternal soil and the external, inorganic nature which was a source of livelihood for the individual, it substitutes itself and subjects the existence of the family as a whole to dependence on itself, that is to say, on contingency. Thus the individual becomes a son of civil society, which has as many claims upon him as he has rights against it (section 238).

When civil society is left to develop unimpeded, then through its own dynamic it is liable to a steady increase in population and to unlimited industrial expansion. As intercourse between men becomes general, the accumulation of wealth intensifies, whilst, on the other hand, there is an equally permanent increase in the subdivision and restriction of particular jobs and with it an increase in the dependence and distress of the class tied to that sort of work (section 243). When the living-standard of a large mass of people falls below a certain subsistence level—a level regulated automatically as the one necessary for a member of the society—and when there is a consequent loss of the sense of right and wrong, of honesty and the self-respect of the man able and willing to exist by his own activity and effort, the result is to create a rabble (*Pöbel*). This in turn makes it doubly easy to concentrate inordinate wealth in a few hands (section 244).

According to Hegel's analysis, therefore, civil society finds itself caught in a vicious circle; it is like a ship parted from anchors and moorings. Hegel sketches the dilemma, without seeing any prospect of a solution within the framework of civil society itself. If the wealthier class were made directly responsible for ensuring the subsistence of the masses who are faced with poverty, then a minimum living-standard for the poor would be guaranteed; but this would go against the principle of civil society and the feeling of independence and self-respect on the part of its individual members. If, on the other hand, the requirements of these paupers be provided for by their being given work to do, that would still further increase overproduction. Hence it becomes apparent that, despite an excess of wealth, civil society is not rich enough, that is, does not possess sufficient resources to check excessive poverty and the creation of a penurious rabble. Hegel concludes this analysis by remarking that these phenomena may be studied on a large scale by taking the example of England and Scotland (section 245).

The insolubility of the dilemma carries Hegel's analysis on to the next step. He notes that this dialectic drives civil society—first and foremost, this particular society—to push beyond its own frontiers (*über sich hinausgetrieben*) and to seek markets outside its own limits among other nations that are more or less on the same economic and industrial level, in order to provide itself with the necessary means of subsistence (section 246).

However, the inner dynamic of civil society is more far-reaching still. Just as the basis for the principle of family life is the land, the soil, *terra firma*, so the natural element for industry is the ocean. In its pursuit of gain, industry abandons the dry land, embracing the element of flux, danger and the risk of destruction. At the same time, by using the sea as its highway it draws the most distant countries into its commercial activity and into a universal system of law. Worldwide commerce becomes the most potent instrument of culture, and through it trade acquires its significance in world history. Within this broad horizon, colonizing activity becomes the means whereby a highly developed civil society supplies itself with a new demand and field for its industry (section 248).

So even in Hegel's *Philosophy of Right*, civil society is driven by its inner contradiction and by the dialectic of its growth beyond its own frontiers. As in the course of its worldwide expansion it proceeds to play a role in world history, it encounters that history as the world's court of judgment (section 340). And as it creates an untenable and insoluble gulf between extreme wealth and extreme poverty on a massive scale, it is faced, as was once the Roman Empire, with the prospect of its own destruction (section 357). In the Christian-Germanic realm Hegel sees the solution of this dilemma in the context of world history: the reconciliation in Christ, prepared for by the people of Israel, with the cross of world history is consummated in the Christian-Germanic state.

Marx's *Critique* breaks open Hegel's solution and exposes it as the saintly form of man's self-alienation. For Germany he completes the critique of religion as a critique of the German state, that is, of Hegel's philosophy of the state. Thus Marx's

Critique is at the same time the critique of the modern state which covers up the inherently impracticable nature of civil society without providing a solution. Friedrich Engels, in an article on Karl Marx (of 1896), puts it like this: "Taking Hegel's philosophy of right as his point of contact, Marx came to realize that the place to look for the key to an understanding of mankind's historical development is not the state envisaged by Hegel as the 'crowning of the building', but rather that 'civil society' he handled in so ill a fashion."

The term which Engels uses here means literally "handled in such a step-motherly fashion". That might lead us to imagine that Marx's role is to be that of the prince who married Cinderella. But really it is Hegel's *Philosophy of Right* that ends with the fairy-tale of a Cinderella "civil society" finally getting its kingdom in the shape of the "Christian-Germanic realm". Marx's role is much more that of the step-mother, dragging Cinderella back to bitter reality and rudely disrupting Hegel's dream version of history. So we cannot do real justice to Hegel's description unless we take a close look at yet another term, namely, the term "key". For Marx, civil society came to be the key to an understanding of mankind's historical development. We may recall the term "key" in the Preface to Marx's dissertation, where he claims to have found in Epicurus' philosophy of atoms the "key" to the real history of Greek philosophy. There again he discovers a key which remained hidden from Hegel's speculative thinking.

I made a point earlier of the connection between Marx's analysis of Epicurus' philosophy of atoms and his (Marx's) analysis of the atomistic "civil society". This characterization of civil society as "atomistic" is Hegel's; but Hegel himself allowed this idea to get lost in his notion of the state. Marx is not deceived by this speculative solution. It is not the state that holds together the atoms of civil society, but they are held together because they are atoms only in a representational sense, in the heaven of their imagination—but in reality creatures enormously different from the atoms: not divine egoists but egoistic men.

And with that we are back to earth, where Hegel's "system of needs" serves to hold together egoistic human beings, the multiplication of that "composite idea we call man", *homo economicus.* Marx detaches civil society from Hegel's *Philosophy of Right* as a whole: and this stone rejected by Hegel he makes the cornerstone of the building of his economic analysis. Not the construction of a new system, but the patient labour entailed by the *Critique of Political Economy.* For "the anatomy of civil society is to be sought in political economy". Critique is anatomy, the scalpel probes the material conditions of life, in which legal relations and forms of state are rooted. The critique of religion takes Marx across the Rhine, to Paris. The critique of politics brings him across the sea—the element that belongs to Hegel's "world history"—to London. So, embodied in Marx's life and in his work, the critique of religion is transferred *via* the critique of politics to that of political economy.

8

Money as Mediator

"A T the entrance to science the same demand is to be made as at the entrance to hell:

Qui si convien lasciare ogni sospetto
Ogni viltà convien che qui sia morta."

With this quotation from the third canto of the *Inferno* in Dante's *Divine Comedy*, Marx concludes the summary of his career up to the year 1859, in the preface to *Zur Kritik der politischen Ökonomie*. With a retrospective look at the excruciating but essential course of initiation into the secrets of the science of political economy, Marx's imagination is transplanted to Dante's journey through hell. Led by the poet Virgil as his guide, Dante follows him through chasms deep and dark as far as the portals of hell, over which is written: "Through me you enter the city of woe . . . Abandon all hope, you who enter here." But Virgil heartens him. He must abandon not all hope but, on the contrary, all irresolution (*sospetto*); here he must slay all his cowardly fear.

To judge by the small number of quotations, the importance of Dante's *Divine Comedy* in Marx's works hardly compares with, for instance, the role which the plays of Shakespeare play in them; and yet the function of the Dante quotations turns out on closer examination to be as strategic as that of the passages cited from Aeschylus' tragedy, *Prometheus Bound*. Just as at the outset of his study—to wit, in his dissertation—Marx identifies himself with Prometheus, so he symbolically portrays his later career in Dante's journey through hell, and through purgatory.

The Preface to the first edition of the first book of *Das Kapital*, written in 1867, also finishes with a quotation from Dante. In it Marx describes the hostile reaction which his *Critique of Political Economy* seems to have aroused. In that particular field, free, scientific enquiry does not meet only the same enemy as it might in all other fields. The peculiar nature of the material it is dealing with arouses the most vehement, pettiest and bitterest feelings of the human heart, all the furies of private interest (*Privatinteressen*). The Church of England, for example, finds it easier to forgive an assault on 38 of the 39 Articles of Religion than on 1/39th part of its monetary income. Even atheism is a *culpa levis*, a venial sin, nowadays, compared with any criticism of the hereditary ownership of property.

In the face of such hostility there is nothing one can do. Every opinion based on scientific criticism Marx is ready to welcome. Faced with the prejudices of public opinion, so called, opinion to which he has never conceded anything, he makes his own the motto of the great Florentine, *Segui il tuo corso, e lascia dir le genti!* (Stick to your course, and let people say what they will!). "The motto of the great Florentine", which Marx appropriated in the introduction to *Das Kapital*, was borrowed, with one tiny alteration, from the fifth canto of the *Purgatorio*. Eight years before, he had ended the preparatory study for his *Critique of Political Economy* with a passage from the *Inferno*. It is as though he has been following Dante's progress from hell to purgatory. In the fifth canto of the *Purgatorio* Dante meets with a company of spirits who (as can be seen from the preceding canto) are enslaved by the sin of Sloth. One of them points at Dante: "See how the light seems not to shine, there to the left below him, and how he seems, a living being, to be beckoned on!" In the spirit realm of the souls awaiting their purification, Dante is the only human being of flesh and blood, the one living person (*vivo*) amid the shades (*ombre*), the only one with a shadow. Virgil enjoins him to "stick to the course" and not let himself be distracted by the amazed reactions of the spirits:

"Why is your mind so troubled, now said the Master, that your steps falter?

Why should you be concerned by what they mutter here?
Keep after me, and let that crowd say what they will.
                                    (*e lascia dir le genti!*)
Stand like a mighty tower whose top no winds can harm,
however hard they blow.
The man whose thoughts are rife, thought against thought,
Always defers his goal,
since one thought spoils the glow of all the rest."

The purpose of this exhortation has to be interpreted in terms
of the start of the preceding, fourth canto:

"Whenever the soul, inextricably linked
to one particular faculty, gripped by delight or pain,
adheres to it and is immersed in it,
each other faculty then leaves unmoved.
This against those who, being in error, hold
that one soul grows in us above the next.
If what appears to sense then keeps the soul
attracted, and its attention held,
then, unobserved by us, time hurries on.
One thing the faculty attached to sense,
another, that infuses all the soul;
one is captive, but the other's free."

Amid the spirits, the souls bound by the senses, Dante's soul
possesses true reality and is therefore free. So too Marx's
Critique makes its own way through the spirit realm of political
economy; amid the fictions of civil society his mind remains
immovably concentrated on the real and essential truth.
Through hell and purgatory he pursues his journey towards
paradise.

The third and final quotation from Dante occurs in the first
part of the first volume of *Das Kapital*, the part we must consider to be the cornerstone of the whole work. The significance
of the quotation can be understood only in the context of the
argument dealing with the connection between value-in-
exchange and money. "The price expresses the value of a
commodity, for instance, of a ton of iron, in this way: by stating
that a given quantity of the equivalent, for instance, an ounce

of gold, is directly exchangeable for iron—but not the converse, that iron is directly exchangeable for gold. In order, therefore, that a commodity may in practice act effectively as exchange value, it must quit its bodily shape, must transform itself from mere imaginary into real gold, although such a transubstantiation may perhaps entail for the commodity an even more radical operation than is involved for the Hegelian 'concept' in the transition from necessity to freedom, or for the lobster in casting its shell, or for St. Jerome in the putting off of the old Adam. Side by side with its actual form—for instance, iron—a commodity may possess ideal value-form or imaginary value-form in the price; yet it cannot at one and the same time actually be both iron and gold. To fix its price it suffices to equate it to imaginary gold. However, if it is to render its owner the service of a universal equivalent, the commodity must be replaced by gold. If the owner of the iron were to go to, for instance, the owner of a commodity designed for mundane enjoyment and were to refer him to the price of the iron as proof that it was already money, then the pleasure-loving owner would answer him as St. Peter in heaven answered Dante, when the latter recited to him the creed:

> *Assai bene è trascorsa*
> *D'esta moneta già la lega e il peso,*
> *Ma dimmi se tu l'hai nella tua borsa.*

The price-form implies that it is both possible and necessary to exchange commodities for money. On the other hand, gold only serves as an ideal measure of value because it already plays the role in the exchange process of the money-commodity. Lurking therefore in the ideal measure of values is the hard cash."

The key to this passage is the term "transubstantiation" that Marx uses to describe the transformation or metamorphosis which a commodity undergoes when it is turned into money. In Marx's analysis an apparently trivial economic event enshrines, it would seem, a mystery which can be adequately described in theological terms alone. A quantity of iron, the moment it enters the process of exchange, turns out to be something more and something other than simply iron. It becomes a market commodity with a price; that is to say, it expresses its value in a given amount of another material, gold. The price is the ideal value-form of the iron, namely, the representation of the equivalent in gold. Evidently, the iron possesses besides its actual form—iron—yet a second, an ideal form, the representation or imaginary presence of a quantity of gold. The real form and the ideal form can exist simultaneously, side by side: actual iron and imaginary gold. But a commodity cannot be at one and the same time actual iron and actual gold. The transmutation of real iron into real gold is nothing more or less than a "transubstantiation". The identical subject of this metamorphosis is the commodity, which is first iron and then gold. For changing one material, iron, into another material, gold, nothing will suffice but the miracle of alchemy. But the subject of the economic metamorphosis is—as opposed to physics—no sort of matter, but what in economics is known as "commodity" or "exchange commodity". In conformity with that, Marx inverts the relationship and speaks, not of a quantity of iron becoming a "commodity" but of a "commodity" that has the substance "iron" as its "natural body", its "bodily shape". Whenever a quantity of iron is converted into money, the commodity puts off its natural body and changes into gold. The commodity acquires another "substance", there takes place a "transubstantiation" of iron into gold. For this "putting off" of the natural body Marx uses the German term *abstreifen*, which means, literally, "stripping off" the skin, "flaying". Hence the comparison with the lobster, which is, as it were, peeled from the burst shell. The analogy can be taken further, because this transition is for the lobster a transition from life to death, from living organism to an article of food. All that remains of the lobster is an "eatable"; it is stripped of the inedible shell, it puts off its natural body, then and only then does it become an "eatable", suitable for consumption. Just as the lobster is required to undergo a "transubstantiation" in order to become part of the process of consumption, so must the commodity which is by nature "iron" undergo a "transubstantiation" in order to be taken into the economic process.

Another analogy is with the transition of the Hegelian "concept" or notion (*Begriff*) of necessity to one of freedom. As a matter of fact, this carries us at once to the conclusion of *Das Kapital*, where on the far side (*jenseits*) of the realm of necessity

Marx sees the realm of freedom appear. Looking for an image to exemplify and illustrate the mystery at the centre of the economic process, namely, the transformation of a quantity of matter in its "natural" form into a quantity of gold, he refers to this complete, qualitative change in the economic order, which his analysis sees as the glimmering dawn of a new day, yonder, on the further side.

A third comparison Marx borrows from a work by St. Jerome, the "Letter to Eustochius: concerning the preservation of virginity". Whereas in his youth Jerome had always to be struggling with the bodily flesh, as is shown by his fight in the desert with the handsome women of his imagination, so in his old age he had to wrestle with the spiritual flesh. "I thought," he says, "I was in the spirit before the Judge of the Universe." "Who are you?" a voice asked. "I am a Christian." "You lie," thundered back the great Judge. "You are just a Ciceronian!"

Set down before God's judgment seat, Jerome had to undergo a transformation. He had to put off the old Adam (*abstreifen*), so as to be able to put on the new Adam. For the youthful Jerome the "old Adam" was the bodily flesh, for the old Jerome the spiritual flesh. This transformation Marx takes as an analogy with what happens in the case of economics. A commodity has a "natural body", iron, and an ideal form, imaginary gold. In order to become actual gold, the commodity has to undergo a transubstantiation, it has to put off the "old Adam", which exists both in the material form of iron and in the ideal form of imaginary gold, so as to be able to put on the "new Adam", namely, actual gold.

These three analogies are still only a preparation for the analogy which Marx takes from Dante's *Divine Comedy*. There is also a climax implied in the order in which the quotations from Dante occur. Whilst the first passage was chosen from the *Inferno* and the second, from the *Purgatorio*, the third and last Dante quotation, which is associated with Marx's *Critique of Political Economy*, is taken from the *Paradiso*. The first two passages quoted contain the guide, Virgil's, exhortation to Dante not to let himself be daunted by the horrors of hell or distracted by the spirits whom he meets on his way through purgatory. Now Virgil is required to hand over the job of

escort, which he is not allowed to continue with because he is a
pagan, to Beatrice, who brings Dante to the gate of heaven,
where Peter waits to give him the test of faith that will decide
whether or not he is to be admitted to Paradise.

So this third quotation, like the first, points to a crucial
moment in Dante's journey. The first referred to the moment
when Dante halted before the gate of hell. In this passage he
was encouraged not to be scared off but to go resolutely forward. Through the length of hell and purgatory Dante is the
only person of flesh and blood amid the spirits. That was the
point of the second quotation. Now Dante has arrived at that
other crucial frontier, the gate of heaven. The third passage
quoted is therefore in a sense pendant and counterpart to the
first. In the place of an exhortation to defy the horrors of hell,
it has the test that is to decide regarding his admission to
heaven.

At this point we are in the 24th Canto of the *Paradiso*. Peter
confronts Dante. "Speak, good Christian, and tell me: What is
faith?" The only thing that can get Dante inside now is a
quality of spirit. Through hell and purgatory it was his
"natural body" that permitted him to go on, when the spirits
were doomed to remain. Now that Virgil has left him, and
Beatrice, the form of spiritual love, has become his escort, the
natural body is no longer enough. Now it is only the spiritual
element, faith, that counts.

Dante replies with the opening words of the eleventh chapter
of the Letter to the Hebrews:

> *Fede è sustanzia di cose sperate,*
> *Ed argomento delle non parventi.*
> "Faith is the substance of things hoped for,
> And an argument for things not seen."

Peter now questions Dante further about the meaning of the
terms "substance" (*sustanzia*) and "argument" (*argomento*),
upon which Dante expatiates:

> "All that in loftier regions
> Goodness unveils before my very eyes
> Down yonder lies in night impenetrable.
> In faith alone can it existence find,

Faith upon which our highest hopes are built,
So that we call it best 'basis' or 'substance' (*sustanzia*).
Based on this faith, with trust alone,
And without actual sight, our inference is made (*sillogizzar*).
Thus we do well to call it 'argument'" (*argomento*).

Dante has testified in words to the true faith; and to that extent he has passed the test that will admit him to heaven. But the test is not yet over. On the contrary, the decisive phase is just now about to begin; for now the final proof is called for. Peter utters the words quoted by Marx:

> *Assai bene è trascorsa*
> *D'esta moneta già la lega e il peso*
> *Ma dimmi se tu l'hai nella tua borsa.*
> "The weight and alloy of this coin
> are tested well enough;
> But tell me if you have it in your purse."

To which Dante is prompt with his reply:

> "Yes, and indeed so glittering and so round,
> I have no cause to doubt the mark it bears."

To Peter's question whence he has obtained this precious joy, the ground of all goodness and virtue, Dante replies that the abundant dew of the Holy Spirit, poured out over the Old and New Testaments, is a syllogism (*sillogismo*) which has led him to such a sharp conclusion (*conchiusa*) that in comparison with it every demonstration (*dimostrazion*) seems to him pointless. Peter then asks him why he considers the proposition (*propozione*) of Holy Scripture, which has led him to this conclusion, to be the "voice of God". Dante answers:

> "The argument that shows the truth to me
> are the ensuing works, for which nature
> could never heat the iron or beat on anvil."

Whereupon Peter asks, "Tell me, what makes you so sure that such works have occurred? You have it on oath from what needs to be proved, and not from anything else."

Dante replies, "Had the world been converted to Christianity without miracles, that would be such a one, the rest would not be one hundredth part of it; for in poverty and fasting you took the field to sow the good seed which, formerly a vine, has now become a thorn-bush."

With that the dialogue provisionally reaches a conclusion. The course it takes is extremely subtle and rests on the identity between faith and that of which it is the "substance" and the "argument". Peter tests Dante's faith by the truthfulness of this identity. If this faith is based on Holy Scripture, how then does Dante know that the Scripture is the Word of God? The reply makes reference to "the ensuing works" (*l'opere seguita*) as proof or "argument" (*prova*). Those works are supernatural; for nature (*natura*) could never have achieved them by heating iron or striking anvil. The metaphor manifestly refers to the coinage which Dante carries in his purse and which he has just been showing to Peter. Such coinage is not manufactured by any natural means. No terrestrial heat would be hot enough to make iron into gold; nor could a die of this sort ever be struck upon an earthly anvil.

This figure of speech is of special importance, therefore, in that Marx seems to have borrowed his illustration from it; for he did in fact choose the example of iron, which undergoes a "transubstantiation" in the exchange-process, "puts off its natural body" and changes into gold.

Dante's argument shows that the coinage of faith, displayed by him, is of supernatural origin. It is emphasized that the voice of Peter, who examines him, "breathes from an ardent flame of love" (line 82) and sounds forth from "the light profound and sparkling" (line 88). The coin of faith is glittering (*lucida*), it radiates the same light (*luce*) in which Peter is veiled; and it is forged in the heat of heavenly love. The stamp (*conio*) is struck upon a heavenly anvil. The coin of faith is a "precious joy, in which all virtue (*virtù*) is grounded". Dante does not in the first instance speak about his own merits, but about the "ensuing works", which are the proof of the divine inspiration of Holy Scripture. This accords completely with the objective character of faith. A little later he declares that again and again the essential being of the Triune God has been stamped (*sigilla*) upon his mind by the gospel teaching. Once more the metaphor is of the coinage struck on an anvil. The coin of faith is the "substance" and the "proof" or "argument" of the divine "works" to which Holy Scripture bears witness.

Peter points out to Dante the circularity of his reasoning. He wants to prove the divine inspiration of Holy Scripture from the divine works to which that selfsame Scripture witnesses; that is to say, he grounds the proof on what requires to be proved. Dante's answer seems to be taken from an argument worked out by Augustine in *De Civitate Dei*: that the whole world should without miracles believe in the apostles' preaching about Christ's resurrection and ascension, that one great miracle would outweigh the recorded miracles. Dante elaborates this argument into a devastating criticism of the history of Christianity. The vine of faith, in the preaching of Peter, who lived and worked "in poverty and fasting", has become a thornbush, a bramble, the bramble of worldly riches and belief in wonders (*miracoli*). The faith that he confesses is the one great miracle, it is the one great "work" that proves the divine character of Holy Scripture. Amidst the field of Christianity (*Cristianesimo*) choked with thorns, the vine of his faith has grown; amid the heap of false coinage is the true coin of his faith, the coin he keeps in his purse, the coin he shows.

This phase of the examination over, the celestial choir strike up the *Te Deum*; yet even now the interrogation is not finished. To end with, Dante must witness to the source whence he has received the faith:

> *Io credo in uno Iddio*
> *Solo ed eterno, che tutto il ciel muove*
> *Non moto, con amore e con disio.*
> "I believe in one God
> sole and eternal, who all the heavens moves
> with love and with desire, himself unmoved."

To this Dante adds that such a faith does not rest simply on physical and metaphysical proofs (*prove fisice e metafisice*), but on the knowledge of truth in the divine inspiration of Holy Scripture. Finally, he confesses his faith "in three eternal persons, who are one essence, one and threefold":

> "The character of godhead (*condizion divina*)
> which here I reverence

214

Is gospel doctrine, stamped (*sigilla*) upon my mind,
not once, but many times.
This the beginning, this the spark of light,
which flares at last in burst of living flame,
and sparkles in me like a star in heaven."

Thus Dante's confession of faith anticipates the apotheosis with which the *Divine Comedy* ends:

"No satisfaction here with wings of mine,
But suddenly my trembling mind was filled
with sense of lightning flash—and eye had
nothing more to ask.
Imagination's yearnings (*fantasia*) now are stilled;
But like a wheel, unwavering and smooth,
My wishing and my willing followed now
The love that moves the sun and all the stars."
(*L'amor che muove il sole e l'altre stelle*).

The entrance fee to Paradise is the precious coin of faith in the Triune God. As the coin bears the stamp or imprint of the ruler, so Dante's mind bears the stamp (*sigilla*) of the divine Being (*condizion divina*). This stamp is the principle (*principio*), the spark, which grows into the glittering light of the stars and thus reflects the reality of the divine Love which moves the sun and the other stars.

The coin of faith has exactly the significance which the open-ing words of Hebrews 11, quoted by Dante, ascribe to faith, *hypostasis* (Lat. *substantia*, Ital. *sustanzia*) and *elenchos* (Lat. *argumentum*, Ital. *argomento*). The two terms have to be used in association with each other. Faith is on the one hand "evidence" or "argument", that whereby we draw from what is visible a conclusion as to the nature of what is not "observable" ("phenomenon", Hebr. 11:3); yet this is not a "physical or metaphysical proof", but it literally represents the things which as yet we cannot see, because they are still hidden in the future. In that sense faith is *substantia*, it is the actuality of the as yet unmanifested reality. The precious coin of faith is the equivalent of that for which it can and will be exchanged in Paradise.

And now we are back with the passage in *Das Kapital* where

Marx quotes from Dante. Marx describes the exchange of a quantity of iron for money as the transformation whereby the commodity (in this case, iron) puts off its natural body and changes from merely imaginary gold into actual gold (*sich aus nur vorgestellten Gold in wirkliches Gold verwandeln*), and he defines this transformation as a "*transubstantiation*". By way of illustration he cites Dante and so posits an analogy between the "transubstantiation" which faith undergoes when Dante enters Paradise and the "transubstantiation" which iron undergoes when it changes from imaginary into actual gold. It is Dante himself who supplies the analogy, in that he compares faith with money (*moneta*). So long as the iron merely has a price, it has only "ideal value-form" (*ideelle Wertgestalt*) or the "form of imaginary gold" (*vorgestellte Goldgestalt*); but in a money-economy this is not sufficient to effect an exchange. For that the iron has to be changed into actual gold. The analogy with Christian faith then goes rather like this: the iron is the natural man, Dante; his faith is the price of the iron, whereby it becomes the equivalent of something else, namely, gold. Gold is a material other than iron, just as heaven is other than earth. But the price makes the iron the equivalent of gold, the price is the "substance" and the evidence or "argument" for what the iron hopes and what it does not yet see—gold; the price is the "faith" of the iron. But for effecting an actual exchange price is no more sufficient than the words of the creed are sufficient to obtain the commodities of heaven and entry into Paradise. For that purpose the iron must undergo a "transubstantiation". The price is the "substance" of the gold-value, just as faith is the "substance" of the "things to come". However, so long as the price, or (as the case may be) faith, possesses this "substance" only in imagination, no actual exchange can occur—the gate of Paradise stays shut, as we might say. Dante has to show Peter the actual money, the hard cash, which he "has in his purse"; but this he would not have been able to do, if the "substance" of things heavenly had not already been present in his faith, just as in the "price" of iron there is present the "substance" of gold. The imaginary "substance" waits to be actualized; the iron and the natural man, Dante, have to put off their natural body, they have to undergo a "trans-substantiation". "Under the ideal measure of values", Marx concludes, "there lurks the hard cash." (*Im ideellen Mass der Werte lauert daher das harte Geld*).

To fathom the full meaning of Marx's train of thought here we shall have to go a little deeper into this analogy. The term *hypostasis* occurs in two other places in the Letter to the Hebrews. In chapter three the brethren are exhorted to offer steadfast resistance to the blandishments of sin, "for we obtain a share in Christ, provided we hold our first confidence (*hypostasis*) firm to the end" (Hebr. 3:14). This exhortation seems to have been the pattern for the words of encouragement addressed to Dante by his guide, Virgil, on his journey through hell and purgatory; the "first confidence" or "beginning" (Greek, *archè*; Lat. *principium*) of the *hypostasis*, which must be held firm to the end, Dante describes as the principle (*principio*), which in the seal (*sigillo*), in the stamp of the divine Essence, in faith is indelibly imprinted upon his mind. This principle is a spark which eventually glitters like the stars. In that way, says the Letter to the Hebrews, "we obtain a share in Christ", that is to say, in it we have the *hypostasis*, the substance (*substantia*) of Christ.

In the opening passage of the Letter to the Hebrews Christ Himself is described as the "reflection" of God's glory and a "copy" or "imprint" (Authorized Version, "express image") of God's *hypostasis*. The reality of faith is made fully apparent here from the fact that the same term is used to define it as is used to define the reality of God Himself. Both have *substantia*, essential being, self-subsistence. The term "imprint" is *character* in the Greek. Just as the coinage bears the stamp of the ruler, represents him, represents his power and glory, so Christ is the visible *character* of God's invisible *substantia*.

Closely related to the term *character* is the term *charagma*. In his speech delivered on Mars' hill (the Areopagus) Paul declares, "Being then God's offspring, we ought not to think that the Godhead is like gold, or silver, or stone, a representation by the art and imagination of men" (Acts 17:29). Gold, silver or stone are *charagma*, a representation by the art (*technè*) and imagination of man. In other words, man expresses in gold, silver or stone the image, the stamp of the Godhead, as he himself envisages it. Furthermore, the term *charagma* occurs repeatedly in the Revelation of John. The reference there is

invariably to "those who had the mark of the beast and worshipped its image" (Rev. 13:17; 14:9,11; 16:2; 19:20; 20:4).
The *charagma*, the mark which men carry on their right hand or
on their forehead, has the same function as the *eikon* (image)
which they worship; both represent the divinized authority of
the Roman emperor. One of these passages is cited by Marx
in the second chapter of the first volume of *Das Kapital*, the
chapter immediately preceding the third chapter, in which
appears the quotation from Dante we have just been discussing.
This second chapter deals with the question of Exchange
(*Austauschprozess*). Marx shows that the special function of
money arises from the fact that a particular commodity,
namely, money, is set apart or excluded by the social action of
all other commodities; it is in this exclusive commodity that all
other commodities whatever express their values. Thereby the
bodily form of this commodity becomes the form of the socially
recognized universal equivalent. To be the universal equivalent
becomes, through the social process, the specific social function
of the commodity excluded by the rest. In this way the excluded
commodity becomes money.

To illustrate this point there follows a quotation in Latin
from the Revelation of John, *Illi unum consilium habent et virtutem
et potestatem suam bestiae tradunt. Et ne quis possit emere aut vendere,
nisi qui habet characterem aut nomen bestiae, aut numerum nominis
ejus.* This is, in fact, a combination of two texts. The first
(Rev. 17:13) comes from the chapter describing the judgment
of Babylon. John sees in the spirit a woman sitting on a scarlet
beast which was full of blasphemous names. "The woman was
arrayed in purple and scarlet, and bedecked with gold and
jewels and pearls, holding in her hand a golden cup full of
abominations and the impurities of her fornication; and on her
forehead was written a name of mystery: 'Babylon, the great
mother of harlots and of earth's abominations'." The woman
was "drunk with the blood of the saints and the blood of the
martyrs of Jesus" (Rev. 17:3–6). The beast on which she was
sitting "had seven heads and ten horns . . . And the ten horns
are ten kings who have not yet received royal power, but they
are to receive authority as kings for one hour, together with the
beast. *These are of one mind and give over their power and authority to*

the beast; they will make war on the Lamb, but the Lamb will conquer them" (Rev. 17:3–14).

The second passage is taken from Revelations 13:17. John describes how he first of all saw a beast rising out of the sea, with ten horns and seven heads (Rev. 13:1). Then another beast rose out of the earth; "it had two horns like a lamb and it spoke like a dragon . . . It . . . makes the earth and its inhabitants worship the first beast . . . Also it causes all, both small and great, both rich and poor, both free and slave, to be marked on the right hand or the forehead, *so that no one can buy or sell unless he has the mark, that is, the name of the beast or the number of its name* . . . Let him who has understanding reckon the number of the beast, for it is a human number, its number is six hundred and sixty-six" (Rev. 13:11–18).

In the Latin translation from which Marx quotes, the Greek word for "mark", *charagma*, is rendered by "character", which brings it more closely into line with the Greek term *charakter*, applied in the Letter to the Hebrews to Christ, the Son of God, the *charakter* of God's *hypostasis* (*substantia*). Marx prefaces this passage, which tells of the "mark" of the beast that is given to men, with the text in which the ten kings give over to the beast the power and authority which they have received for one hour, together with the beast. The terms "power" (Greek *dynamis*) and "authority" (Greek *exousia*) in the New Testament are terms applied also to God and Christ. Thus the kings receive divine authority and "hand it over" (Latin *tradunt*) to the beast.

In combining these two passages, what Marx is plainly interested in is the combination of the handing over of a delegated divine authority to the beast with the command issued by the beast that everyone must bear its mark as precondition for the licence to buy and sell. The next chapter of the Revelation of John spotlights the close connection between the "merchants of the earth" and the "kings of the earth". "Babylon the great" falls because "all nations have drunk the wine of her impure passion, and the kings of the earth have committed fornication with her, and the merchants of the earth have grown rich with the wealth of her wantonness" (Rev. 18:3). "The merchants of the earth weep and mourn for her, since no one buys their cargo any more, cargo of gold, silver, jewels and pearls", and so forth (verse 11). No light of any lamp will shine in fallen Babylon any more; her merchants were the great ones of the earth, for all nations were deceived by their sorcery (verse 23).

Just as "Babylon the great" gets its worldwide authority from economic control over the world market, so, conversely, the economic process is anchored in political power. The exclusive bond between economics and politics is expressed in the stipulation that it is essential to bear the mark of the beast and to worship its image if one is to be allowed to take part in the economic process. The total, divinized authority which politics and economics have handed over to the beast is in contrast to the authority of the Lamb, the "Lord of lords and King of kings" (Rev. 17:14). Seduction by the sorcery of economic idolatry is set over against the genuine gold that is to be bought from the Son of God. John writes to the congregation at Laodicea: "For you say, I am rich, I have prospered, and I need nothing; not knowing that you are wretched, pitiable, poor, blind and naked. Therefore I counsel you to buy from me gold refined by fire, that you may be rich" (Rev. 3:17 f.). The elect have been "ransomed for God" by the blood of the Lamb (Rev. 5:9), they have been "redeemed from the earth . . . redeemed from mankind as firstfruits for God and the Lamb" (Rev. 14:3 f.).

As the "mark" (*charagma*) of the beast is set over against Christ, who is the "stamp" or "imprint" (*character*) of God's nature (*hypostasis, substantia*), so the "image" (*eikon*) of the emperor is set over against Christ, who is "the image of the invisible God" (Col. 1:15). The "god of this world" has blinded the minds of the unbelievers, "to keep them from seeing the light of the gospel of the glory of Christ, who is the likeness (image) of God" (2 Cor. 4:4). The functions of the "mark" and the "image" are united in the effigy (likeness) and the legend (inscription) on the tribute-money. Because it bears the likeness (*eikon*) of the emperor, Jesus says, "Render therefore to Caesar the things that are Caesar's, and to God the things that are God's" (Matt. 22:20 f.).

Bearing the "mark of the beast" (which means bearing the *charagma*, the *character*, the "image" (*eikon*) of the beast) is contrasted with bearing the image of Christ. The elect are predestined to "conformity" to the image of God's Son; there is a "metamorphosis" (2 Cor. 3:18) : as they have borne the image of the man of dust ("the first Adam"), they will also bear the image of the man of heaven ("the second Adam") (1 Cor.'15:49).

The passage which Marx chooses to quote from the Revelation of John has a special significance, because it is the one occasion on which explicitly, and in the express form of a word for word quotation, reference is made to the Bible. Reminiscences of the Bible, a primarily ironical use of biblical expressions in attacks on bourgeois Christianity and comments on biblical injunctions or customs do occur here and there in Marx's writings. The present quotation from the Revelation of John, on the other hand, was carefully chosen and put together to illustrate and undergird his argument regarding the social function of money and the origin of that function.

Moreover, he had been using the term *character*, which in this passage is the Latin rendering of "mark", only a little while before in the context of the same argument, in the expression *Charaktermaske*. In the economic exchange-process there arises a legal relation in which the owners of commodities behave towards one another as persons, and mutually recognize one another as private proprietors. The subject-matter of this juridical relation is given by the economic relation itself. The persons here exist for one another merely as representatives of, and therefore as owners of, commodities. Marx sums up the outcome of the argument he has still to develop by saying that "the characters who appear on the economic stage are only the personifications of the economic relations that exist between them" (*dass die ökonomischen Charaktermasken der Personen nur die Personifikationen der ökonomischen Verhältnisse sind, als deren Träger sie sich gegenübertreten*). What in economico-juridical relations, therefore, is called a "person" (*Person*) is in fact the "personification" (*Personifikation*) of an economic relation. Marx resolves the term "person" here into the original meaning of the Latin word *persona*, that is, the mask worn by the actor. The evolution of the term would then be from the stage mask to the dramatic role being played and hence to the social role that somebody plays and the character he has. The term *Charaktermaske* takes us back to the source. The mask that the actor wears imprints upon him the "character" of what he represents; the mask is the "personi-fication" of what is being represented. We should remember in this connection, therefore, that originally, in Greek tragedy, the gods were themselves present behind the mask worn by the performer; the mask is the "personification" of a god.

It is precisely with the original meaning of concepts like "person" and "character" in view that Marx turns to the Revelation of John. Those who take part in economic exchange, bear the "character" of the beast; their economic function is the personification of a divinized, absolutized power. The "image" of the beast that is worshipped is money, in which the economic exchange of goods assumes a duplicated form, namely, the duplication (*Verdopplung*) of the commodity into commodity and money. "At the same rate, then, as the conversion of products into commodities is being accomplished, so also is the conversion of a commodity into money."

And with that we find ourselves back with the argument which the quotation from Dante was used to support: the transformation, conversion or "transubstantiation" of a commodity into money. In fact, Marx has recourse to a primitive terminology in which "person" and "substance" were still identical; in ancient thought the Greek term *hypostasis* is synonymous with the Latin *persona*; in the mask the "essential nature", the *substantia* itself is present.

In summing up, the conclusion we come to is that the two passages quoted enshrine the antithesis between the two extremes. The passage from the Revelation of John points us to the one extreme: money is the "mark" or "character" of the great beast, the power of the world state and the world market, treated as though it were divine. In the Dante passage, on the other hand, money is the representative of the other extreme, of Christian faith in the Triune God. Money is a symbol of the *substantia* or *hypostasis* in which the heavenly "good things to come" are already present to faith. At the entrance to Paradise Dante "trades in" this precious coin for the glory that awaits him. In hope of the good things to come, in that context, faith is already the "substance" and the "argument" (proof) of what lies hidden behind things visible (*phainomena*, Hebrews 11:3). Through the spirit realm of hell and purgatory Dante's progress carries him towards the true reality of Paradise.

Against the background of the two previously quoted passages from Dante, which I considered earlier, what Marx is getting at now starts to become clear. The *Critique of Political Economy* has taken him through the spirit-realm of civil society as far as the portals of reality, the new world in which man will really be man again. Just as in the Revelation of John there is revealed a vision, the vision of a new heaven and a new earth, of the Paradise that is to come when the great beast has been cast into the abyss, and just as Dante's journey through hell and purgatory leads to Paradise, so Marx's critical journey goes steadily forward, his view focused on the reality which lurks behind the imaginary forms and quasi-relationships of political economy. His scientific analysis is indeed a disclosure of what was hidden. Behind all the philosophical self-reflection, the term *Kritik*, which in Marx's case enshrines the very heart and centre of his life's work, turns out to have a fundamental connection with the Greek term *Kritikos*, used in the Letter to the Hebrews. In chapter four the prospect is held out of the coming "sabbath rest for the people of God". There follows an exhortation in the same vein as that of Marx's first and second Dante quotations, namely, the exhortation to make every effort to enter into that coming sabbath rest, that no one should fall by imitating the disobedience of those who have not entered (Hebr. 4:9–11). "For the word (*logos*) of God is living and active, sharper than any two-edged sword . . . and it is a *kritikos*, a discerner of the thoughts and intentions of the heart. And before Him no creature is hidden, but all are open and laid bare to the eyes of Him before whom we have to render account (*logos*)" (verse 12 f.). The word for "thoughts" is the same term (*enthumèseis*) that Paul uses in his speech on the Areopagus, where he argues that the Godhead is not like gold or silver or stone, a representation (*charagma*) by the art (*technè*) and imagination (*enthumèsis*) of man (Acts 17:29). The term *logos* is employed both for the "word" of God and for the "account" which we human beings have to render. In this objective-cum-subjective sense Dante renders an account of his faith before Peter. The same function is fulfilled in Marx's work by his critique; in the *Kritik der politischen Ökonomie* there is at work the *logos* of reality.

The similarity to Dante extends even further, in that in

Dante the critical method is itself already present. After all, the criticism which Dante has to undergo before the judgment-seat of Peter is turned against Peter himself. If Dante's appeal to the "works", that is, the miracles, to which Holy Scripture witnesses, as proof of the divine inspiration of that same Scripture is refuted by Peter as *petitio principii*, then Dante parries this objection by twisting the sword of criticism round and pointing it at Peter himself. The truth is that on earth Peter has not a single "work" to show. The vineyard of Christianity, which in poverty and fasting he once worked to create, is now completely choked by thorns and brambles. Keeper of the keys he may be at the gate of heaven; but on earth his work has miscarried. From this Dante takes his indirect proof. As over against a Christianity plunged in worldly riches and belief in marvels, Dante himself stands destitute before the gate of heaven; and the proof of his faith in the Triune God is that one great miracle, which puts all miracles in the shade: the very fact of his faith, a miracle as great as the faith of Peter and the faith of those converted by the apostolic preaching. So the examination which Dante has to endure at the entrance to Paradise becomes a "critique of earth", a devastating critique of historical Christianity.

It is in the light of all this that the curious function of Marx's third and last quotation from Dante is to be understood. The "money in the purse" that Dante has to show to Peter is the real faith which is barely to be met with on earth. Just as in the price iron possesses an "ideal value-form" (*ideellen Wertgestalt*) or "the form of gold in imagination" (*vorgestellte Goldgestalt*), so it is with nominal Christianity; it is an iron faith, which only "ideally" or in "imagination" possesses the reality of God. A commodity cannot at one and the same time be actual iron and actual gold. In fact, Marx is implying, bourgeois Christianity is centred in a quite different "transubstantiation" from the transmuting of real faith into the believed in and hoped for reality of the coming Kingdom of God. In point of fact, money has taken the place of the Triune God, and it is this displacement of God by Mammon that is denoted by the passage from Dante. As surely as Dante's faith had to be transformed into the glory and splendour of Paradise, with the same sort of inevitability the commodity is converted in the economic process into money; for "under the ideal measure of values there lurks the hard cash". Bourgeois Christianity believes in the exchange value of commodities; and it sees this belief come true. A commodity is transmuted into cash.

The profound irony of this analogy between Dante's faith in the Triune God and money eventually assumes a somewhat surprising guise in the structure of *Das Kapital*—not so much in the construction in three books as in the way the third book ends up by analysing what Marx calls the "trinitarian formula" or the "economic trinity": "capital-profit (employers' profits plus interest), land-rent, labour-wages, this is the trinitarian form that embraces all the secrets of the production-process in society". This analysis is incorporated in the final section of the third book of *Das Kapital*, entitled *Die Revenuen und ihre Quellen* (Revenues and their Sources.) Curiously enough, an analysis of the "economic trinity" closely akin to this is provided in a similarly named essay with the English title of *Revenue and its Sources*, added as an appendix at the end of the *Theorieën über den Mehrwert*. These were written before *Das Kapital*, but are incorporated in it as Book Four. Thus Marx's major work is twice climaxed with an analysis of the "trinitarian formula". Just as the three parts of Dante's major work, *The Divine Comedy*, lead up to the meeting in Paradise with the Triune God, so Marx's main work, also in three parts, issues in the "economic trinity". And there we have the transition from the religious realism of the Middle Ages to a modern "critique of earth".

The analogy between the critique of the "theological trinity" on the one hand and the critique of the "economic trinity" on the other does indeed run like a golden thread through the whole of Marx's work. As early as the *Critique of Hegel's Philosophy of Right*, written in 1843, Marx is drawing a parallel between the critique of theology and the critique of politics, and in doing so he explicitly takes the dogma of the Trinity as his starting-point. On the one hand, Hegel is blamed for interpreting the contrariety of the appearance as a unity in essence, in the idea. Because of that he remained blind to the fundamental contradiction between the political state and civil society, the conflict of the abstract political state with itself; therein lies, for example, the root of the intrinsic contradiction within the legislature.

Without actually introducing the term, Marx deploys here the modern doctrine of the *trias politica* as the theory of the political trinity. That becomes evident from the sequel to his argument in which he arraigns the popular criticism for falling into precisely the opposite error to that which had ensnared Hegel. Thus the popular criticism criticizes the constitution, for instance; it points to the contrast between the powers (that is, of the *trias politica*: legislative, executive and juridical); it finds conflict and contradiction here, there and everywhere. In itself, this is still a dogmatic critique, battling against its object, just as at an earlier period people employed the contradiction between one and three to confute the dogma of the Holy Trinity. A proper critique, on the other hand, shows the inner genesis of the Holy Trinity occurring within the human brain. It describes how it came to birth; and so a truly philosophical critique of the present-day constitution not only demonstrates the existence of contradictions but explains them, understands their genesis, their necessary character. It grasps them in their unique and peculiar significance. This process of understanding, however, does not entail, as Hegel believes it does, a general recognition of the peculiar attributes of the logical concept; it does mean grasping the inherent logic of the peculiar object.

Marx has already formulated here, à propos of the critique of politics, the fundamental principles that will assist him again with the *Critique of Political Economy*, in which he carries out the "anatomy of civil society". The *Critique* explains the inner contradictions (*Widersprüche*) through an understanding of how they were engendered (*Geburtsakt*), their inner genesis. That genesis is both the inner genesis within the human brain (*die innere Genesis im menschlichen Gehirn*) and the peculiar logic of the peculiar object (*die eigentümliche Logik des eigentümlichen Gegenstandes*), that is to say, the anatomy is at one and the same time an analysis of the subject and of the object; for the event being analysed is indivisibly subjective-objective.

This analytical method Marx applies to the "economic trinity". In one of the last chapters of *Das Kapital*, chapter 48 of Book III, he discusses the trinitarian form that embraces all the mysteries of the production-process in society: capital-profit, land-rent, labour-wages. In this formula is defined the interconnection between the components of value and of wealth in general, on the one hand, and the sources of value and wealth, on the other. The mystification of the capitalist mode of production, the conversion of social relations into things (*Verdinglichung*), the direct coalescence of the material production relations with their historical and social determination —all this is brought to completion in the economic trinity. It is an enchanted, perverted, topsy-turvy world, in which Monsieur le Capital and Madame la Terre do their ghost-walking as social characters (*soziale Charaktere*) and at the same time directly as mere things. Marx sees it as the great merit of classical economy to have achieved the dissolution of this false appearance and illusion, this mutual self-sufficiency and ossification (*Verknöcherung*) of the various social elements of wealth, this personification of things and conversion of production relations into entities, this religion of everyday life (*Religion des Alltagslebens*). Classical economics has after all analysed the economic trinity. Interest it reduced to a portion of profit, and rent to the surplus above average profit, so that interest and rent converge in surplus value. The process of circulation it represents as a mere metamorphosis of forms. And finally it reduces value and surplus value of commodities to labour in the direct production process. Nevertheless, even the best spokesmen of classical economy remain more or less in the grip of the world of illusion which their own criticism had dissolved—from a bourgeois standpoint it could not be otherwise—and thus they all fall more or less into inconsistencies, half-truths and unsolved contradictions. On the other hand, it is just as natural for the actual agents of production to feel completely at home in these estranged (*entfremdeten*) and irrational forms of capital-interest, land-rent, labour-wages; for these are precisely the forms of illusion in which they have their being and find their daily occupation. The vulgar economy (*Vulgärökonomie*) in its turn is nothing but a didactic, more or less doctrinaire translation of the ordinary conceptions of the actual agents of production, into which it introduces a certain, to ordinary intelligence understandable, order. It is therefore equally natural that a vulgar economy should see precisely in this trinity, from which every trace of inner cohesion has been effaced, the natural and unquestionable basis for its shallow self-importance. This formula at the same time tallies with the interests of the ruling classes, in that it proclaims the physical necessity and eternal justification of their sources of revenue and elevates them into a dogma.

In some comments appended to the end of the *Theorieën über den Mehrwert* (that is to say, to the end of the fourth book of *Das Kapital*) Marx expressly examines the analogy between the theological trinity and the economic one. Whereas, he argues, classical and therefore critical economists see a problem in the form of alienation (*Entfremdung*) and attempt by the use of analysis to strip this away, a vulgar economy is completely at home only with the strangeness in which the various portions stand over against one another in value. Precisely as a scholastic is on familiar ground with God-the-Father, God-the-Son, God-the-Holy-Ghost, so is your exponent of vulgar economy with land-groundrent, capital-interest, labour-wages. After all, this is exactly the form in which to outward appearance (*Erscheinung*) these relations would seem (*scheinen*) directly to cohere and thus also live in the imaginations and in the consciousness of the agents of these relations, obsessed with capitalistic production.

It might seem that in the trinity of land-groundrent, capital-profit (interest), labour-wages, the last member is the most rational. After all, the source from which wages derive is explicit enough. But in fact this last form is the most *irrational* and the basis of the other two, just as working for wages generally presupposes land as *landed property* and product as *capital*. Only when labour is confronted with its preconditions in this form is it paid labour, work for wages. Because the wages appear here as the specific product of labour, its sole product (and indeed for the wage-earning worker they are the sole product of his labour), the other portions of the value—landrent, profit (capital interest)—appear just as necessarily as arising from other sources; and precisely as the portion of the product-value that is resolved into wages should be envisaged as the *specific* product of the labour, so the portions of the value which are absorbed in interest and profit must be taken to be specific results of the agencies (*Agentien*) for which they exist, to

which they accrue, that is to say, as the offspring of the earth
and of the capital, respectively.

The vulgar economy which keeps conceptions of this sort on
the go believes in its own simplicity, naturalness and general
usefulness, which is and remains far removed from theoretical
niceties; and this claim is all the more obvious in as much as it
indeed does nothing but translate these ordinary notions into a
doctrinaire kind of language. The more alienated, therefore,
the form in which it envisages the formations of capitalistic
production, the closer it approximates to the element of the
ordinary conception, and the more it finds itself moving in its
natural element. Then again, that answers very well the
purposes of apologetic; for in land-rent, capital-interest,
labour-wages the various forms of surplus value and the forms
of capitalistic production are not mutually estranged (*ent-fremdet*), but alien (*fremd*) and indifferent, simply differing,
without contrast or opposition. The various revenues arise from
quite different sources, one from the land, another from capital,
another from labour. Thus there is no antagonistic relation
between them, because there is no intrinsic relation at all.

So Marx sees a fundamental analogy between the scholasticism operative in theology and the scholasticism operative in
the economy. Just as it is the function of the critique of theology
to analyse the alienated forms of the outward show of things
and so reveal the true reality lying hidden behind it, the
critique of political economy does the same thing at the level of
the critique of earth.

From the very outset of his study of economics, this analogy
with theology was a guiding principle for Marx. One of his first
exercises during his stay in Paris, in what was for him this
unfamiliar territory, was an attempt to précis the work by the
British economist, James Stuart Mill, entitled *Elements of
Political Economy* (1821). The manuscript was written in the first
half of 1844. As is usual with Marx, it not only contains a large
number of quotations but follows them up with a searching
commentary. Having first criticized the method of the political
economy, because it formulates abstract laws whilst ignoring
economic activity in practice, he then gets to the positive
merits of Mill's work. Mill indeed hits the nail on the head and
reduces the essence of the thing to a single notion when he

describes money as the instrument (*Vermittler*—that which mediates) of exchange. The essential thing about money is not in the first instance that in it ownership, the possession of property, becomes alienated (*entaüssert*), but that the mediating (instrumental) activity or movement, the human, social action which ensures that man's products mutually complement and supplement one another, is alienated (*entfremdet*) and becomes the property or attribute of a material thing outside of man, namely, of money. Because this intermediary activity itself alienates man (*entaüssert*), he is active here only as man lost and abandoned, man dehumanized (*entmenschter Mensch*); the proper relation between things, the human operation carried out in this way, becomes the operation of something outside man and above man. Because of this alien intermediary (*fremden Mittler*), instead of man himself having to be the intermediary for man, man sees his will, his activity, his relationship to other people, as a power independent of him and of them. Thus his enslavement reaches a climax. Clearly, this intermediary, this instrument, has now become the real God, since the intermediary is the real authority over that with which it reconciles me. Its cult becomes an end in itself. Objects, divorced from this instrument, lose their value. Only in so far as they represent it do they have value, whereas originally it looked as though it only had value in so far as it represented them. This reversal of the original relationship is inevitable. This intermediary is therefore the essential substance of private ownership that has lost itself, the alienated substance, a private ownership that has become alien, external (*aüsserlich*) to itself, an alienated, externalized (*entaüsserte*) substance; just as money is the alienated mediating factor between one human production and another, the alienated (*entaüsserte*) activity of the human species (*Gattungstätigkeit*). All the attributes proper to that activity, therefore, are transferred to this intermediary. Thus man becomes all the poorer as man, that is to say, in separation from this intermediary, the richer the intermediary itself becomes.

The term "intermediary", "mediator", prompts Marx to turn his thoughts from J. S. Mill's economic definition of money as the instrument or "mediator" of exchange to the heart of Christology, in fact to a direct analogy between the mediator-

ship of Christ and the function of money. Christ represents
initially (1) people before God (*vor Gott*); (2) God to the
people (*für die Menschen*); (3) people on behalf of people (*dem
Menschen*). Similarly, in accordance with the notion of money,
money represents initially: (1) private ownership on behalf of
(*für*) private ownership; (2) society on behalf of (*für*) private
ownership; (3) private ownership on behalf of society. But
Christ is God estranged and man estranged (*entaüsserte*). God
continues to have value only in so far as he represents Christ,
man only in so far as he represents Christ. It is the same with
money.

Why is it that private ownership has to go over to a money
system? Because man as a social being has to resort to exchange
and because exchange, under conditions of private ownership,
is bound to change over to value. The mediating activity of
man as the agent of exchange is in fact not a social, not a
human activity, not a human relationship, but it is the abstract
relation of private ownership to private ownership; and this
abstract relation is the value, which has no actual existence *qua*
value except as money. Because the people engaged in the
process of exchange have no human relationship to one
another, the thing loses the significance attaching to human
ownership, personal ownership. The social relation of private
ownership to private ownership is already one in which
private ownership is alienated (*entfremdet*) from itself. The
consciously explicit (*für sich seiende*) existence of this relation,
money, is therefore the alienation (*Entaüsserung*) of private
ownership, the abstraction of its specific, personal nature.

So Marx concludes that the opposition of modern political
economists to the monetary system cannot ensure us the
decisive victory, notwithstanding their intelligence. The un-
educated economic superstition of the people and of governments clings to what the senses can observe, the tangible,
visible money-bag, and so to the absolute value of precious
metals, just as they believe in their possession as the sole manifestation of real wealth. Then the enlightened, sophisticated
political economist comes along and shows them that money is a
commodity like any other, so that the value of money, as of any
other commodity, depends on the relation of production costs
to supply and demand, to the amount or competitiveness of the

other commodities. But our enlightened economist is fairly answered when it is said that the real value of things is their exchange value and that in the final instance this consists in money, just as money consists in precious metals, so that money is the true value of things and therefore the thing most to be desired in itself. In the end, the theories of the political economists themselves boil down to this piece of profundity; only they possess the power of abstraction, so that they are able to recognize money as existing under every form of commodity and do not believe, therefore, in the exclusive value of its official, metallic existence. The metallic existence of money is merely the official, sensory expression of that pecuniary soul which lurks in every joint and article of the productions and activities of civil society.

The opposition of modern political economists to the monetary system is simply this: that they have grasped the money business, the world of finance, in its abstraction and generality, and through their enlightened insight have managed to rise above the sense-ridden superstition which believes that this thing exists exclusively in precious metal. In place of this uninstructed, ill-informed superstition they put their own refined version. However, because they both depend essentially on one and the same root, the enlightened form of the superstition cannot altogether oust the unenlightened, sense-ridden form of it, since the enlightened version does not get to grips with the essence of the thing, but only with the particular form of that essence.

In the *Economic and Philosophical Manuscripts*, dating from the same year (1844), Marx brings this argument round to a striking definition, when copying Friedrich Engels he describes the British pioneer of modern political economy, Adam Smith, as the Luther of political economy (*den nationalökonomischen Luther*). This enlightened political economy discovered the subjective essence of wealth, within the framework of private property; it therefore regards the partisans of the monetary and mercantilist system, who consider private property to be simply an objective being for man (*ein nur gegenständliches Wesen für den Menschen*), as fetishists and Catholics. Luther recognized religion, faith, as the essence of the external world, in opposition to Catholic paganism; he annulled external religiosity by making religiosity the inner essence of man; he disclaimed the priest, who exists outside the layman, because he transferred the priest into the heart of the layman. In the same way, the wealth that is external to man and independent of him (and thus only to be acquired and conserved from outside) is annulled. That is to say, its external and mindless objectivity (*aüsserliche, gedankenlose Gegenständlichkeit*) is annulled by the fact that private property is incorporated (*sich inkorporiert*) in man himself, and man himself is recognized as its essence. But, as a result, man himself is brought into the determinative sphere (*in der Bestimmung . . . gesetzt*) of private property, just as with Luther he is brought into the determinative sphere of religion.

With this analogy Marx completes the circle of his critique. In the "Introduction" to the *Critique of Hegel's Philosophy of Right*, likewise dating from the year 1844, the critique of politics refers back to the critique of religion, and specifically of Germany's theoretical revolution, the Reformation; the critique of Germany sharpens and narrows into the critique of Luther. The critique of politics, the anatomy of civil society, leads to the critique of political economy; the critique of France and in particular of Britain becomes most acute in the critique of Adam Smith. Yet once more the critique here returns to the critique of religion. Adam Smith is the Luther of political economy: a fact which once again confirms that the critique of religion is the premise of every critique.

9

Critique of Political Economy

WHEN in 1866 Marx was busy preparing for publication of the first Book of *Das Kapital*, he compared his work in a letter with a new-born animal, licked into shape by its mother "after so many birth-pangs". Marx's biographer, Franz Mehring, therefore gives the first section of the chapter in which he deals with the creation of *Das Kapital* the title of "Birth-pangs"; and he begins by remarking that these birth-pangs had lasted for about twice as many years as physiology requires months for bringing into the world a fully-formed human baby. Even in 1851 Marx had thought he would be finished within five weeks; and in 1859 he again saw the completion of his work as being less than six weeks away. In point of fact it was the end of 1865 when an enormous manuscript lay to hand, from which material, from the beginning of 1866, Marx managed over a period of fourteen months to compile the first Book of *Das Kapital*, although continually plagued by disease and by financial difficulties. It was with good reason that in a letter dating from this period Friedrich Engels wrote of "this accursed book", the cause of Marx's unhappiness, "this never-to-be-finished thing" that was threatening to crush him physically, mentally and financially.

Between 1842, the year of Marx's first analysis of economic conditions in the article concerning the legislation on wood-stealing, and 1883, the year of his death, there is an interval of about forty years. If one goes by the fact that Marx's economic ideas had taken shape so early on (in 1842 he was twenty-four, and the Communist Manifesto appeared in his thirtieth year) then four decades should have afforded plenty of time for the systematic unfolding of fundamental ideas, formed at an early age. As a systematic work in several parts, the product of mature study, *Das Kapital* would fit splendidly into this picture. However, the picture is a misleading one and conflicts with the course which Marx's work in the economic sphere actually took. Ludwig von Beethoven testified towards the end of his life that he had only just begun to discover what composing is really all about. In the light of that declaration, Beethoven's development becomes something quite different from the organic ripening of the seed into the final fruit; it resembles more the surprisingly successful and yet abortive expedition of a Columbus, or the fruitless effort of a medical research-worker to track down the cause of cancer. Marx's economic anatomy is impelled by the insatiable flair of the scientific investigator and fired by the creative urge of the composer; and in these two together we can recognize the rational-irrational passion of the alchemist.

In 1859, when Marx is writing the Preface (*Vorwort*) to *Zur Kritik der politischen Ökonomie*, he looks back over the way he has come, and in a matter of a few pages sums up the result, the conclusion, of his economic studies: a conclusion which "once reached, continued to serve as the leading thread in my studies". He then sketches the main features of historical materialism, leading up to his thesis regarding the bourgeois relations of production as the last antagonistic form of the social process of production, constituting the closing chapter of the pre-history of human society. The impression created here by Marx's development is indeed that as early as in 1844 and 1845, the period he spent in Paris and Brussels, his economic philosophy was already settled in principle, so that all it needed was to be worked out in greater detail. Friedrich Engels said himself that, with the composition of the *Thesen über Feuerbach* in February 1845, the main features of Marx's materialistic theory of history had already been completed.

This view of Marx's development is certainly not wrong; and it is supported by Marx's autobiographical account. Nevertheless, it is misleading, if one takes it to be the whole truth. It is a half-truth, crossed by another interpretation. After all, a term such as "materialistic theory of history" (*materialistische Geschichtstheorie*) suggests that Marx's life's work consisted mainly in battling against idealistic theories and replacing them with his own materialistic theory; the antiquated and dilapidated buildings are demolished and a huge, brand-new construction is run up in their place.

Marx himself was all along opposed, and radically opposed, to any such scheme. If these lectures have the title, *Critique of Heaven and Earth*, the assumption is, of course, that the essence of Marx's whole work resides in critique. In his letters to Arnold Ruge of 1843, Marx had already described the replacement of one theory by another as the "setting up of a dogmatic banner" (*eine dogmatische Fahne*); and in the *Critique of Hegel's Philosophy of Right* he also dismisses the vulgar critique that does battle with its object (*mit ihrem Gegenstand kämpft*) as "dogmatic critique". A true critique describes the process of birth, the inner genesis within the human brain, the peculiar logic of the peculiar object. That is why his motto is reform of the consciousness, not by means of dogmas but through analysis of the mystical consciousness which has not attained to clarity regarding itself, whether in its religious or its political form of manifestation. To put it in a nutshell: the *Selbstverständigung*, the enlightenment of the age regarding its own struggle and its own desires. Instead of confronting the world on a doctrinaire basis, he wants to develop new principles for the world out of the principles (elements) of the world. That is critical philosophy.

In the light of this critical method, Marx's development is not simply that of a "materialistic theory of history"; it assumes a different appearance. Again, in Marx's auto-biographical *Vorwort* to *Zur Kritik der politischen Ökonomie* (1859), the term *Selbstverständigung* plays an important role. The term is implicitly enshrined in the thesis that "mankind always takes up only such problems as it can solve (*stellt sich die Menschheit immer nur Aufgaben, die sie lösen kann*), since, looking at the matter more closely, we will always find that the problem itself arises only when the material conditions necessary for its solution already exist or are at least in the process of formation." This proposition is a product of the critical-analytical

method that distinguishes sharply between the material transformation of the economic conditions of production, which can
be determined with the precision of natural science, and the
legal, political, religious, artistic or philosophical—in short,
ideological—forms in which men become aware of this conflict
and fight it out. Just as our opinion of an individual is not based
on what he thinks of himself, so we cannot judge such a period
of transformation by its own consciousness. On the contrary,
critical analysis operates the other way round. It explains the
consciousness by reference to the contradictions of material life
and in terms of the existing conflict between the social forces of
production and the conditions of production. No social order
ever disappears before all the productive forces for which there
is room in it have been developed; and new conditions of
production never appear before the material preconditions
for their existence have matured in the womb of the old
society.

The critical method which operates in this way achieves
precisely what the letter of 1843, addressed to Ruge (the letter
we quoted earlier) defines as *Selbstverständigung*, the capacity of
the period for clarifying the question about itself, an ability to
comprehend its struggle and its yearnings; in other words,
critical analysis of the opaque, cloudy consciousness, whence it
will appear that humanity is engaged not in any new enterprise
but in the conscious completion of the old one. This *Selbstverständigung*, this clarification, is the fulfilment at the conscious
level of the task, and the solution of the problem which, at the
level of material life, is resolved by the forces of production that
develop within the womb of bourgeois society and also create
the material conditions for resolving the antagonism within the
social process of production. With the resolution of this
antagonism, which is at the same time the dissolution of the
ideological consciousness, the prehistoric stage of human society
is brought to an end.

Having summarized these insights as the product of his
economic studies, Marx proceeds with the account of his
development. He describes how Friedrich Engels, with whom
he had maintained a continuous correspondence ever since the
publication of Engels' ingenious outline for the critique of
economic categories (the article *Umrisse zu einer Kritik der*

Nationalökonomie in the *Deutsch-Französischen Jahrbücher* of 1844), had come by a different road to the same conclusions as himself. When they were both staying in Brussels, in the spring of 1845, they decided to work out together the contrast between their views and the ideological notions of German philosophy and thus to settle accounts with their earlier philosophical conscience. The outcome of their collaboration was a critique of post-Hegelian philosophy, set out in *Die deutsche Ideologie*. When it turned out to be impossible to get the bulky manuscript into print, "we abandoned it to the gnawing criticism of the mice, the more readily because we had accomplished our main purpose—*Selbstverständigung*—the business of clarifying the question for our own benefit." Having referred to a few writings published during the years that followed (primarily, the *Manifesto of the Communist Party* and the anti-Proudhon tract, *Misère de la philosophie*), Marx rounds off the sketch of this period with a mention of his essay, *Lohnarbeit und Kapital*, the publication of which was prevented by the February revolution of 1848 and his expulsion from Belgium.

Thus in the *Selbstverständigung* which was his purpose in writing *Die deutsche Ideologie* his career, the development of his economic studies and the tumultuous events unfolding on the political stage are inextricably intertwined. The *Critique of Ideology* is no private concern of a few philosophers, any more than is the construction of a new philosophical theory, now called "materialistic"; but in the *Critique* there occurs the *Selbstverständigung*, the dissolution of the ideological consciousness that goes hand in hand with the resolution of the social antagonism. That is why he could calmly yield the manuscript of the *Critique of Ideology* to the gnawing criticism of the mice. If the work had been intended as a philosophical enterprise in its own right, then its going to waste would have meant serious frustration for the two authors. In point of fact, Marx treated the manuscript with such lack of care that it has been preserved more or less by accident and was not even published until 1932. The same fate awaited the *Economic and Philosophical Manuscripts* of 1844, likewise published only in 1932. Of them too it could be said that they were written for the purpose of *Selbstverständigung*, of "sorting oneself out", and had therefore fulfilled their function.

What Marx calls "settling accounts with our earlier philosophical conscience" is defined more closely in *Die deutsche Ideologie*, where he criticizes the "philosophical phraseology" of his two articles in the *Deutsch-Französische Jahrbüchern* (the Introduction to the *Critique of Hegel's Philosophy of Right* and the article on the Jewish question). But he goes on at once to say that this philosophical phraseology itself definitely points the way to the materialistic view of the world, that is, the view which is not based on reasoning without premises from an *a priori* (*nicht voraussetzungelosen*) but, on the contrary, examines empirically the actual material premises as such and is therefore *really* critical. In other words, Marx's *Critique of Ideology* is necessarily also a critique of political economy; and taken together, the two comprise the *Selbstverständigung* that Marx achieved in his economic studies during the eighteen-forties, as the attainment of self-consciousness by the "prehistoric stage of human society" which is ending and is pregnant with the real history to come. The economic critique is not a self-supporting formulation of theory, but a function of the "pre-history" of which it is itself a part. So we find Marx at the close of the eighteen-fifties looking back on his studies during the eighteen-forties: the compendious economic studies of that period in which the broad features of the economic insights set out in *Das Kapital* had already taken shape become part and parcel of the emergence of "pre-history" into self-consciousness.

The years 1848 and 1849 bring with them the pause which Marx describes as the interruption of his economic studies by the publication of the *Neue Rheinische Zeitung* and the events which ensued later. In May 1849 he is exiled from Germany; and not until the next year is he able to pick up the threads of his study of economics in his new place of residence—London. But the continuity has been broken. Revolutionary events have brought the period of the eighteen-forties to an abrupt end; and emigration entails a transition to a new environment. Just as emigrating from Germany and settling in Paris had been both a drastic and a definitive step and set a seal upon the critique of religion—which was at the same time the critique of Germany —so did his expulsion from France set a seal on the critique of politics. In London the *Critique of Economy* begins really in earnest for the first time; or as Marx himself says, it is there

that he was obliged to start completely from scratch, all over
again. He mentions three reasons for this: the enormous
amount of material on the history of political economy which is
stored in the British Museum; the convenient vantage-point
which London offers for examining bourgeois society; and
finally the new stage of development upon which the latter
seemed to have entered with the discovery of gold in Cali-
fornia and Australia. Furthermore, a critical study of the new
material led him into the area of other sciences, specifically of
history and of the physical sciences.

Indeed, these factors were more than enough to warrant a
course of scientific labours spread over very many years,
especially as Marx was still obliged to earn his living as a
correspondent of the Anglo-American paper, the *New York
Daily Tribune.* Yet Marx would seem to have something else in
mind, when he uses such a radical expression as "needing to
start all over again from scratch" (*ganz von vorn wieder anzu-
fangen*). The turn of phrase does seem highly exaggerated,
when one takes stock of what he had been doing during the
eighteen-forties. From the *Economic and Philosophical Manuscripts*
on (that is, from 1844), Marx is engaged in elaborating the
basic elements of his economic critique, and in the *Misère de la
Philosophie* of 1847 he displays a thorough knowledge of the
classical economists, in particular of Adam Smith and Ricardo.
The *Communist Manifesto* of 1848 enshrines the ground-plan of
historical materialism. No doubt the remaining task—the
completion of the whole building—is an enormous one; but
that is something basically different from a totally new start.
On the contrary, one's impression is that Marx is all the time in
pursuit of a mystery, a secret which he has been vainly trying to
unravel, and that he is now endeavouring with renewed
determination to pick up the scent.

In the eighteen-fifties too a restless passion for research and
exploration continues to goad him into activity. With the
arrival of an economic crisis in 1857 comes a quickening of the
pace. With the possibility of a revolution in view, Marx wants
at any rate to finish marking out clearly the main contours of
his economic *Critique.* Between August 1857 and March 1858,
working chiefly through the night hours, he writes the *Einleitung zur Kritik der politischen Ökonomie* and several Cahiers in

which he builds up an enormous stock of analyses and detailed studies.

The work advances but slowly, he writes in a letter of February 1858 to Lassalle, "because subjects which one has made a principal object of study over many years are always revealing new aspects and raising new problems. Moreover, I am not master of my own time, but more of a lackey. I have only the nights to myself; and besides, frequent attacks of a liver complaint disrupt these hours of nightly toil."

His plan is still to work away at the *Critique of Political Economy* in a number of Cahiers to be published in due order, one by one, to oblige the public. He is far from happy with this way of doing things; for he has always preferred the method of condensation. His primary concern in this enterprise, as he goes on to explain to Lassalle, is with "a critique of economic categories or, if you like, a critical exposition (*Darstellung*) of the bourgeois economy as a system. It is at one and the same time an exposition of the system and a critique of it . . . The exposition, I mean the manner, is wholly scientific and therefore not in conflict with police in the ordinary sense. The whole is divided into six Books: (1) On Capital; (2) on land-holding; (3) on wage-labour; (4) on the state; (5) international trade; (6) the world market. Of course, I cannot avoid taking up a critical posture from time to time towards other economists, especially in argument against Ricardo, in so far as even he, as a citizen, is compelled to commit blunders, looking at it even from a strictly economic standpoint. Taken as a whole, however, the critique and history of political economy and of socialism must constitute the subject of a different enterprise. Finally, the brief historical outline of the development of economic categories and relations: a third undertaking. After all, I have a presentiment that now—now that after fifteen years of study I have got so far as to begin to get a grip on the thing—various outside tumults and commotions will very likely get in the way. Never mind. If I get finished too late to find the world still interested in such matters, then the fault will obviously be my own."

In April 1858 Marx's iron constitution gave way under the excessive strain. Because of overwork, he was obliged temporarily to give up. In sheer volume the result of his work was enormous, but for that very reason not ripe for publication. It is typical of Marx's way of working that the *Einleitung zur Kritik der politischen Ökonomie* was only discovered among his papers in 1902 and was first published in the following year in the journal *Die Neue Zeit*. So far as the seven Cahiers are concerned, these were first published in 1939 under the title "Outlines of the Critique of Political Economy" (*Grundrisse der Kritik der politischen Ökonomie*), comprising about 700 printed pages. How far the manuscript was from being ready for publication is clear, for instance, from the fact that Marx had not himself given it any title. This had to be concocted from references in his letters of that period. I shall refer to this work from now on as *Grundrisse*.

Strictly speaking, the *Grundrisse* comprises only an opening section of the first Book of the outlined plan of six Books, which he had unfolded in the letter to Lassalle already quoted, that is to say, of the Book on Capital. In the *Grundrisse* we find various draft plans for this first Book; from which it appears that, during the time he was writing it, Marx was continually occupied with the basic structure, and within a few months had gone over to a new scheme for this first Book. But, in addition, the manuscript contains abundant material for the subsequent chapters as envisaged by him in the first Book, as well as for the five other Books. He had, of course, already decided to limit himself to basics in the last three Books (State; International trade; World market), and to go into detail only in the first three (Capital; Land-holding; Wage-labour). But he did not get anywhere near achieving even this more summary exercise.

In the course of 1858 a publisher was found in Germany who was prepared to publish the entire work in successive stages, in a run of what looked like being fifteen Cahiers, or thereabouts. At the beginning of June, having sufficiently recovered from his period of depression, Marx started to prepare for the publication of the first Cahier. He had systematically to select the relevant material for that purpose from the enormous manuscript in which everything lay jumbled together (*wie Kraut und Rüben durcheinandergeht*). What resulted was a manuscript of which only the closing part has survived. "In all that I have written," he complains in a letter sent in November to Lassalle, "the style bespeaks my liverish affliction.

And I have a dual reason for not letting this document be spoilt and wasted on medical grounds: (1) It is the result of fifteen years' scientific investigation, that is to say, of the best years of my life; (2) It is the first scientific presentation of an important view of social relations . . . I have not aspired to elegant presentation, but am only trying to write in my run-of-the-mill fashion—a thing that during the months of suffering was impossible for me on this subject."

Eventually, in the early months of 1859 a finished manuscript was ready for the press and was published under the title *Zur Kritik der politischen Ökonomie*. This was, in fact, the title under which the whole series of Cahiers was to appear. The work published in 1859 contains the first two chapters of the first part of the first Book on Capital. This first part was meant to deal with "Capital in general", subdivided into three chapters, the first two of which had as their subjects "Commodities" and "Money or elementary circulation", respectively.

Marx's plan was to prepare the third chapter, dealing with "Capital", for publication, as he had already announced at the end of the printed edition of the first two. This third chapter was arranged under three heads: (1) The production process of capital; (2) The circulation process of capital; (3) The union of these two, or capital and profit, interest.

Had the third chapter been published, that would have served to complete only the first of the four parts of the first Book. According to the plan worked out during the ensuing years, three more parts should have followed (Competition; Credit; Nominal (share) capital (*Aktienkapital*)). Meanwhile, however, the basic plan was altered. In the early months of 1859 Marx devised a scheme for this third chapter, giving it the title of "Capital", with a view to publication. This scheme he took as a guiding principle for a new manuscript, extensive enough to include 23 Cahiers. On this enormous manuscript, which again bore the title *Zur Kritik der politischen Ökonomie*, he set to work in the summer of 1861. In the course of the following year he decided not to give this manuscript the form initially intended for it, as the third chapter of the first part of the first Book on capital, but to bring it out as an independent work, with the title *Das Kapital*. The title *Zur Kritik der politischen Ökonomie*, originally intended to cover all six Books as a whole, became in this new and considerably reduced design the sub-title of what, viewed in the context of the original scheme, was in fact only the third chapter of the first part of the first Book.

Das Kapital was actually published in accordance with the new scheme, devised in 1862. Marx laboured from 1861 to 1863 on the above-mentioned manuscript of 23 Cahiers, which dealt principally with subjects that were to be taken up later in Book I of *Das Kapital*. In the next two years he was working on the manuscript from which a great part of Book III was compiled; and only after that did he get down to preparing for the publication of Book I, which eventually came out in 1867. It is the only Book of *Das Kapital* which Marx was able to prepare for publication and personally see published. Between 1867 and 1870 he was at work on manuscripts, the material from which turns up in Books II and III. Then came an interval when sickness made it practically impossible for him to write. In 1877 and 1878 he renewed his attempts to apply himself to the preparation of Book II; but he gradually realized that he would never see it completed.

A part of the manuscript of 23 Cahiers, which came into existence between the summer of 1861 and the summer of 1863, was devoted to one particular subject, namely, "theories of surplus value" (*Theorieën über den Mehrwert*), ten Cahiers in all, comprising more than half the total manuscript. In the letter of February 1858 to Lassalle, in which Marx unfolds his basic plan for six Books, he talks about a separate work, the subject of which is to be the critique and history of political economy and of socialism, and then also of a third work which will present a brief historical outline showing the development of economic categories and relations. In fact, these second and third works were not drawn up individually; but the material for them turns up in the manuscript we have already referred to, in the form of "theories of surplus value". Indeed, it was a feature of the original scheme that this special subject was to form only a constituent part of the whole. Marx described this as the historical, historico-critical or historico-literary part of his work, as distinguished from the theoretical part. In the document *Zur Kritik der politischen Ökonomie* of 1859 there are indeed three special sections on this subject occurring in the course of the work (A. Notes on the history of the theory of commodities; B. Theories of the unit of measurement of money; C. Theories of the means of circulation and money). The same kind of procedure was envisaged for the subsequent Cahiers. But during the actual writing this historical and critical part grew far beyond the proportions of the basic plan. This expansion was also bound up with the fact that his critical analysis of the classic representatives of political economy in part preceded the writing of the theoretical portion in which he developed his own ideas, and formed an important stimulus and challenge to them.

So, we find in Marx's letters from 1865 onward indications that he wanted to set aside this historico-critical part for Book IV, which was to follow the three Books of *Das Kapital*. On the other hand, he proceeds on the assumption that in substance he has already completed this part. It is obvious that the "Theories of Surplus Value" are indeed part and parcel of the total design of *Das Kapital*. "Indeed," runs a letter of 1877, "I privately began *Das Kapital* in exactly the reverse order to that in which it is being presented to the public." The historico-critical part was, the pre-requisite and premise for the emergence of Books I to III, the theoretical part of *Das Kapital*. When in 1861 Marx set himself to prepare all this, and started to edit the manuscript of the *Grundrisse* on which he had begun four years previously, he needed a fresh confrontation with the bourgeois economy, in particular that of the British classicists, to clarify his ideas. The sub-title, *Kritik der politischen Ökonomie*, given to *Das Kapital*, applies in the first instance as a critical analysis of politico-economic theories.

In line with Marx's own intention, it was Friedrich Engels' plan to publish the "Theories of Surplus Value" as Book IV of *Das Kapital*; but though he had mentioned this in the Foreword to the edition of Book II as being what he meant to do, he was unable to carry it further. The material was first published between 1905 and 1910 by Karl Kautsky, but as a separate document, and without any grasp of the distinctive structure of Marx's work, in which historico-critical analysis is inextricably interwoven and bound up with theoretical exposition and argument. Only during the nineteen-fifties did a Russian edition appear, arranged according to Marx's original scheme, to be followed in 1965 by an edition of the original German text, connecting up with the three Books of *Das Kapital*.

It was more than a century, therefore, before Marx's historico-critical work, incorporating the cornerstone of his *Critique of Political Economy*, was published in a scientifically responsible edition and in the original language. The circumstance typifies the very arduous way in which his economic analysis developed. The "birth pangs" were so protracted and so painful that even the greatly reduced and condensed form in which the original plan of the *Kritik zur politischen Ökonomie* was transposed into the design of *Das Kapital* proved almost too much for the author to cope with. When he did eventually manage to bring out Book I of *Das Kapital*, it was as though giving birth to this one and only child very nearly cost the mother her life. In a letter written in April 1867 he describes how he "was all the time hovering on the edge of the grave. I was therefore obliged to employ every moment available to me in an effort to finish the work; and I have sacrificed to it my health, my happiness and my family . . . I laugh at so-called 'practical' men and their sagacity. If one wanted to be a brute beast, one could of course turn one's back on all the sufferings of mankind and save one's own skin. But I would have thought myself really unpractical to peg out without having fully completed my Book, at any rate in manuscript."

To find an explanation for the "birth pangs" of the *Critique of Political Economy* one could, of course, adduce the "fantastical" strain in Marx's character; but a psychological explanation of that sort in fact depends on a circular argument; and, what is more, it conflicts with the speed and apparent ease with which the same man produced other works, such as the *Communist Manifesto*. One has to look for the explanation more in the peculiar character of Marx's critical method itself.

Friedrich Engels points the way to it in the Foreword to Book II of *Das Kapital*, which he himself published, when he asks what is really new in Marx's theory of surplus value, compared with the theories put out by various predecessors and contemporaries. How is it that Marx's theory struck home like a bolt from the blue—in every civilized country too—whereas those of all his socialist predecessors went up in smoke, leaving not a wrack behind? He finds the answer in an illustration taken from the history of chemistry.

The theory that received general support up to the end of the eighteenth century was the phlogistic theory, according to which combustion consisted essentially in this: that a certain hypothetical substance, an absolute combustible named phlogiston, separated from the burning body. This theory sufficed to explain most of the chemical phenomena then known, although it had to be considerably strained in some cases. But in 1774 Priestley succeeded in producing a certain kind of air which was free from phlogiston. "Dephlogisticated air", he called it. Shortly after, Scheele obtained the same kind of air in Sweden and demonstrated its presence in the atmosphere. He also found that this kind of air disappeared, whenever some body was burned in it or in ordinary air and therefore he called it "fire-air". He drew the conclusion that the combination arising from the union of phlogiston with one of the components of the atmosphere (that is to say, from combustion), was nothing but fire or heat which escaped through the glass.

Priestley and Scheele had produced oxygen without knowing what they had in front of them. They remained imprisoned within the phlogistic categories, as they had encountered them. The element destined to upset all phlogistic views and to revolutionize chemistry remained barren in their hands. But Priestley had immediately communicated his discovery to Lavoisier in Paris, and Lavoisier, with the help of this new fact, now analysed the entire phlogistic chemistry. He first discovered that this new kind of air was a new chemical element; that in combustion the mysterious element does not vanish from the burning body, but that this new element combines with that body. Thus he put the whole of phlogistic chemistry, which in its phlogistic form had stood on its head, squarely on its feet. And although he did not produce oxygen simultaneously and independently of the other two, as he claimed later on, he nevertheless is the real discoverer of oxygen vis-à-vis the others who had only produced it, without having the least suspicion of what it was they had produced.

Well now, says Engels, proceeding with his argument, as Lavoisier relates to Priestley and Scheele, so does Marx to his predecessors. The existence of that part of the value of a product which we now call surplus value had been ascertained long before Marx; it had also been stated with more or less precision what it consisted of, namely, the product of the labour for which the person acquiring command of the product had paid no equivalent. But there was no getting any further. Some (the classical bourgeois economists) investigated at most the quantitative proportion in which the product of labour was divided between the worker and the owner of the means of production. Others (the socialists) found this division unjust and looked for utopian means of abolishing the injustice. Both parties remained prisoners of the economic categories as they had encountered them.

Now Marx appeared on the scene; and he took a view directly opposite to that of all his predecessors. Where they had seen a solution (*Lösung*), he saw only a problem. He saw that he was dealing neither with dephlogisticated air nor with fire-air, but with oxygen. He discovered that it was not here simply a matter of baldly stating an economic fact or of pointing out the conflict between this fact and eternal justice and true morality, but of explaining a fact which was destined to revolutionize all economics and offered to the one who knew how to use it the key to an understanding of all capitalist production. With this fact as his starting-point he examined all the economic categories, the whole body of categories employed up to then, just as Lavoisier, with oxygen as his touchstone, had examined the categories of phlogistic chemistry in current use.

In order to understand what surplus value was Marx had to find out what value was. He had to criticize above all Ricardo's theory of value. Hence he analysed labour's value-producing property and ascertained for the first time what labour produced value, and why and how it did so. He found that value is, in fact, nothing but condensed labour of *this* kind. Next, he examined the relation of commodities to money and demonstrated how and why commodities and commodity-exchange are bound to engender the opposition between commodity and money—and that because of the attribute of value intrinsic to commodities. The theory of money he based on this is the first exhaustive theory, which, Engels adds, has now been tacitly accepted everywhere. Marx further analysed the transformation of money into capital and demonstrated that this is based on the purchase and sale of labour-power. By substituting labour-power, the value-producing property, for labour he solved at a single stroke the difficulties which had proved the downfall of the Ricardian school: the impossibility of harmonizing the mutual exchange of capital and labour with Ricardo's law that value is determined by labour. By establishing the distinction between constant and variable capital he was the first to succeed in tracing (*darzustellen*) the process of the formation of surplus value in its real course and in the minutest detail, and so to succeed in explaining it (*erklären*)—a feat which none of his predecessors had achieved. In other words, he established a distinction within capital itself; neither his socialist predecessors nor the bourgeois economists knew what to do with this distinction, although it does in fact furnish the key to the solution of the most complicated economic problems. On analysing surplus value yet further, he found its two forms: absolute and relative surplus value. And he showed the differing but in both cases decisive role played by surplus value in the history of capitalist production. On the basis of this surplus value he developed the first rational theory of wages we have, and for the first time drew up an outline of the history of capitalist accumulation, with a sketch of the course its history has taken.

Thus far, the argument presented by Engels. We have followed it here quite deliberately, step by step, because it opens a way to the heart of Marx's critical method. Although he does not actually say so, Engels is making advance use here of an analogy which Marx uses himself in Book III of *Das Kapital*. As about nine years elapsed between the publication of Book II (1885) and Book III (1894), in both cases by Engels, he was perhaps not even aware of having borrowed the comparison from Marx himself. At all events, it is to Engels' credit that by using it he was able to get at the core of Marx's critical method and give us a clearer picture of it than Marx himself was able to do.

In Book III, which is entitled "The United Process of Capitalist Production", the subject of the first chapter is "Cost Price and Profit". Marx first argues that profit is the same thing as surplus value, only in a mystified form that is none the less a necessary outgrowth of the capitalist mode of production. He then shows that the excess value realized in the sale of a commodity (the surplus value) appears to the capitalist as an excess of its selling price over its value as a commodity, whereas in reality the surplus value is the excess of the value over the cost price of the commodity. Because of this mystification, the capitalist imagines that the surplus value incorporated in a commodity springs out of the sale itself, whereas in fact the surplus value is only realized through the sale. The bourgeois economy, because it remains the prisoner of this mystification, is unable to offer any real explanation of how profit is formed, because on its false assumptions profit can only appear to be a "creation out of nothing". He then comments critically on Malthus in particular, and concludes that Malthus is unable to explain the sale of commodities above their value, "since all arguments of this sort never, in effect, fail to be reduced to the same thing as the once-famed negative weight of phlogiston". Marx also takes Proudhon into his *Critique*, particularly the idea that the cost-price of a commodity constitutes its actual value, and that, on the other hand, surplus value springs from selling the product above its value. This "thoughtless conception . . . has been heralded . . . as a newly discovered secret of socialism by Proudhon with his customary quasi-scientific charlatanry."

So here is Marx himself drawing a parallel between both a bourgeois and a socialist economy on the one hand, and on the other the phlogistic theory of eighteenth-century chemistry, exploded by the discovery of oxygen. But this is not the first time that Marx has ventured into such terrain. The first chapter of *Zur Kritik der politischen Ökonomie* (1859) starts with an analysis of the distinction between use-value and exchange-value. Use-value as such lies beyond (*jenseits*) the horizon of political economy. Use-value only comes within its purview as the material basis which directly underlies a definite economic relation called exchange-value. Only the latter has an economic significance. Thus, entirely apart from their natural forms and without regard to the specific kind of wants for which they serve as use-values, commodities in certain quantities equal each other, take each other's place in exchange, pass as equivalents, and in spite of their variegated appearance, represent the same entity. Use-values are primarily means of existence. Conversely, however, these means of existence are themselves products of social life, the result of an expenditure of man's vital power, labour materialized (*vergegenständlichte*) or turned into an object. As the embodiment (*Materiatur*) of social labour, all commodities are the crystallization of the same entity.

Basing himself on this analysis, Marx now goes on to examine more closely the character of this entity, that is to say, of labour, which is expressed in exchange value. In this context he chooses an analogy from the field of chemistry, namely, the existence of oxygen. Let us suppose that one ounce of gold, one ton of iron, one quarter of wheat and twenty yards of silk represent equal exchange-values. As equivalents, in which the qualitative difference between their use-values has been eliminated, they represent equal volumes of the same kind of labour. The labour which is equally embodied (*sich vergegenständlicht*) in all of them must be uniform, homogeneous, simple labour; in the case of this labour it makes no difference whether it be manifested in iron, gold, wheat or silk, just as it makes no difference in the case of oxygen whether it appears in the rust of iron, in the atmosphere, the juice of a grape or human blood. But the digging for gold, the extraction of iron from a mine, the raising of wheat and the weaving of silk are so many kinds of labour, differing in quality. Indeed, what appears from a realistic viewpoint (*sachlich*) as a diversity of use-values, from the standpoint of the productive process (*prozessierend*) appears as a variegation of the activity that engenders the use-values. Since the labour which creates exchange-values is neutral *vis-à-vis* the particular material of the use-values, it is also neutral *vis-à-vis* the particular form of the labour itself. Furthermore, the different use-values are the products of the activity of different individuals, and thus the result of instances of labour differing individually the one from the other. But as exchange-values, they represent the same homogeneous labour, that is, labour from which the individuality of the workers has been eliminated. Labour which creates exchange-value is therefore abstract general labour.

In the first chapter of Book I of *Das Kapital* we find this piece of exposition recurring almost word for word, with an interesting illustration. The mutual exchange of quantities of different commodities presupposes that in so far as they constitute exchange-values, those quantities must be reducible to a third factor. A simple illustration from geometry will make this clear. In order to calculate and compare the areas of rectilinear figures we decompose them into triangles. But we reduce the triangle itself to a formula totally different from its visible figure, namely, half the product of the base into the altitude. In the same way the exchange-values of commodities must be reducible to something common to them all, of which thing they represent a greater or less quantity. This common "something" cannot be a geometrical, physical, chemical or any other sort of natural property of the commodities. Such material properties claim our attention only in so far as they affect the utility of those commodities, that is, make them use-values. But the exchange of commodities is evidently an act characterized by a total abstraction from use-values . . . As use-values, commodities are, above all, of different qualities, but as exchange-values they can only be of different quantity, and so do not contain an atom of use-value. Discounting, then, the use-value of commodities, they have only one common property left, that of being products of labour. Of their material existence there is no residue other than the same spectral objectivity (*gespenstige Gegenständlichkeit*), no more than a congelation of homogeneous human labour. Looked at as crystals of this social substance, which they all have in common, these things are values, that is to say, commodity-values.

Taken together with the analysis provided by Engels, the arguments expounded by Marx offer in principle a sufficient basis for grasping the essence of his critical method. Nevertheless, there remains even now the fundamental difficulty that whilst the analogy with the field of the natural sciences is totally adequate and indeed provides the key to the secret of Marx's analysis, even then one cannot begin to get anywhere (as Engels puts it) so long as one does not know how to use the key. The fact is, an analogy with scientific research only takes us part of the way, since the whole area of economics is substantially different in kind from that of the physical sciences. Not until we understand this distinction are we in a position to open the door to which the analogy furnishes the key. Then again, Marx himself adds to the difficulty by at the same time drawing a parallel with the field of geometry, which itself is essentially different from that of the physical sciences, even though up to a point both areas do admittedly apply the same sort of method to the solution of problems.

In order to find our way through this complex nexus of problems, we shall start from the analogy Marx has given between the labour which creates exchange-values and oxygen. That analogy presupposes a knowledge of what oxygen is; and this concept in turn assumes the previous analysis first completed by the chemist, Lavoisier. The fact that labour creates exchange-values was known before Marx, just as oxygen was known and had been produced by investigators like Priestley and Scheele prior to Lavoisier's discovery. But before Lavoisier's discovery there was no possibility of understanding *what* had been produced, or in other words, *what* oxygen is, as the categories of phlogistic chemistry were barring the way to such an understanding. Similarly, prior to Marx's critical analysis the possibility had been denied to economics of grasping the essential nature of exchange-value and so of reaching any real understanding of surplus value. Phlogistic chemistry explained the nature of combustion by postulating a hypothetical substance, phlogiston, which escapes from the burning material. When it had been established that the weight of metals heated in the atmosphere increases, some champions of the theory ascribed a negative weight to the phlogiston. Marx compares the way in which in the field of political economy people were trying to explain surplus value with these phlogistic hypotheses which, as he puts it, more or less amount to assuming a creation *ex nihilo*.

The analogy with Lavoisier's work points the way to an understanding of Marx's analytical method. Just as Priestley and Scheele had already produced the element which Lavoisier was to call "oxygen", at the same time they had no idea of what they were doing. First, a revolution in phlogistic chemistry was necessary. Whilst the production of oxygen provided an opening for this, it was not in itself enough to set such a radical change in motion. That required a fundamental renovation of chemistry, the creation of new categories. Although both his predecessors had produced "oxygen", Lavoisier was the first to *discover* oxygen, because he replaced the inadequate categories of phlogistic chemistry with adequate ones, thus making possible the notion of oxygen as a new element that combines with the burning substance. Similarly, Marx's analysis of surplus value signified a revolution in economic science. Although surplus value was known to exist, it was he who *discovered* it, because his was the first analysis capable of creating adequate categories for understanding the origin and nature of surplus value.

As Lavoisier, using Priestley's observations to help him, had subjected the whole of phlogistic chemistry to investigation, so Marx did the same with the current "theories of surplus value"; but this investigation was inseparably bound up with an analysis of the economic process itself. Just as in the illustration from geometry, which he himself employed, a comparison of the areas of rectilinear figures only becomes possible when these are decomposed into triangles, and the triangle itself is then reduced to a mathematical formula, so Marx analysed the economic process first into exchange-values, which he then reduced to abstract, general human labour, in so far as that labour creates exchange-values. This abstract, general labour he compares, on the one hand, with a mathematical formula, and, on the other with, oxygen. The correspondence between the two analogies is this. Both the mathematical formula and the chemical element, oxygen, can be the common denominator for a comparison of very different things: in the first instance, every possible sort of triangle; and in the second case, all substances whatever, containing oxygen. Yet there is, on the other hand, a fundamental difference between the two analogies. In geometry the mathematical formula is a pure abstraction, whereas oxygen is a chemical element which experiment can detect and establish.

Now, by using both analogies, Marx reveals the distinctive character of his method, which, on the one hand, is purely analytical and, on the other, is engendered by the encounter with the empirical terrain of the economic process, the phenomena of which demand an analysis that will make it possible to understand and explain them. This brings us close to the heart of the problem. For it consists in the fact that the so-called empirically ascertainable phenomena of the economic process at the same time have a specific character directly akin to that of the mathematical analysis of geometrical figures. Once again we must hear what Marx has to say. Entirely in keeping with the geometrical illustration, he puts it in the first chapter of *Zur Kritik der politischen Ökonomie* like this: "In order to measure commodities by the labour-time contained in them, the different kinds of labour must be reduced to uniform, homogeneous, simple labour, in short, to labour which is qualitatively the same, and therefore differs only in quantity." This is paralleled in every respect by the illustration of the reduction of all possible triangles to one and the same mathematical formula.

But then comes a passage of crucial importance: "This reduction appears to be an abstraction; but it is an abstraction which occurs daily in the social process of production. The conversion of all commodities into labour-time is no greater abstraction nor a less real process than the chemical reduction of all organic bodies to air." In this utterance we can recognize the combination of analogies: there is the geometrical-cum-mathematical abstraction or reduction, and also the abstraction or conversion (*Auflösung*) which occurs in chemical reduction. But the most important element in this passage is embodied in the proposition that an abstraction which would appear to be the preserve of the geometrical-mathematical method, occurs in reality, nay, takes place daily in the social process of production. "Labour, thus measured by time, does not appear (*erscheint*) in fact as the labour of different individuals, but the various working individuals appear rather as no more than organs of labour." This applies not only to unskilled labour but to skilled labour as well. "This kind of labour resolves itself into composite unskilled labour . . . This is not the place to consider the laws which regulate this reduction. It is clear, however, that such reduction does take place; for as exchange-value the product of the most skilled labour is in certain proportions equivalent to the product of unskilled average labour." In other words, analogously to the reduction of complex rectilinear figures to triangles.

The central problem now is this: that the crucial abstraction in the economic process is the reduction to a unity (or entity) of a basically different order, just as the reduction of areas in geometry to a mathematical formula is likewise a transition to another order, namely, from a visible figure to a mathematical expression, which abstracts from all representational extension. Analogously, this transition occurs in the economic process where exchange-value is determined by labour-time. The following three aspects are crucial in this regard: (a) the reduction of labour to simple (unskilled) labour, devoid of any quality; (b) the specific way in which labour, which creates exchange-value and so produces commodities, becomes social labour; (c) the distinction between labour as producer of use-values and labour as the creator of exchange-values.

If we equate the visible geometrical figure to the use-value of a product of labour, then the mathematical formula is equivalent to the exchange-value. This abstracts from the geometrical, physical, chemical or other kind of natural properties of a commodity. Yet it is precisely through the exchange-value that the labour of the individual, which creates use-values, becomes social labour. The heart of the problem resides in the fact that the labour of the individual becomes social labour only by taking on the form of its direct opposite, the form of abstract universal labour.

Exchange-value is, in fact, a social relation between persons; but in its manifestation this reality appears as it were in reverse (*sich gleichsam verkehrt darstellt*), namely, as a relation in the disguise of a thing (*unter dinglicher Hülle verstecktes Verhältnis*). Just as a pound of iron and a pound of gold represent the same weight in spite of their different physical and chemical properties, so do two use-values, as commodities containing the same quantity of labour-time, represent the same exchange-value. Exchange-value thus appears as a social property naturally inherent in use-values, as a property which they possess by virtue of being things. Appearing in this form, use-values can be exchanged for one another in definite proportions or form equivalents, just as simple chemical substances combine in certain proportions, and form chemical equivalents. In commodities this mystification is as yet very simple; but in higher productive relations this semblance of simplicity disappears. That, Marx concludes, is why the modern economists who sneer at the illusions of the monetary system exhibit the same illusions as soon as they have to deal with higher categories—capital, for example. "These illusions appear in the expression of naive astonishment, when what they have just thought to have defined with great difficulty as a thing suddenly appears as a social relation and then reappears to tease them again as a thing, before they have barely managed to define it as a social relation."

It must by now be clear to what a complicated analysis Marx was committed in the cause of probing and searching out the specific nature of the economic process. His critical method is *sui generis*, with a character all its own. On one hand, it is analogous with the abstractive and reductive method used in the mathematical analysis of geometrical figures, but for a surprising reason—because of the method of abstraction which the social process itself employs in the reality of everyday life. On the other hand, his method is analogous to the way in which in the history of chemistry oxygen is discovered as a new element—yet with this crucial difference, that the analogous "element" which Marx discovered, namely, the specific character of surplus value, is the direct opposite of a physical element. A fundamental aspect of his discovery is the very fact that he tore the veil from the mystification which perverts a social relation between human beings into a natural property inherent in things as such.

The multidimensional character of Marx's critical method offers a real obstacle to a full comprehension of it. The comparison with Lavoisier properly puts it in the succession of scientific revolutions. The historian, Thomas S. Kuhn, in *The Structure of Scientific Revolutions* (1962), analyses Lavoisier's discovery as a classic example of the way in which revolutions in the history of the natural sciences come about. What Engels calls "categories" in Kuhn's terminology is a "paradigm": it is a "paradigm change" that activates a scientific revolution. Kuhn also argues that this entails a combination of two closely interrelated factors, namely, "discovery", the demonstrating of new facts ("novelties of fact") and "invention", the creation of a new theory ("novelties of theory"). An analogous distinction is made by Engels, when he distinguishes between Priestley's work which "produced" (*dargestellt*) oxygen and Lavoisier's work as the "discoverer" (*Entdecker*) of oxygen. The conformity between Engel's analysis and Kuhn's goes one stage further, where the latter concludes that after a scientific revolution the scientist not only uses another "paradigm" but finds himself in another world ("after a revolution scientists are responding to a different world"). This he illustrates with the aid of *Gestalt* experiments, first written up by Stratton in 1897, in an article entitled *Vision without inversion of the retinal image*. In our own century these experiments have been taken further. The subject of the experiment is given a special pair of spectacles which invert the image. At first he sees everything upside down, because the organ of sight functions as it had learnt to function without the spectacles. After an initial phase in which the subject is totally disorientated and undergoes an acute personal crisis, he learns slowly but surely to feel at home in this new world. Usually after a transitional phase in which his vision is simply confused, he begins to see things as he used to before the spectacles were put on. The assimilation of a previously anomalous visual field has changed the field itself. Literally as well as metaphorically, the subject has undergone a revolutionary transformation of vision.

Indeed, Engels expresses himself in very much the same way when he says that Lavoisier was the first to place all chemistry, which in its phlogistic form had stood on its head, squarely on its feet. Without actually saying so, Engels returns to a simile already found in *Die deutsche Ideologie*, which he and Marx had written together: "Consciousness (*Bewusstsein*) can never be anything else but conscious being (*das bewusste Sein*) and the being of men is their real life-process. If in the whole of ideology men and their relations appear upside down as in a *camera obscura*, this is due as much to their historical life-process as the inversion of objects on the retina is due to their immediate physical life-process." There follows an explication of Marx's critical method: "In direct opposition to German philosophy, which comes down from heaven to earth, here there is ascension from earth to heaven ... At the point where speculation ceases —that is, with real life—actual, positive science, the representation (*Darstellung*) of real activity, the practical process of human development begins. When the vapourings of consciousness cease, real knowledge must surely take their place. With the representation of reality a self-sufficient philosophy loses its means of existence."

In the postscript (*Nachwort*) to the second edition (1873) of

Book I of *Das Kapital*, again without actually referring to it, Marx elaborates upon these views when he explains the specific character of his critical method as distinct from Hegel's. "Of course, the method of presentation (*Darstellungsweise*) must differ in form from that of enquiry (*Forschungsweise*). The latter has to appropriate the material in detail, to analyse its different forms of development, to trace out their inner connection. Only after this work has been done can the actual movement be presented in conformity with it. If this is done successfully, if the life of the subject-matter is ideally reflected as in a mirror, then it may appear as if we had before us a mere *a priori* construction. My dialectical method is not only different from Hegel's, but fundamentally its direct opposite. To Hegel . . . the process of thinking, which under the name of 'the Idea' he even transforms into an independent subject, is the demiurge of the real process, which itself is only the external, phenomenal form (*Erscheinung*) of the Idea. Conversely, for me the ideal is nothing other than the material, transmuted and translated in the human brain (*das im Menschenkopf umgesetzte und übersetzte Materielle*) . . . The mystification which dialectic suffers in Hegel's hands by no means prevents him (however) from being the first to present its general form of working in a comprehensive and conscious manner. With him dialectic is standing on its head. It must be turned right side up (*umstülpen*, i.e., literally, 'to turn it inside out') again, if one is to discover the rational kernel within the mystical shell."

So far the analogy between Marx and Lavoisier would still seem to be totally applicable. Just as Lavoisier set to rights phlogistic chemistry, so Marx did the same for Hegel's dialectic. But as we have already seen, between the critique of political economy and the method used in the natural sciences there is a fundamental point of difference, in that the sphere of economics is not nature but the human and social process of production. The "inversion" occurs not only on the retina and in the brain of the scientific investigator but in the actual thing being investigated, that is, in the very process by which the object of economics, the commodity, comes into existence. As soon as a natural product of human labour begins to function as a commodity (so Marx argues in the first chapter of *Das Kapital*) it changes into something still sensory yet transcendent (*sinnlich übersinnliches*). It stands, not just with its feet on the ground, but in relation to all other commodities it puts itself on its head.

This is why the critique of political economy calls for a more complex method than do the physical sciences. There is an extra dimension, as it were. Lavoisier became the discoverer (*Entdecker*, or, in Kuhn's terminology, "inventor") of oxygen. After it had been produced (*dargestellt*, or, in Kuhn's terminology, "discovered") by another chemist, Priestley, Lavoisier created the theory, the categories, the "paradigm", calculated to enable us to understand what oxygen is. Marx's investigation of surplus value, on the other hand, required a quite different approach; for surplus value was not, like oxygen, something produced (*dargestellt*) by earlier economists, but is being produced (*dargestellt*) day by day in the social process of production itself—produced, indeed, by a process which stands on its own head. It is not enough to put on a special pair of spectacles so that one can watch this process inverted, that is, right side up; but we must invert the process itself, if our analysis is to be an adequate one. Marx's mode of presentation really means that by his use of critical analysis *he* must produce, must present (*darstellen*) the truth and reality of the object. The reality being investigated is a perverted world (*verkehrte Welt*), which gives rise to a perverted world consciousness (*verkehrtes Weltbewusstsein*). It is the task of a critique to present (*darzustellen*) an inversion of that perverted world, to present it, that is, "normal side up"; and in so doing it at the same time "rights" the inverted consciousness. The critique of political economy follows no other road than the critique of religion.

10

A new heaven and a new earth

Now that the end of this series of lectures is in sight, it is expedient for me to pick up the threads once more from the beginning. In fixing upon the central theme, my intention was to operate within the field defined by the Trust Disposition and Settlement of the Gifford Lectures as "natural theology". The critical theology, which is what I have in mind in these lectures, I see not just as a possible interpretation of natural theology, but as even a worthy descendent of it, qualified and competent to be its legitimate heir and successor. If the idea underlying the tradition of natural theology is not to become a dead letter, then it must be translated and extended in categories adapted to the questions of our time.

And in this connection the thing itself—what it is all really about—is of more importance than the terminology. If the meaning of the term "natural theology" is open to varying interpretation, and indeed in the course of tradition has signified many different things, the term "critical theology" would seem to be equally vulnerable; it threatens to fall, as it were, between two stools.

On the one hand, an attempt to continue the tradition of natural theology, according to whatever interpretation, runs the risk of falling back behind the radical critique of Karl Barth, who rejected natural theology as an inherently contradictory aim to propose, a contradiction in terms. In the Introduction to his Gifford Lectures he rightly rendered his account of this. Indeed, a "critical theology" is only justifiable if and when it has fully assimilated a critique based on a "dialectical theology".

On the other hand, there seems to be an unbridgeable gulf between a critical theology and the "critique of heaven and earth" as projected by Karl Marx. To the extent that such a theology comes within the scope of Marx's thinking, it would appear to fall under the withering judgment pronounced in *Die Heilige Familie* upon the crypto-theological *kritischen Kritik*, the "critical critique", of Bruno Bauer and his associates. Can a critical theology contain anything but a theological, i.e., a speculative, critique, a specimen of the reprehensible *deutsche Ideologie*?

All things considered, the scheme presented by this series of lectures seems doomed from the start to miscarry and to be quite unacceptable to the judgment of Lord Gifford, Karl Barth and Karl Marx in turn, or indeed of all three together. The justification for the choice of my central theme can only lie therefore in my settled conviction that theology today has an imperative need for such an enterprise. The critical theology I have in mind is a risky venture, but a necessary one; for what is at stake is nothing more or less than the future of theology itself. Furthermore, it is no blind venture, because there is most certainly a compass; and when it comes to mapping out a course a number of obstacles and unnavigable zones may in any case be noted. It will be enough to recall some of the aspects already considered.

In the lecture in which a start was made with the "Critique of Heaven" I characterized the genesis of Marx's critique as the transformation of theology. At the same time I instanced Karl Barth's total disregard of Marx in his work on the Protestant theology of the nineteenth century as a symptom of the dilemma with which Marx confronted the theological tradition. The dilemma was accentuated in the first lecture on the "Critique of Earth"; and the conclusion was that Marx's *Critique of Political Economy*, in particular, cannot be adequately comprehended and accommodated within the traditional framework of theology. In other words, because Marx's *Critique*, historically and in principle, can only be understood as a transformation of theology, it therefore confronts theology with the inescapable need for a transformation. This cycle of lectures can and is intended to do no more than indicate the direction in which such a theological transformation must come about. When theology steers in the direction of Marx's "critique of heaven and earth", that in itself will mark the beginning of the transformation which must precede any adequate understanding of Marx's critical method. These lectures are meant to help shape a course; they are prolegomena to the navigation that is still to come.

From this kind of transformation of theology I would expect a new prospect to emerge for the tradition of a "natural theology"; for there can be no future for it along any familiar path. In my opening lecture on the "critique of earth" I have already pointed to the context to which "natural theology" continued to be assimilated, along with ethics, jurisprudence and the social and political sciences, including economics, right up to the first half of the nineteenth century. I also pointed out, in Marx's historical account of British materialism, certain obvious traces of a vision of an all-round materialism, which slowly but surely disappeared, when from the seventeenth century onwards the world came to be envisaged more and more on a mechanical and mathematical basis. Again, in Marx's account of the history of political economy in Britain we find the same sort of vision of a lost totality, a lost wholeness. In the postscript to the second edition of the first Book of *Das Kapital* Marx pays his respects to the "classical political economy" of which he sees David Ricardo as being the last great representative. He takes 1830 to be the year in which that economy finally expired. "In France and England the bourgeoisie had seized political power. From then on the class struggle, in practice and in theory, took on more and more outspoken and threatening forms. It sounded the knell of scientific bourgeois economy. From then on the issue was no longer whether this or that theorem was true; the crucial question now was whether a given theorem was useful to capital or harmful, expedient or inexpedient, politically dangerous or not." Marx's premiss is that "political economy can remain a science only so long as the class struggle is latent or manifests itself only in isolated and sporadic phenomena."

Without whittling down this assertion we may wonder whether it is wholly satisfactory from Marx's own standpoint.

I would simply recall the broad context of "Moral Philosophy" within which Adam Smith developed his specialized economic studies; the *Wealth of Nations* still has a relation to the classical system of natural law that was rooted deep in European history. When Marx discourses with Adam Smith, he is in a sense in dialogue with the classical tradition which Adam Smith had kept alive. Even from this point of view, the *Critique of Right* and the *Critique of Political Economy* run in the same groove. Not without reason does Hegel's *Grundlinien der Philosophie des Rechts* bear the sub-title *Naturrecht und Staatswissenschaft*. Through Hegel as its last great representative, Marx is in dialogue with classical natural law. Moreover, the term *Staatswissenschaft* (political science) also embraces political economy; and the *Staatsökonomie* of Adam Smith and Ricardo is treated explicitly by Hegel, in the introductory section (section 189) to the "System of needs" in his *Philosophy of Right*, as the typical science of the "Understanding", which by analysis extracts the simple rudiments from an infinite number of facts. Hegel's contemporary, Ricardo, is discussed by Marx as the last great representative of the classical political economy. Ricardo "in the end, consciously makes the antagonism of class interests, of wages and profits, of profits and rent, the starting-point of his investigations, naively taking this antagonism for a social law of Nature. But by this start the science of bourgeois economy had reached the limits beyond which it could not pass."

Marx's attitude to Ricardo's "naivety" would have been less indulgent, had it not been integral to the "classical" nature of Ricardo's notion of the "social law of nature" (*gesellschaftlichse Naturgesetz*). He can still recognize in Ricardo's idea of the matter the definition, traceable right back to scholasticism, which, equates natural law (*lex naturalis*) (*justum naturale*) both with reasonable truth (*ratio recta*), and, with what is socially useful or necessary (*expediens et necessarium*). After Ricardo, that unity falls apart: not truth (*ratio recta*) but only usefulness, utility, that matters to the capitalist (*expediens et necessarium*. Marx is really saying in so many words that with the political asendancy of the bourgeoisie, i.e. with the complete breakthrough of "civil society" (*bürgerliche Gesellschaft*), the classical system of natural law and with it the classical political economy was dead and buried. The "impassable limits" *unüberschreitbare) Schranke)* of the science of bourgeois economy are none other than those of the natural-law system. Hegel confronts Marx with the same problem as Ricardo: there is absolutely no way in which the advent of bourgeois (civil) society can be made to square with the classical rules of the natural-law system. The year 1830 is the historical landmark (Hegel's death occurred in the next year; Ricardo had died in 1823). Like Athens' own Themistocles, Marx sees himself faced with the task of grounding society upon a new basis, a "new element". That is possible only by means of a critique: radical analysis of the primary principles on which the new period of world history must depend. A return to the classical system of natural law is out of the question; and yet what Marx sees in his mind's eye is a totality of thought which is as significant for the new period as the classical system of natural law had been throughout a bygone period of Europe's history.

In this perspective it really does make sense to think in terms of a continuation or "implementation" of natural theology. Just as the tradition of "natural theology" is inseparably bound up with that of "natural law", in which political economy also had a place, so the collapse of that tradition entails at the same time the collapse of "natural theology"—just as on the other side it sounded the knell of the classical political economy. To that extent Lord Gifford was simply too late when in 1887 he founded a Lectureship on natural theology. Indeed, from a strictly theological viewpoint, Karl Barth's radical opposition to natural theology is the right answer to the questions posed by the modern period of history. And yet, if Barth had chosen not the Scottish Confession but Scottish political economy as the subject of his Gifford Lectures, he would have had a much broader view of the total context of "mental" and "social" sciences within which natural theology was included. From within a perspective of this kind Barth might well have made an important contribution to a radical transformation of natural theology. But as I pointed out in my first lecture, he stops short at that very point. In Barth's history of Protestant theology in the nineteenth century Karl Marx is the great absentee. Marx's "critique of heaven and earth" is the eye of the needle through which the theological tradition will have to squeeze if it is to enter the modern period. On the horizon of Marx's critical analysis the prospect looms of a transformed theology able to take a specific but authentic and real position within the total spectrum of the sciences.

The direction in which such a theological transformation will lead us can be inferred from the difference between Karl Barth and Karl Marx where the critique of religion is concerned. In Barth's dogmatics religion is subject to the radical critique of "God's revelation as the superseding (*Aufhebung*) of religion". Religion is unbelief. Religion is defined by Barth as "the attempt by man to justify and sanctify himself *vis-à-vis* an image of God projected by his own reason and his own authority" (*Church Dogmatics*, 1/2, section 17). That definition is a radical one in so far as this aspiration on man's part could embrace every dimension of his existence. But when we examine the way in which Barth actually handles the definition, it turns out that his whole treatment of it is pursued from the very outset at the level of "religion" in the stereotyped sense which the term has acquired in modern usage. His account of the field of religion takes its material from the arsenal furnished by the history and phenomenology of religion; and it is enough to have read Chantepie de la Saussaye's *Lehrbuch der Religions-geschichte* to be able to follow Barth's exposition. Certainly, Barth is too skilled a dialectician to ignore the critical limits of positive religion—mysticism and atheism—but even there he sees these negative phenomena exclusively in the plane of "religion" in the currently accepted sense of the word. Ultimately, his concern with the problem of religion turns out to be engrossed by the dogmatic question of how the "Christian religion" can be liberated from the fatal toils in which the modern concept of "religion" has ensnared it. His radical critique runs parallel to Marx's radical critique of the philosophers to this extent: that Barth also exposes original sin as being a confusion of subject and predicate. "Christianity" or "the Christian religion" is a predicate of a subject which may have other predicates, a species within a genus to which other species also belong. The saving answer to the problem of religion in general and of the "Christian religion" in particular lies therefore in a return to the definition of *religio christiana* as identical with God's revelation in Christ. Subject and predicate are returned to their original position; revelational religion is indeed tied to God's revelation, but God's revelation is not tied to revelational religion.

Measured against nineteenth-century Protestant theology Barth's critique of religion is certainly radical; it might even be regarded as the very spearhead of his whole critique of that theology. The radical character of Barth's critique pales, however, in the light of Marx's critique of religion. Hence the significance of the fact that Marx is deliberately left out of Barth's account of the Protestant theology of the nineteenth century. In that way Barth ensured that there would be no question of discovering and striking at the Achilles' heel of his own theology; for, measured by the yardstick of Marx's critique, Barth's concept of religion remains trapped within the magical ellipse of which Hegel and Feuerbach constitute the focal points.

The critique which Marx directs at Hegel's speculative dialectics in general, and at his speculative philosophy of right in particular, can also be applied to Barth's critique of religion. Let God's revelation be posited as the "superseding" (*Aufhebung*) of religion; but in that case religion is being endorsed just as much on a dialectical-theological basis as it is endorsed in Hegel's philosophy of religion on a dialectical-philosophical one. This parallel remains unaffected by Barth's critique of Hegel's philosophy, which substantially coincides with his critique of religion. For if on Barth's criterion religion is given a higher sanction in Hegel's philosophical "supersession", then Barth's theological "supersession" of religion falls in its turn under Marx's stricture that religion is here acquiring a superior, that is, a theological, sanction; a theological dialectic which closer inspection shows to be akin to philosophical dialectic—for the roots are to be found in speculation.

On the other hand, Barth seems not to pass by Feuerbach's position. Barth apparently presents a lethal critique of Feuerbach by exposing the atheistic critique of religion as itself having been engendered in the womb of religion. In the engagement with Feuerbach, this method works in so far as it hoists the opposing party with his own petard; whereas Feuerbach unmasks theology as concealed anthropology, conversely the atheistic mask of Feuerbach's critique of theology is torn away by Barth, and its true visage, its religious visage, brought to light. But with all this Barth is still in the same arena as Feuerbach and with him falls under the judgment of the *Deutsche Ideologie*: they remain inside the "sphere of influence" of speculative theology and abstract anthropology.

Marx's "critique of heaven and earth" is conducted at three different levels. The first is the level of "religion" in the conventional sense of modern usage. The second level is that of law and politics. The third is the level of political economy. On each of these three levels Marx presents a radical critique of religion. It is radical inasmuch as it defines religion as "a roundabout way of acknowledging man, through an intermediary". The nature of religion, and with it the nature of the critique of religion, changes according to whether we happen to be on the first, second or third level; but on all three he is concerned with religion in the sense of this definition.

Considered from this standpoint, Barth's critique of religion would seem to remain on the first level. At first sight, this might appear to be a very unfair thing to say, if one takes into account the essentially political dimension of Barth's theology. The fact is, apart from the radical-theological opposition to the ideology of National Socialism, formulated in the Barmen Declaration and made concrete in the sufferings of the German "Confessing Church", Barth's theology is at most a brilliant continuation of a familiar theological tradition. Again, Barth's refusal after the second world war to let himself be hustled into an anti-communist ideology goes along with his political-cum-theological resistance to the "twentieth-century myth" of National Socialism and to the "Hitler or Moscow" alternative. In its political dimension, therefore, Barth's theology would rather seem to be an endorsement of the demand voiced by Marx that the critique of religion be transmuted into the critique of politics. In other words, Barth's theology would appear really to proceed on the second level of Marx's critique of religion.

Let us look rather more carefully, therefore. This series of lectures opted for a starting-point in Marx's *Critique of Hegel's Philosophy of Right*, which Marx himself described as a critique of Germany. In my first lecture, I recalled that just a century later this critique of Germany was confirmed with a demonic accuracy in Hitler's Third Reich. The political and theological opposition offered by Karl Barth to the National Socialist myth did in fact pronounce on Germany's situation the judgment formulated by Marx almost a century before. It was a sentence passed upon the mythology of the *Heilige Römische Reich deutscher Nation*—the Holy Roman Empire of the German nation—which persisted in the Christian-Germanic idea of the state and found its absurd outcome in Hitler's Third Reich. This political mythology-cum-critique functions all the time at the first level of Marx's critique of religion. When Marx posits the need to move over from the critique of religion to that of politics, he has in view more than a critique of the idea of the Christian state and of the pagan mythology lurking at the back of it. His critique of Hegel's constitutional law is aimed at the hybrid monstrosity of constitutional monarchy, which he exposes as an impossible amalgam of two impossibilities. So his critique of Hegel's constitutional law proceeds at one and the same time on the first and on the second level. Its target is Hegel's philosophical justification of the Germano-Christian monarchy, as well as Hegel's philosophy of the French Revolution and of the modern, atheistic, constitutional state. Now on this second level of the critique of religion—the critique of the "heaven" of the modern political state—Marx is not followed by Barth. One looks in vain to Barth's theology for an unmasking of the Swiss state, of which he was and always remained a loyal citizen, or even for a critique remotely comparable with his devastating critique of the idea of the Christian-Germanic state and of Hitler's Germany. In this respect Barth's is indeed a "Swiss theology" *par excellence*. His theology simply lacks the categories and the organization for such a critique; and so the third level of Marx's critique of religion lies wholly beyond the purview of this theology.

A theological critique of religion which does not command an analytical method for pushing through from *homo religiosus via* the citizen (*citoyen*) to the *bourgeois*, naturally lacks the equipment for a critique on this third level, the critique of political economy. Whereas the German Karl Marx's critique of religion crossed first the Rhine and then the Channel, the Swiss Karl Barth's critique of religion failed to draw the line from Christian theology and religion *via* the modern state to the modern economy. It stayed on the first level.

As Barth's critique of religion may be regarded as the most basic and radical yet produced by Christian theology, one can gauge from the distance which separates Barth from Marx just how far behind theology is lagging, and what the transformation will be when theology is at last drawn through the gate of Marx's critique of heaven and earth. To illustrate this, I have chosen a central element of Marx's *Critique of Political Economy*, that is, the so-called "economic trinity". At first sight this curious expression, to which I have already pointed, *en passant*, in earlier lectures, looks to be no more than an ironic play on words. Even were it no more than that, the word-play is worth closer investigation; for in the course of these lectures we have not infrequently come across this sort of figurative use of language by Marx, which seemed to contain a fundamental analogy. In this particular case, however, there is a cogent reason anyway for taking Marx's remarkable phrase seriously: namely, in virtue of the central position which the "economic trinity" occupies in his work as a whole. As I indicated on a previous occasion, we find this expression at the close of the third Book of *Das Kapital* and again at the end of the *Theorieën über den Mehrwert*, that is to say, of the fourth Book of *Das Kapital*. In this phrase Marx sums up concisely the basic structure of his work. We may recall that originally Marx had projected a basic scheme in six parts, which was later reduced to *Das Kapital*. Of this sexpartite scheme the "economic trinity" forms the first half, the basis on which the *Critique of Political Economy* rests.

Since the second half of the plan follows the scheme of Hegel's *Philosophy of Right* and of his *Philosophy of History*, it is natural to assume a similar relationship where the first half of the plan is concerned. Indeed we do find in Hegel's *Philosophie der Geschichte* a trinitarian structure, notably in his treatment of the history of the Christian-Germanic world. Hegel divides this into three successive periods. The first ends with Charlemagne, whilst the transition from the second to the third period is the reign of Charles the Fifth in the first half of the sixteenth century. The third period is ushered in by the Reformation. This threefold division supports a trinitarian structure. The

three periods may be distinguished as successively the King-
doms of the Father, of the Son and of the Spirit. On the
analogy of this division, Hegel applies the same trinitarian
principle to the preceding periods of world history. The
Germano-Christian Realm is, in fact, the last in a succession of
four Realms in world history, and in its trinitarian rhythm is,
as it were, a summing up of that world history. The oriental
world, in particular the Persian empire, is the Realm of the
Father, the Greek world is the Realm of the Son, the Roman
world the Realm of the Spirit.

The division into four Realms is something we find in
the closing chapter of Hegel's *Philosophy of Right*, where "world
history" is the subject. When in the *Vorwort* (Preface) to his
Zur Kritik der politischen Ökonomie of 1859 Marx is describing the
outcome of his revision of Hegel's *Philosophy of Right*, he arrives
at a rough subdivision of mankind's history into four periods,
successively determined by asiatic, ancient, feudal and modern
bourgeois relations of production. These four periods or epochs
he characterizes as "so many epochs in the progress of the
economic formation of society". With the period of bourgeois
production-relations "the prehistoric stage of human society"
comes to an end.

It would be of interest in itself to make a comparison of
Marx's fourfold division and Hegel's. In so doing we would be
doing the journey in reverse, as it were, and *via* Hegel's
Philosophy of History translating Marx's consideration of
economic history back into the terms of a trinitarian theology.
What is more, a method of this sort can make direct contact
with the clear traces of a trinitarian structure in Marx's thought,
which I have indicated as being present already in his most
youthful work. We come across such traces again in the preliminary studies for his dissertation; namely, in the triad:
visible heaven, sealed Word, unsealed Word.

This triple division is based on a "trinitarian" philosophy of
history in which the pre-Christian period, the epoch of the
Father, is dominated by the visible heaven; the Christian
period, now approaching its end, is the epoch of the Son, the
sealed Word; and now history awaits the unsealing of the
Word, the coming Realm or Kingdom of the Spirit. What
Marx's dissertation signifies against this background we saw as

an identification with Epicurus' revolution *versus* the visible heaven, which should now be repeated in the revolution *versus* the sealed Word. When we looked more closely at Marx's first economic treatise on the legislation against wood-stealing, this turned out to reflect a trinitarian train of thought in its invocation of the state's inalienable duty to protect the rights of the poor.

This kind of evidence can be further supplemented with data in Marx's economic writings that postulate an analogy between economic and religious history. The contrast between the modern bourgeois economy and that of the preceding period is compared with the paired concepts "protestantism-catholicism" and, parallel to that, with the polarity "Christianity-paganism". This sort of analogy provides some indication of the relationship between Marx's fourfold division of economic history and the similar division that we find in Hegel's *Philosophy of History*. We know from his dissertation that Marx endorses the analogy Hegel posited between the advent of the bourgeois period of modern Europe and that of the Roman period of ancient civilization. All these things together serve to suggest a bipartite pattern underlying Marx's view of economic history, that is, a division into a pre-Christian period and a Christian one, making the main emphasis fall, just as Hegel had done, on the Christian period. Of Hegel's threefold partitioning of Germano-Christian history we find Marx retaining the second and third periods, that is, the feudal period and the modern bourgeois one. These, in Hegel's trinitarian definition, represent the Realm of the Son and the Realm of the Spirit.

When I was discussing Hegel's *Philosophy of Right*, I pointed to a contradiction between two distinct lines of development. One of them issues in the idea of the Germano-Christian state as the fulfilment of world history; but, as against that, there is another one which, *via* bourgeois society and its global expansion, issues in a world history that is the world's court of judgment on states as particular entities. We have seen that Marx's *Critique of Hegel's Philosophy of Right* entails a radicalizing of this second line. If we look at Hegel's trinitarian view of history from within the perspective towards which this second line is pointing us, then the inner contradiction in Hegel's

Philosophy of History stands revealed at its climactic point, that is in the Realm of the Spirit. Not only does Marx's critical analysis bring this contradiction out into the open, but his scalpel also probes down to its roots, that is, to the inherent contradiction in bourgeois society, mirrored in Hegel's philosophy. The dissecting of this interrelationship is carried out in the *Critique of Political Economy*. It subjects Hegel's trinitarian view of history to remarkable and critical exposure, which is clearly evident in the structure of the sexpartite plan of the *Critique of Political Economy*.

Remember that this plan consists of two halves, the first of which comprises the economic trinity: capital, land-holding, wage-labour. In the second half, Marx pursues the line that I referred to as the second line in Hegel's *Philosophy of Right*. This second half is made up of the trinity: state, international trade, world market. If we now look at the sexpartite plan in its entirety, then the *Critique of Political Economy* emerges as the economic critique of Hegel's trinitarian *Philosophy of History*. The critique concentrates on the period characterized by Hegel as the Realm of the Spirit, the modern bourgeois period. Marx radically extends the second line of Hegel's *Philosophy of Right* and projects it on to the field of economics. The economic trinity engenders the Realm or Kingdom of the economic Spirit "unto the ends of the earth": the world market. Christian history approaches its fulfilment when the bourgeoisie, like the eleven disciples at the end of Matthew's Gospel (Matt. 28:16–20), baptize the nations in the name of the economic trinity. The bourgeoisie, says the *Communist Manifesto*, plays a very revolutionary role over the whole surface of the globe, it compels all nations to adopt the bourgeois mode of production. In short, it creates a world after its own image. That is the *Creator Spiritus* of the economic Realm of the Spirit.

These somewhat sketchy pointers must suffice for the present to lend real plausibility to a theological background to the notion of an "economic trinity". Before looking more closely to see what analytical method is applied to this central notion, we now turn first to the theology of Karl Barth. Our purpose here is, by comparing the one with the other, to get an impression of the kind of transformation theology may expect, if and when it is found to be ready to submit itself to Marx's critical method.

Within the tradition of Christian dogmatics as a whole, Barth's revolutionary act was to begin his dogmatics with God's revelation as the root of the doctrine of the Trinity. This took theology from the very start out of the orbit of a generally philosophical type of speculation and concentrated it upon the witness of Scripture. Although Barth takes it as self-evident that the doctrine of the Trinity is not to be found in the Bible directly, in the form of a dogmatic formulation, he does not see that as preventing him from making it the starting-point of his *Dogmatics*. On the contrary, his method entails his seeking the roots of the trinitarian doctrine in God's revelation, to which Scripture is witness. He finds it rooted in the three elements of unveiling, envelopment and proclamation. These elements he further defines as form, freedom, historicity; or Easter, Good Friday, Pentecost; or the Son, the Father, the Spirit.

Because Barth developed the doctrine of the Trinity on the basis of God's revelation, he refers in as many words to a term that stems from the tradition of dogmatics, "economic trinity". This has long served to mark the distinction between the revealed Trinity and the Trinity as the mysterious being of God "from eternity", the "immanent Trinity". It is a principle of Barth's dogmatic method that he starts from God's revelation, that is to say, from the "economic Trinity" and only on *that* basis discourses upon the "immanent Trinity". This dogmatic tradition goes back to the Fathers of the second century A.D. Tertullian's theory regarding the trinitarian economy links up with the Greek word *oikonomia*, which in the New Testament denotes God's eschatological action in history through His Son (Ephes. 1:10; 3:9). With Irenaeus the purpose of the Incarnation, of God's becoming man, namely, "that we may become godlike", is unfolded in the "economy" of salvation history. Thus the term focuses directly on the relation between God's revelation and history. Furthermore, there is a close connection with the technical term "economy" as currently employed in general discourse. In the New Testament the terms *oikonomia* and *oikonomos* usually denote "stewardship" and "steward" respectively (e.g., Luke 12:42; 16:1 ff.); and Paul too understands the term in that sense when he refers to himself as *oikonomos*, steward, of the mysteries of God (1 Cor. 4:1 f.). Indeed, as an apostle he identifies the stewardship entrusted to him with God's "economy" or plan (Ephes. 3:9; Coloss. 1:25). Implicitly, that identification confirms the "economic" origin of the theological terminology as well as the close relationship with the history of events after Pentecost.

Barth does not delve into the tradition of the terminology; but he does offer a radical critique of the theological tradition which claims to discover everywhere—in nature, history, religion, in the human soul—traces of the Trinity (*vestigia trinitatis*). Of course, Barth rejects this idea root and branch, as it represents a typical instance of natural theology. On the one hand, he sees the theology of trinitarian history, inaugurated by Joachim of Flora in the Middle Ages, having its outcome in the secularized mythology of Moeller van den Bruck's *Das dritte Reich*. On the other hand, he draws a line from Augustine's trinitarian interpretation of the structure of human consciousness to modern philosophy, which by way of Descartes, Kant, Schelling and Hegel eventually arrives at Feuerbach. The line is not extended through to Marx; but in such a sketchy survey of the varieties which trinitarian speculation has to offer this would seem unnecessary. The political dimension of Barth's theology gives marked emphasis to his unbending refusal to go in for any sort of speculation. I believe that I reflect what Barth had in mind when I see speculations of this sort, in so far as they take the form of a philosophy of history, as resulting in one or another ideology, whether it be National Socialism, the Soviet ideology, or that of the "free West".

An unconditional "No" to every form of ideological view of history is theologically necessary and justified; but the reverse side of Barth's resistant attitude is his inability to take seriously the problem which the philosophy of history tries to answer. It is the problem of what the relation is between God's revelation and our history, more especially our "Christian" history. Although the aspect or element of the Spirit is described by Barth as historicity (*Geschichtlichkeit*), it says a great deal that this is precisely the aspect he does not persist in exploring further. In the relevant section (section 12) the holy Spirit is discussed only under the aspect of redemption, whereas about historicity nothing is said. The superficial reduction of the notion of religion that is "superseded" by revelation is something I have already matched against the depth of Marx's critique of religion. Since the passage in question (section 12) forms part of the third part, dealing with "the outpouring of the Holy Spirit", here is an indication that the inability to relate the Spirit to history is taking its toll in an inadequate anatomy of religion as a historical reality; and behind that lies the central question of what capacity to analyse this theological method has. In the second part, which has to do with the "incarnation of the Word", Barth attacks the tendency to make revelation a predicate of history. No; on the contrary, history is a predicate of revelation (section 14). Nowhere, however, are we told what this means concretely. Again in the first chapter, which grounds the doctrine of God's revelation in the Word of God, the freedom of God's activity is so absolutely divorced from everything that has to do with our notion of nature and history that the character of history-as-predicate remains an empty concept (section 5). When we have sought in vain for some more concrete representation in the doctrine of God's Providence (section 48–49), in the end even the last volume to appear does nothing to enlighten us. In the section on "the Holy Spirit and the mission of the Christian community" (section 72) "the people of God in world history" are committed to the guiding utterance *Hominum confusione et Dei providentia regitur*; but nowhere can one find any trace of a concrete analysis of this perplexity and disorder among men.

The theology which has made its appearance in the twentieth century as "dialectical theology" or as the "theology of crisis" has as a "critique of heaven" had a refining function; but as a "critique of earth" it has not filled the bill. If the critical format, the strictness of method and the classical structure of Barth's theology turn out to be unable to command sufficient analytical power in this respect, then that puts a fundamental question-mark against the analytical method of theology as such. I would think it a backward step if we were to invoke the aid of other methods of theological approach, whose "critique of Heaven" cannot measure up to the sheer weight and radicality of Barth's critique. Theology as a whole stands confronted here with the still virgin task of a radical critique of heaven *and* of earth.

All this brings us back to Marx's critical analysis of the "economic trinity". It is time we formed a more detailed impression of the method applied there. A fundamental correspondence with the method of Barth's theology is implicit in the diagnosis and the therapy conjoined with it. Marx and Barth alike expose as the original sin of philosophical theology or of theological philosophy, the confusion of subject and predicate. Each man's method consists in a fundamental inversion of this wrong relationship, so that subject and predicate are returned to their right place; and in both their methods the diagnosis is achieved in and through the therapy. The correspondence extends even further and is literally applicable to the "economic trinity". Barth's thesis that revelation is not the predicate of history but, on the contrary, history is a predicate of revelation, holds good also of Marx's critique. The "economic trinity" is not the predicate of history, explained first in some other way, but the "economic trinity" is the subject of history, the substance apart from which history is not to be understood.

It is precisely this far-reaching correspondence that enables us to register, with the greatest possible clarity, the radical difference between the methods of Barth and of Marx. When Barth succeeds in inverting and setting right the wrong relation between subject and predicate, this is a theological leap that transposes the *circulus vitiosus* of the false relation into the *circulus salutis* of the true one. Religion, history as determined by the Fall, these are "superseded" by God's revelation. The possibility of such a crucial leap cannot by definition have its ground in the *circulus vitiosus*; it can only derive from the reality of the *circulus salutis* and only within that be comprehended by faith, in the power of the Holy Spirit. It is a leap from total darkness into total light, a *creatio ex nihilo*; but a leap in which history is "superseded". It is a tremendous merit of Barth's *Dogmatics* that in them the doctrine of God's revelation is developed out of the history of the Incarnation of the Word, and the doctrine of the Trinity derives from that. Yet this gain also becomes a loss, because no real relation is established with our history. The dialectic, it would seem, is not able to overcome the dualism.

Marx's method is basically dialectical. To put it in theological terms, it follows neither the *gratia non tollit, sed perficit naturam* ("grace does not abrogate nature, but perfects it") of natural

277

theology, nor the *gratia tollit naturam* ("grace abrogates, or supersedes nature") of Barth's theology. It neither assumes the possibility of a "leap across" from sin to grace, nor posits a *vicious* (i.e., intractable) impossibility. The *circulus* of sin is in fact not a *circulus vitiosus*; but it does contain an intrinsic impossibility which *because* of its impossibility is destined to supersede itself. The circle is bound sooner or later to explode, it is *per se* non-viable. The moment at which the closed circle bursts apart is the *exodus* from the intrinsic impossibility. The *principium contradictionis* has then demonstrated its truth and its reality, the contradiction is self-destroying. Yet this dialectic has a positive side too, for the *principium contradictionis* is not only a self-annihilating principle but an active principle as well; it acts as a source of motive energy. Marx's analysis lays bare the hidden contradiction in which the visible phenomena are rooted, and thereby at the same time reveals the dynamic engendered by the historical process. Thus he opens the *Critique of Political Economy* by analysing the contradiction between exchange-value and use-value, and then concludes, "The differentiation of commodities (into commodities and money) does not sweep away these inconsistencies, but it creates a form in which they can exist side by side. This is generally the way in which real contradictions are resolved. For instance, it is a contradiction to depict one body as constantly falling towards another and as at the same time constantly flying away from it. The ellipse is a form of motion in which this contradiction is simultaneously realized and resolved."

The mathematical analogy which Marx calls in aid here brings us back once more to the astronomy of Kepler, whose discovery I compared in an earlier lecture with Marx's discovery of what was so original in Epicurus. The point at issue here is not the character of astronomical or atomic motions, but the "circulation" of commodities (*Warenzirkulation*) and the "currency" (*Umlauf*) of money. The terminology of the economic process plainly corresponds to the celestial motions and so automatically, as it were, puts us on to the astronomical track. This in itself is a clue to the connection between Marx's "critique of heaven" and his "critique of earth"—an indication powerfully underlined by the analogy with the mathematical figure of the ellipse. "The circulation of commodities is the starting-point for capital . . . The modern history of capital dates from the creation of worldwide trade and a world market in the sixteenth century." So begins the chapter on "the conversion of money into capital". The growth in the circulation of commodities, in other words, is the point from which began the global expansion described in the latter three parts of Marx's sexpartite plan for the *Critique of Political Economy*. In this world-embracing movement "economic trinity" describes the dynamic movement of Hegel's "world history".

It is highly significant in this context that in the Introduction to his *Philosophy of History*, where he discusses the particular nature of the course taken by world history and historical progress, Hegel himself refers to the method of astronomical research developed by Kepler. The dialectical course of world history, in which the consciousness of freedom on the part of the Spirit is evolved, is so structured that each rung on the ladder of this development has a principle all its own, and quite distinct from other rungs, which principle Hegel defines as "a particular national genius", that is to say, the genius or spirit whereby a people succeeds in expressing its actual, concrete existence as an entity. The peculiar nature of this can only be understood by applying a method of enquiry in which there is constant interaction between abstraction and empirical observation, the principle and the infinite multiplicity of detailed data, the "idea" and the concrete facts. It was in accordance with such a method that Kepler made his revolutionary discoveries. Because he was familiar *a priori* with mathematical figures like ellipses, cubes and squares, therefore he was able to discover "from the empirical data those immortal laws of his".

Marx associated himself very closely indeed with this Hegelian exposition; but he transposed it into economic history. Hegel's "particular national genius" is transposed into the "particular mode of production" that is dominant in this or that particular historical form of society, the special quality of lighting, as it were, in which all the other colours are bathed, the special "ether" which determines the specific gravity of everything that appears in it. So far as the method of enquiry is concerned, Marx accepts the interaction between abstract

and concrete, as Hegel described it; but Marx bases his fundamental critique on this methodological principle, as Hegel had
himself disavowed it. It is indeed the right scientific method for
analysing a concrete totality into abstract qualities and then
describing the concrete totality as though it were made up of
these abstract qualities. To our thinking, therefore, it does
indeed look as though the concrete totality is the result of a
process that combines the several abstract qualities; and Hegel's
speculative philosophy confuses this semblance with reality. In
point of fact, though, things happen precisely the other way
round. That is why, when it comes to the study of society, "in
the employment of the theoretical method the subject, society,
must constantly be kept in mind as the premise from which we
start". Marx realized very well what problem this interaction
entails. It is this: that at the end of a successful investigation
which first analyses (*Forschung*) and then describes (*Darstellung*)
the concrete totality being investigated, the "life of the subject-
matter is ideally reflected as in a mirror, so that it may appear
as if we are dealing with an *a priori* construction". His critique,
which brings Hegel's dialectical method back from mere
semblance to reality and turns it right side up, as it were, has no
other aim than to discover the rational kernel within the
mystical shell. For the method is correct: Hegel was the first to
present dialectic's general form of working in a comprehensive
and conscious manner.

From this viewpoint a clear light is shed upon Marx's
account of the dialectic of the economic process on the analogy
of elliptical motion. He is applying here the method Hegel has
described by reference to Kepler's astronomical discoveries.
An application of the ellipse-model did indeed play a revolutionary role in Kepler's investigations. In calculating the path
described by the planet Mars, Kepler as a scientist had the
courage to part company with the Platonic axiom requiring all
celestial bodies to follow a uniform, circular motion. Prompted
by an almost endless series of laborious calculations, an
irrepressible doubt arose in Kepler's mind regarding this
ancient axiom, which till then had always been the incon-
trovertible foundation of astronomy. When he had racked his
brains over the problem *pene usque ad insaniam* (until it had
nearly driven him mad), suddenly the scales fell from his eyes

when he realized that the formula he had worked out for the Martian orbit fitted exactly one particular pattern of an ellipse. It is not so much the formulation of Kepler's law, according to which a planet will describe an ellipse with the sun in one of the focal points, but the irreparable break with the Platonic axiom of uniform, circular motion that marks Kepler's discovery as a revolutionary moment in the history of science. In Dijksterhuis's words ("The mechanizing of our world view"), we see here "as it were the door separating the hall of ancient and medieval science from that of the classical (modern) variety turn upon its hinges; and with the man who opened it we may go into the newly unlocked area of thought."

In its revolutionary importance the way that Marx makes use of the mathematical properties of the ellipse is on a par with Kepler's own application. It goes without saying that the use Marx makes of this differs as much from Kepler's as economics differs from astronomy; but the correspondence lies in the break which both of them made with the circular model. In the case of Marx this break occurs at two levels—the first being the historical one. By transposing the economic "circulation"-model into an elliptical model governed by the contradiction between two focal points—use-value and exchange-value—he discovers the key to the description of a historical process which through its immanent contradiction simultaneously propels itself forward and contrives its own ruin. To the "eternal" economic "laws of nature" which go with the classical economy, Marx opposes a fundamentally historical model of a historical phase, of which he can explain the historical origins *and* the historical end, genesis and crisis too.

At the same time this model is operative at a second, theological level. From Hegel, Marx learnt a historical method which he transposed on to the economic reality of man's history. That entailed, on the one hand, a break with a theological method which we might call Platonic. We have seen that in Barth's theology this method is implemented in a new form and with extreme consistency: the *circulus vitiosus* of sin is "superseded" or annulled in the *circulus salutis* of God's revelation. Hegel's historico-dialectical method carries within it the possibility of transposing this circle-model into a historical model in which justice is done to the reality of human history as a developing process moving towards a goal; but for Hegel the Platonic tendency proves too powerful. Marx discovers the *principium contradictionis* to be the dynamic *and* critical principle of earthly, that is, material history. Whilst that does not in itself make world history "the world's court of judgment", the latter is effected in and through world history. Marx is fundamentally opposed to pseudo-theological constructions of a primordial, paradisal situation or a terminal, utopian situation, which in economic analysis merely cloak the inability to provide a real explanation of the contradictions in economic history. To express it in theological terms, he concentrates on actual history *after* the expulsion from Paradise and before the dawning of the End; for *prior* to that there was as yet no history and after it history will have ceased. In Marx's dialectical critique the *principium contradictionis* is the principle of the *peccatum originale*; only with the Fall does man's history, as we know it, begin, and at the same time with the Fall the final judgment on history is in principle carried out; in both a positive and a negative sense the Fall is the supremely human and the supremely historical category, because it sets its limits to history, limits without which history could not be real history at all.

Actual history as we know it and as we ourselves make it from day to day—that is, *sub specie peccati originalis, sub conditione principii contradictionis*—is the "*pre*-historic stage of human society" (*Vorgeschichte der menschlichen Gesellschaft*). It is in the prefix, in the "pre"-, that we can feel the very heartbeat of Marx's critical method. Here the bloodstreams coursing through his critique flow together. The process he is investigating is one which has entered its final and decisive phase, and that final phase bears the marks of both extinction and resurrection: the death throes are at the same time birthpangs. In the final phase the temptation to anticipate has become almost irresistible. Thus, Hegel makes the Realm of the Spirit start with the Reformation. But anticipation is the great perversion; and it is so in a dual sense: it confers on *pre*-history the predicate of real history and in that way wraps sin in the garment of salvation. In that final phase occurs the twofold perversion which the New Testament calls the manifestation of Antichrist: Satan masquerades as an angel of light (2 Cor. 11:14;

1 John 2:22; Matt. 24:5; etc.). It is this perversion which Marx describes as the speculative play of *Schein* ("mere semblance" or "sham") and *Widerschein* ("reflection"), of a *verkehrtes Welt-bewusstsein* (a perverted world consciousness) and a *verkehrte Welt* (a perverted world). It is this perversion which he refers to as "religion". Just as the cry of John the Baptist, "Repent, for the Kingdom of heaven is at hand", starts from the assumption that this is a perverted, a topsy-turvy world, so is Marx's critique directed at the perverted world of modern, Christian society. And the term *"pre-*history" echoes the biblical "is at hand".

Marx's critique is at once anatomy and analysis, because the final phase is both a process of dying and a process of birth. The anatomy of political economy, that is to say, of civil society's "material conditions of life", conditions of life which have become also conditions of death: pathological anatomy, the cutting open of a dying root. Anatomy is an-atomy, an exposing of the atomistic character of modern society. The anatomy of the last phase of *pre-*history and, on that basis, of the earlier periods of history. In that sense Engels' posthumous tribute to Marx as the Darwin of human history is apt—but then only in the specific sense of "a Darwin in reverse". "The anatomy of the human being is the key to the anatomy of the ape"; the bourgeois economy furnishes a key to the preceding periods. As anatomy, notice; that is to say, as a critical exposing of the *last* phase, the phase of dying. Yet the final phase is also the supreme one, just as man's existence is the outcome of a preliminary process which organic life has undergone. The process whereby the capitalist mode of production is formed (*Bildung-sprozess*) is also the process which brings about the dissolution of an earlier mode of production in society (*Auflösungs-prozess, Scheidungsprodukt*).

In that sense, critique is also analysis. Scientific analysis, which transfers the method of modern astronomy to the economy. The an-atomy of civil society is carried out in an analysis that uncovers the inner nature of capital beneath the outer appearance and understands that nature, "just as the apparent motions of the heavenly bodies are intelligible only to the person familiar with their real motions—motions not however directly perceptible by the senses". Scientific analysis, that is to say, by means of abstraction, in the same way that a natural scientist uses tubes and retorts in order to study a chemical process but abstracts from the apparatus when it comes to his analysis. The analysis serves to dissect the complex, concrete totality into its several elements. If the analysis of processes in nature is difficult, the analysis of historical processes is even more exacting. The specific problems involved are described by Marx in the *Vorwort* to the first Book of *Das Kapital*. In the study of organisms in general, the body as an organic whole is easier to study than is the separate cell. In the analysis of economic forms there is the added disadvantage that one has neither microscope nor chemical reagent to help one. In their stead, one has to employ the force of abstraction (*Abstraktionskraft*). To the layman this analysis has the appearance of becoming embroiled in mere niceties of detail. It does indeed deal in minutiae, but in the same way that micrological anatomy does. Marx sees this high degree of abstraction as explaining why the fundamental analysis performed by him had never been carried out before, so that the first chapter of *Das Kapital*, devoted to the analysis of the commodity, is also the most difficult. "The value-form, the fully developed shape of which is the money-form, is very elementary and simple. Nevertheless, the human mind has for more than 2000 years sought in vain to get to the bottom of it." Why did Marx succeed where no one had ever succeeded before? Because history had itself advanced to this high degree of abstraction. "For bourgeois society the commodity-form of the product of labour—or the value form of the commodity—is the economic cell-form." Only in this final phase of the "prehistoric stage of human society" does economic development itself make such an analysis possible. The simplest abstraction, namely, abstract general labour, "appears in this abstraction truly realized only as a category of modern society". Moreover, this analysis can only succeed where modern society has attained such a high degree of development. The physicist examines natural processes and conducts his experiments under conditions that reduce disruptive influences to a minimum. This is why Marx chooses for his study of the capitalistic mode of production and the conditions of production and exchange corresponding to it the "classic ground" of his day, England. So his dissecting knife probes down to the roots of the formation of modern society, on the basis of which earlier formations and less well-developed situations in other countries can be understood. From England he can conduct the critique of Germany and cry out to what had been his fatherland, *De te fabula narratur*, just as from the most advanced phase of development in man's history a revealing light shines upon the preceding phase, the "bestial stage in the history of mankind". So the aim proposed for his analysis is "to reveal the economic law of motion in modern society". Not in the illusion that it will be able to leap over or ignore phases that conform with its natural development (*naturgemässe Entwicklungsfasen*). What the analysis does permit, on the other hand, is "shortening and lessening the birth pangs".

Thus scientific analysis becomes *ana-lusis*, becomes a work of deliverance and release applied to society and history, rather in the wake of Socrates' "maieutic" critique, which assists truth at the moment of birth. The birthpangs, however, are also death throes; indeed, pre-history must first die of its own non-viability before the true human society can dawn. England, pioneer of the Industrial Revolution, is at the same time the industrial hell "in which Dante would have found the worst horrors of his Inferno surpassed". The anatomy of political economy must follow in Dante's footsteps through Inferno and Purgatorio, must pick its way through the wraithlike fictions civil society has produced. In the final phase of the pre-history of human society the real state of affairs is stood on its head, truth is mirrored in chimerical notions, the realm of the living is a spirit-world of shades, the world is a perverted world. Just as through the physical process that takes place in the eye an inverted image of reality appears on the retina, so does the historical life-process produce within the *camera obscura* of pre-history, in the last phase of civil society, a perverted world consciousness. It is the task of an anatomical critique to analyse the relation between the historical life-process and the perverted consciousness and so "to develop out of the actual conditions of life their corresponding celestialized (*verhimmelte*) forms". Then this perverted consciousness must be dissected so that its roots can be seen.

This critical analysis is the task of the *Critique of Political*

Economy. The perverted consciousness of the bourgeois economy expresses itself most succinctly in the formula of the "economic trinity". In the same way that a scholastic theology can obfuscate the doctrine of the Trinity by reducing it to a conglomerate of three divine persons, a similar fate awaits the "economic trinity" in the vulgar economy. The classic bourgeois economy does make a serious attempt at an analysis that will bring out the oneness within the threeness; but any such attempt is bound to misfire because the classical economy is powerless to unmask the illusory forms of civil society. Marx's critical method positions the knife just at the spot where the classical economic analysis stops short. Then again, it follows exactly the opposite path to theology. It is precisely this inverted method that conforms with the character of the "economic trinity" as the *credo* of the perverted world consciousness, the reflection of a perverted world. Whereas Karl Barth's theological dogmatics try to present the classical structure by starting with the doctrine of the Trinity as the essence of God's revelation, the "economic trinity" only turns up at the end of *Das Kapital* as a typical surface-phenomenon, a bogus form, which is only seen as a real one by the superficial consciousness of the run-of-the-mill capitalist and by the vulgar economy which is his mouthpiece. Whilst the theological Trinity represents the essential being of God from eternity, the "economic trinity" is the particular structure of the latest phase of the "prehistoric stage of human society", the civil or bourgeois form of society; it belongs not to the beginning but to the end of history. In other words, the "economic trinity" is a specific illusion standing in the same inverted relation to the actual condition of "human society" as the Antichrist has to Christ: a pseudo-anticipation. That is the very reason why the basic plan of the *Critique of Political Economy* is built on this trinitarian scheme; for the job of the *Critique* is after all to expose the sham.

The classic formula, *una substantia, tres personae*, summarizing the theological doctrine of the Trinity, is reflected in the economic illusion. I pointed to this connection in my eighth lecture. Behind the masked characters appearing on the economic stage Marx analyses the one substance. Just as in the theological doctrine of the Trinity the pivot is formed by

Christology as the theory concerning the Mediator, the Second Person, so in the "economic trinity" capital functions as "the active middle" (*Kapital muss immer als die tätige Mitte erscheinen*), to such an extent, in fact, that the original sexpartite plan is eventually reduced to *Das Kapital*. Closer analysis shows that the concealed *una substantia*, the single "substance", is constituted by surplus value. If we then proceed to read the first Book of *Das Kapital* from back to front, then *via* the "production of (absolute and relative) surplus value" we get to the analysis of the "transformation of money into capital" in order finally, *via* the analysis of "money or the circulation of commodities", to end up with the first chapter, "Commodities and money". It is in the closing section of this same first chapter that we find the epitome of Marx's critique of heaven and earth: "The fetishism of commodities and the secret thereof".

Here is where the dissecting knife touches the very root; here is that conjunctive point at which all the threads I have been following through this series of lectures come together. There is a profound and most probably deliberate irony in Marx's choice of the term "fetish", which remains constantly in attendance right through the course of *Das Kapital*. After all, in Hegel's *Philosophy of World History* (*Philosophie der Weltgeschichte*) fetishism is placed on the bottom rung, where the developing process of world history has not as yet really begun. In fact, the African negro "exhibits the natural man in his completely wild and untamed state. We must lay aside all thought of reverence and morality—all that we call feeling—if we would rightly comprehend him; in this character nothing is to be found that can remind us of any human quality". For in what is the typical African character the "category of universality" is entirely absent. The negro has not yet attained to the consciousness of any settled, objective reality such as, for instance, God or Law. Actually, he has not yet got as far as religion; for "religion begins with the consciousness that there is something higher than man". The negro is still living in a world of sorcery, where there is no idea of a God, of a moral belief. Sorcery "exhibits man as the highest power, regarding him as alone occupying a position of command over the power of nature". In this sorcerer's-religion, Hegel goes on to tell us, the negroes give a visible form of expression to this arbitrary power of theirs, projecting it outside themselves and making themselves images of it. "What they envisage as their power, therefore, is not an objective or substantial reality that is different from themselves, but usually the first object to present itself, which they raise to the dignity of *genius*, whether it be animal, tree, stone or figure of wood. This is the fetish, a word first given currency by the Portuguese, and deriving from *feitizo*, sorcery. Here, in the fetish, a kind of independence as contrasted with the caprice of an individual does seem to assert itself, it is true; but as the objectivity (*Gegenständlichkeit*) is nothing other than the individual caprice making a graphic representation of itself, the individual caprice remains master of the projected image."

This piece of exposition by Hegel makes an excellent introduction to Marx's use of the terms "fetish" and "fetishism". Only Marx's interpretation penetrates behind the Portuguese term to the Latin source. The word *factitius* ("factitious" in English) actually means "artificial" (as opposed to "natural"), "copied", "simulated" (as opposed to "original", "genuine", "real"). The commodity, which is the foundation-element of economic exchange, is in that sense "factitious", *factitius*, created by man. It is this character of the economic process as historically determined, as determined by man's thinking and behaviour, which in the "fetish-like character" of the commodity forms the starting-point of Marx's analysis. The field of his enquiry is civil society, the latest and highest phase of world history, as the terminal phase of Hegel's *Philosophy of History* included under the Germano-Christian empire, characterized as the realm of the Spirit. Quite deliberately, on this highest rung of mankind's history, Marx's action is to select the term central to Hegel's description of the bottommost rung, the subhuman level, the term "fetishism". Once more we see the character of the "economic trinity" being confirmed, as an illusion on the analogy of the Antichrist. *Corruptio optimi pessima*: the corruption of the best is the worst corruption of all. It is in the final phase of the "prehistoric stage of human society", and precisely there, that the *corruptio originalis* finds its fullest expression. On the highest rung is revealed the vanity of "progress" in the final result, which is exactly like the position at the start.

With that, the circle of the critique of heaven and earth is indeed closed once more. The critique of theology is transformed, *via* the critique of law, into the critique of political economy, the outcome of which is the critique of fetishism, that is, the critique of theology. The critique of religion becomes the critique of Germany, that is to say, of Hegel's Germano-Christian end-phase of world history; but this philosophy turns out, on closer analysis of the economic roots of law, to issue in the most primitive religion, fetishism.

So it is that Marx's analysis leaves us uncertain whether it belongs to the critique of earth or to the critique of heaven. Our doubt is bound up directly with the nature of the object being investigated. After all, a commodity appears at first sight a very trivial thing, and easily understood. But further analysis shows that a commodity "is a very queer thing, full of metaphysical subtleties and theological hair-splitting". In so far as it is a value in use, there is nothing mysterious about the commodity; but "so soon as it begins to function as a commodity, it changes into something at once accessible and inaccessible to sense, something transcendent (*sinnlich übersinnliches*). It not only stands with its feet on the ground; but in relation to all other commodities it puts itself on its head". Then an ordinary wooden table evolves "out of its wooden brain fancies much more grotesque than any impulse it might have to dance a jig".

"The mysterious thing about a commodity is simply this: that in it the social character of men's labour appears to them as an objective character stamped upon the product of that labour, as a matter of social attributes accruing to it in the course of nature. In contrast to the physical process which converts the impact of light upon the retina to the image of an object which is itself outside the eye, the commodity-form and the value-relation between the products of labour have nothing to do with the physical nature of the commodity. It is only the particular social relation between men themselves which here assumes in their imagination the fantastic form of a relation between things. If we want to find an analogy, we shall have to ascend into the misty regions of religion. There the products of the human brain seem endowed with a life of their own, self-subsistent forms having a relation to one another and with human beings. So is it in the world of commodities with the products of men's hands." Marx calls this the "fetishism inseparably bound up with the products of labour, so soon as they are produced as commodities, a fetishism therefore which cannot be divorced from the production of commodities".

Thus, this fetishism differs essentially from that described by Hegel as being the religion of the African negroes. There indeed it is in the traditional sense of the word a phenomenon of "religion" that can be analysed by the traditional critique of religion. Marx's critique, on the other hand, not only discovers this religion on the highest rung of world history, but religion here is identical with the economic structure of the actual form of society, the fetishism is implicit in the actual conditions of production. The paradox consists in the fact that the fetishism, which by Hegel's account is marked by the complete absence of any capacity for abstraction, here turns out to be inherent in a most highly developed form of society, which *is* characterized by a perfected capacity for abstraction. The fact that forms of society develop to a higher stage is precisely what forces the critique of religion to transform itself into a critique of political economy. The truth is that at a lower stage of development, where "the umbilical cord of the natural cohesion of men's social existence", which binds individual people together, has not yet been cut, this natural restraint is ideally reflected in the ancient worship of nature and in other popular religions. In earlier modes of production, typical of asiatic, ancient and feudal forms of society, we find the conversion of products into commodities, and therefore the conversion of people into the producers of commodities, playing a subordinate role. "Trading nations exist in the ancient world only in the interstices (*intermundia*), like the gods of Epicurus or like the Jews in the pores of Polish society."

With this analogy Marx resumes the thread of his dissertation. I spoke in an earlier lecture of the connection Marx establishes between Epicurus' philosophy of atoms and the atomistic structure of civil society. Like the atomistic deity of Epicurus, the modern citizen is autonomous and completely independent, but precisely because of this autonomous activity also creator and sustainer of the process of reciprocal attraction and repulsion between the atoms. Putting it in terms of modern civil society, the private and totally self-sufficient bourgeois mode of existence is also the activating principle of the *bellum omnium contra omnes*, the free play of economic elements, the atomistic world of capitalist competition. Epicurus' atheistic philosophy is in fact the atheistic religion of the modern citizen (the member of "civil society"). A form of society that in the ancient world was the exception has now become the all-prevailing one. Epicurus' gods no longer exist in the *intermundia*, the interstices of the world of the nations, but they swarm across the globe, compelling other peoples into their magic circle, creating the entire world after their own image, the image of the modern "private citizen".

Epicurus had the nerve, as a lone apostate, to repudiate the ancient religious cult of the celestial bodies. The modern citizen, on the other hand, venerates the circulation, the cyclical movement, of the modern economic process with the same sort of religious naivety as the ancient Greeks did the celestial motions. But since then there has been a fundamental change. The religion of the "visible heavens" has made way for that of the "sealed Word". Christianity has cut the umbilical cord which united man with the cosmic powers; the religion of modern man has become abstract, it has been embodied in the modern fetishism of commodities. Christianity has become the economic religion. "For a society of commodity-producers whose relation to social production in general is that they relate to their products as commodities, that is, values, producers who in this material form reduce their individual labour to the standard of homogeneous human labour—for such a society Christianity, with its *cultus* of abstract man, more especially in its bourgeois developments, Protestantism, Deism, etc., is the most adequate form of religion."

In this way the critique of Christianity, which with Barth remains on the level of religion in the received sense of the word, ends up on the level of the economy. The "cultus of abstract man" is certainly inaugurated by the Reformation and is translated by Hegel into philosophical language; but it takes a proper shape in civil society only in the political economy of Adam Smith, the "Luther of national economy". This is why at the very centre the *Critique of Political Economy* is a critique of the Christian religion in its actual form as the spirit, the "genius", of society's history, on the very highest rung of its development.

But the *Critique* goes deeper than that. It bears upon the tendency to envisage the world more and more in mathematical and mechanical terms, against which Marx's vista of an all-round, humane materialism is a gesture of revolt. On the modern development of the physical science the physicist, C. F. von Weizsäcker, has made the following observations which, put in terms of the critique of political economy, read like a sort of commentary on Marx's analysis.

"When it comes to the physical sciences, we find ourselves nowadays in a state of disillusionment about as extreme as we are able to conceive; and we look back today over the way we have come. Through all the centuries the world has stood for God, albeit in very divergent ways. At one time it was itself divine. Later, it pointed to its creator. In recent times it has become a surrogate for God. But we have not thereby returned to the view of pagan antiquity, which was itself divine or, as it has been strikingly put, full of gods. It is only as a beautiful, if usually ill-comprehended, memory that this world re-emerges for our day. The road back to it has been barred by a more powerful urge: the urge towards the infinite. The gods of the pagan world are the forces of nature in and around us. The world of our natural existence, however, is finite and relative. Christianity has made the infinite and absolute the goal of our endeavours. Secularized, modern man has not given up this aspiration, but is seeking to realize it only in another plane. Essentially, therefore, his attitude to nature comes down to this: that he is exceeding the limits and the scope of his original, natural existence. He is penetrating—to use the language of antiquity—into a country without gods or into one whose gods are strange, are alien to us. And as he does so, he obtains a knowledge and a power which every earlier period would have held to be both unlawful and impracticable. Knowledge and power have become our gods; and they have been surrounded with a halo of the infinite and the absolute."

Being both a physicist and a Christian, von Weizsäcker does not stop short at this diagnosis, but searches for an answer. We have to start "by seeing the abyss and facing up to the void". The surrogate-symbolism has collapsed like a pack of cards.

Not because it was symbolical, but because it was a surrogate. The void with which we are confronted is no end but the summons to a decision. "Everything depends on whether we are really willing to listen to God. Not where we would be glad to hear his voice, but where he is really speaking to us." It is here the dilemma really becomes inescapable. For if we are prepared to listen, shall we not find ourselves standing irrevocably outside science? "Does not our life then fall apart into two worlds: that of real, authentic existence *qua* man, and the unavoidable but intrinsically meaningless technical-cum-physical world? Can we set aside the fact that the external world is bereft of all meaning without indulging in self-deception?"

For Marx, this question is already answered by the actual structure of civil society. The self-deception is inherent in the "cult of abstract man"; and the meaninglessness of the technical and natural world is one which that society has itself produced and reproduces all the time in its "religion of every-day life" (*Religion des Alltagslebens*). It is the meaninglessness of the "realm of necessity". How deeply Marx felt the barb of this is evident from the fact that at the end of *Das Kapital*, in the chapter on "The Trinitarian Formula", he is obliged to resort to a term which in his works is usually a technical term for the idea of religion, the term *jenseits*, "yonder", "away and beyond". "In point of fact, the realm of freedom begins only where the kind of labour that is determined by sheer need and by an extrinsic expediency ceases; in the nature of the case, therefore, it lies *beyond* (*jenseits*) the sphere of actual material production. Just as the savage must contend with nature to satisfy his wants, and provide for and reproduce the means of subsistence, so too civilized man has to wrestle with nature, and do so in every form of society and under every possible mode of production. As he develops, this realm of physical necessity expands, as his wants multiply; but at the same time the forces of production which satisfy those wants also multiply. Freedom in this area can only consist in socialized man, the associated producers, rationally regulating their interchange with nature, bringing it under their common control, instead of being ruled by it as by a blind force; and achieving this interchange with the least expenditure of energy, and under conditions most worthy of their human nature. But it still remains a realm of necessity. Beyond it (*jenseits*) begins that development of human energy which is sensible of being an end in itself, the true realm of freedom, which yet can only blossom and flourish with this realm of necessity as its basis. The shortening of the working day is its fundamental prerequisite."

At this point we are back once more with the *Vorwort* of *Das Kapital*, where Marx defines the ultimate purpose (*letzte Endzweck*) of the *Critique of Political Economy* as being to reveal the "law of economic motion" of modern society, with a view to "shortening and lessening the birth-pangs". The English language preserves the connection between heavy work and the pangs of giving birth, in the words "labour" and "travail". The "shortening of the working day" and the "shortening of the birth-pangs" are very closely akin to each other, in the sense that work, labour, within the realm of blind necessity, without the dawning light of the realm of freedom anywhere in view, resembles a false pregnancy or an abortion. Work, comprehended within the total context of our human mode of being, means working for the completion of the "prehistoric stage of human history". Marx sums up the genius of Hegel's philosophy when he says that Hegel "grasps the self-creation (*Selbsterzeugung*) of man as a process . . .; and that he therefore understands the nature of labour, and comprehends the human being of flesh and blood (*gegenständlichen Menschen*), real and therefore true man, as the result of his own labour". That is Hegel's philosophy stood right side up, as it were. That is the labour which triumphs over the "cult of abstract man". Labour means labouring for the completion of history; it lies in the constellation of birth.

Yet the birth-pangs are at one and the same time death-throes. The awareness of this dialectic permeates Marx's critique of heaven and earth. The work of completing history threatens to be unavailing. At the beginning of this series of lectures, I reminded you of the theological problem of the Fall. It is not devoid of significance that the story of Paradise ends with the "pain and sorrow of child-bearing", the "eating of bread in the sweat of your face" and with "you are dust, and to dust you shall return". Paul bases himself on this in the eighth chapter of the Letter to the Romans: the whole creation is subject to futility—but in hope; it is in travail. This chapter I have put alongside the *Magna Charta* of the critique of religion, the Introduction to the *Critique of Hegel's Philosophy of Right*, which forms the background to this series of lectures. The remarkable ambiguity of analogy and contrast between the two texts is even now, at the close of my lectures, not removed. That ambiguity belongs to the historical period in which we live. The dilemma is different from the one that the earliest Christian community had to face. Marx himself compared the "cult of abstract man" with the worship of the beast described in the Revelation of John. The essential difference, however, is that in the worship of the beast it is the death-throes of ancient paganism that are taking shape, whereas in the modern "cult of abstract man" what is in its death-throes is the history of the *Corpus Christianum*. It is all about us now: *de te fabala narratur*!

For that very reason it is a life-and-death matter for Christian theology whether or not it is willing and able to submit to the critique of heaven and earth. When it speaks of history, the Bible speaks of "births". "This is the history (Hebrew *toledöth* = births, generations) of heaven and earth, when they were created" (Genesis 2:4). John on Patmos surveys a new heaven and a new earth, "for the first heaven and the first earth had passed away" (Rev. 21:1). Its own past burdens Christian theology with the temptation to flee from the passing away of the first earth to the first heaven. It suits its convenience to overlook the fact that, *along with* the first earth, that first heaven is also passing away. Heaven and earth are created together: our earth has the heaven that befits it, that belongs to it. Heaven and earth stand in crisis together, "under critique" together. We are forbidden to take our flight from earth to heaven. The command to us, and the promise, is that we take the road to a new heaven and a new earth. On that road theology is subject to the critique of heaven and earth; for if it has no part in the "passing away" of pre-history, it will surely have lost the way to the new heaven and the new earth whose birth-pangs bear the name of "history".